I Promise You I'll Be Home

I Promise You I'll Be Home

*Korean War Letters
of a U.S. Marine*

AL MARTINEZ

Edited by SARA S. HODSON

McFarland & Company, Inc., Publishers
Jefferson, North Carolina

Library of Congress Cataloging-in-Publication Data

Names: Martinez, Al, author. | Hodson, Sara S., 1949– editor.
Title: I promise you I'll be home : Korean War letters of a U.S. Marine / Al Martinez ; edited by Sara S. Hodson.
Other titles: Korean War letters of a U.S. Marine
Description: Jefferson, North Carolina : McFarland & Company, Inc., Publishers, 2024. | Includes bibliographical references and index.
Identifiers: LCCN 2024004659 | ISBN 9781476693163 (paperback : acid free paper) ∞ ISBN 9781476652146 (ebook)
Subjects: LCSH: Martinez, Al—Correspondence. | Korean War, 1950–1953—Personal narratives, American. | United States. Marine Corps. Marine Regiment, 7th. Battalion, 2nd. Company F | Marines—United States—Correspondence. | United States. Marine Corps—Military life. | Korean War, 1950–1953—Campaigns. | Korean War, 1950–1953—Participation, Mexican American. | Korean War, 1950–1953—Regimental histories—United States. | BISAC: HISTORY / Wars & Conflicts / Korean War
Classification: LCC DS921.6 M378 2024 | DDC 951.904/2092 [B]—dc23/eng/20240206
LC record available at https://lccn.loc.gov/2024004659

British Library cataloguing data are available

ISBN (print) 978-1-4766-9316-3
ISBN (ebook) 978-1-4766-5214-6

© 2024 Estate of Al Martinez. All rights reserved

No part of this book may be reproduced or transmitted in any form or by any means, electronic or mechanical, including photocopying or recording, or by any information storage and retrieval system, without permission in writing from the publisher.

Front cover image: Al Martinez, 1951. The Huntington Library, UDID 324238.

Printed in the United States of America

McFarland & Company, Inc., Publishers
Box 611, Jefferson, North Carolina 28640
www.mcfarlandpub.com

To the memory of Joanne Martinez,
who walked in grace and beauty

Table of Contents

Acknowledgments	ix
Chronology	xi
Preface	1
Introduction: A Hole in History Three Years Wide	8
One—Come 4 A.M.—Reveille!	19
Two—Through Mud, Mortars and Hell	69
Three—Cpl. Al Martinez, Combat Correspondent.... How About That!	144
Afterword	215
Glossary: People, Places, Events, Phrases, Abbreviations, Military Terms	219
Further Reading	227
Index	229

Acknowledgments

This book has been a labor of love and I am delighted to see the publication of Al's letters, which he had hoped to accomplish himself. To Al, I give my gratitude for writing the extensive body of remarkable letters from which this book springs. To his wife Joanne, I give my deep thanks for giving me permission to embark on this project and for providing both encouragement and help, as she endeavored to recall people and events from 70 years in the past to answer my questions. Much appreciation goes to Al and Joanne's son and daughter, Allen (Marty) Martinez and Linda Bach, for granting permission for this work after Joanne passed away. Their joy and excitement in the project have been an inspiration, and I could not have asked for better support and encouragement.

To Clay Stalls goes my gratitude for introducing me to E.B. Sledge's book, *With the Old Breed*, one of the finest war memoirs ever written. In relating his combat experiences, Sledge documents the profound depth and meaning of the comradeships formed by men in battle. I hope that Al's accounts of his own war-time friendships will resonate with Clay almost as much as Sledge's.

To Susan Phillips a hearty thank you for spending time she didn't have to read my book proposal and make helpful suggestions to improve it. In addition, at a crucial moment, she introduced me to Nathan Lu, who created the superb map of Korea that appears in the book. Kudos and thanks to Nathan for a map that is not only exactly right but also a handsome artistic work.

The Huntington Library, as holder of Al Martinez's papers, played a crucial part in the work on this book. The Reader Services Department performed essential and exceptional service in providing access to the letters in the Ahmanson Reading Room, ably answering my questions, no matter how odd or arcane, and providing assistance in many other ways. The department members are Anne Blecksmith (department head), Hector Acosta, Morex Arai, Stephanie Arias, Lisa Caprino, Nathaniel de Gala, Mark Fleming, Leslie Jobsky, James Kitahara, Mina Marciano, Kevin Miller, Frank Osen, Jazmin Rew-Pinchem, and Erica Wofford. Morex Arai deserves special recognition for his kind and patient assistance with aspects of the library's online systems that challenged my limited technological capabilities. The Photographic Department performed its customary visual miracles with the images I requested; a grateful tip of the hat to photographer Manuel Flores and to former staff members Brian Moeller, John Sullivan, and Devonne Tice. Jon Sims and Rob Studer of the IT Department rescued me more than once as I headed down a wrong technology path. Krystle Satrum, in the Research Division, has a significant technology feather in her extensive cap of expertise and bailed me out with several essential tips.

Librarians in other institutional settings also provided essential assistance. Dorothy Lazard, in the History Room of the Oakland Public Library, replied promptly and helpfully to my queries, and Alisa Whitley, Branch Head and Archivist for the Historical Resources Branch, Marine Corps History Division, provided quantities of photocopies that answered a number of questions.

Several people made important comments for improving my book proposal, and my thanks go to Colleen Dunn Bates, Paddy Calistro, Chuck Rankin, and Nancy Stauffer.

Steve Padilla, an editor at the *Los Angeles Times*, searched a *Times* database and located a number of Al's columns on Korea that I would not have found on my own, and he put me in touch with former staffers who knew Al and shared reminiscences. He has my gratitude.

Hye Ok Park is, as ever, an interested and supportive friend and also an invaluable resource for information and understanding of Korea and its people. I owe her my thanks as well for referring a query to Dr. Jai-hoon Shim. He kindly identified a location in Taiwan that Al and Joanne visited during their 1992 Revisit Korea trip.

Most important, to my husband, Peter Blodgett, I give my deep love and my abiding gratitude for his encouragement and unwavering support for this enterprise. His devotion and confidence in me enabled me to reach further and venture more than I thought I could. He answered my neophyte queries about military matters and practices and shared his extensive historical knowledge. In all things, Peter is my trusted companion, valued advisor, and best friend.

Chronology

1929

July 21—Al is born.
December 11—Joanne Cinelli is born.

1949

July 30—Al and Joanne marry.

1950

June 25—The conflict begins when North Korean forces attack South Korean positions south of the 38th Parallel. The United Nations Security Council adopts a resolution calling for the withdrawal of North Korean forces to the parallel.
July 21—Al's 21st birthday.
August 2—First U.S. Marine Brigade reaches Korea.
September 15—First Marine Division makes a successful amphibious assault on Inchon.
September 22—Al is on the train from San Francisco en route to San Diego for USMC induction and basic training.
September 29—MacArthur enters Seoul with President Syngman Rhee.
November—At the Chosin (Changjin) Reservoir, X Corps is attacked by 10 Communist China divisions. The First Marine Division completed a successful fighting withdrawal through 78 miles of mountain roads to reach the port of Hungnam.
September–October—Al begins boot camp.
End of November or beginning of December—Al completes boot camp.

1951

March 15—Al embarks for Japan and Korea aboard the U.S.S. *Thomas Jefferson*. He is a member of E Company, part of the seventh draft.
April 2—Al arrives at Pusan, Korea. He is assigned to Fox Company, 2nd Battalion, 7th Regiment, 1st Marine Division.
May 23 to June 17—Hwachon Reservoir fighting.
May 31—Birth of Cinthia Louise Martinez, Al and Joanne's first child.
June 3—Al learns of his child's birth but doesn't learn her gender until June 14.
July 21—Al's 22nd birthday.
July 31—Al and Joanne's second anniversary.
August–October—First Marine Division is engaged in hard fighting near the "Punchbowl," a ridgeline overlooking a deep circular valley in the Korean mountains.

August–September—Battle of Bloody Ridge, west of the Punchbowl.

September–October—Battle of Heartbreak Ridge, northwest of the Punchbowl.

October 15—Al is transferred to regimental PIO.

November 10–176th birthday of the U.S. Marine Corps.

1952

April 8 or 9—Al departs Korea, bound for home, on the *General William Wiegel*.

April 27—Al's ship arrives in San Diego.

1953

July 27—Armistice is signed at Panmunjom.

1956

Al and Joanne's daughter Linda is born.

1964

Al and Joanne's son Allen is born.

1976

Al creates a television series, *Jigsaw John*, starring Jack Warden, based on a profile Al had written for the *Los Angeles Times* about John St. John, a one-eyed Los Angeles homicide detective.

1992

Al and Joanne travel to Korea on a trip put together by the Korea Revisit Program, sponsored by the U.S. Navy League, Korean Air, and Dynasty Tours to send Korean War veterans and their loved ones back to the sites of the conflict. After the trip, Al wrote about it in several columns and essays.

Al receives an Emmy nomination for *Out on the Edge*, a television series starring Rick Schroder.

2009

January—The *Los Angeles Times* lets Al go in a cost-cutting effort. He soon begins writing a column for the *Los Angeles Daily News* and continues until March 2013.

2011

March 29—Cinthia dies of cancer.

2012

The Huntington Library presents a major exhibition on Al's life and career titled "Al Martinez: Bard of L.A."

2015

January 12—Al passes away from congestive heart failure and COPD (chronic obstructive pulmonary disease).

2021

April 5—Joanne dies of lung cancer.

Preface

War memoirs and collections of war-time letters hold an essential place in the historical record. Such first-person accounts relate the real-life experiences of participants in the tumult and upheaval of military conflict. Stories of living through battle and its aftermath enable the rest of us to understand the experiences of those who were directly involved. Wars effect profound changes to national boundaries, to economies, to governmental systems, and to the lives of the people who live through the conflict.

In the twentieth century, three wars have exerted a strong influence on the American people. These include the two world wars and, in its own category, the Vietnam War. The Korean War, not officially a war at all, but a "police action," occupies a smaller space in the historical record. Coming just five years after the end of the Second World War, this conflict met a war-weary American public that did not understand why the United States was at war and could not muster the energy to embrace or support the war effort. As a result, the Korean conflict has received less attention than the other wars that occurred in our recent history. But this inattention has begun to be corrected. As Hampton Sides, author of *On Desperate Ground: The Marines at the Reservoir, the Korean War's Greatest Battle*, observed in 2018, "The men who bled and died in Korea are now taking their bows.... They're unassuming, uncomplaining men who answered the call and fought for a principle, long ago and far from home, in a war that was not 'officially' a war—a war that curiously became a dormant account in our public memory bank."[*]

This volume presents selected letters from the correspondence written home by Al Martinez during his time with the U.S. Marine Corps during the Korean War. It is not a history of the war, nor is it an account of the role of the U.S. Marine Corps in the war. This book endeavors to bring one important story from the Korean War to readers who are interested in military history and in a narrative of human drama. Al Martinez, who unexpectedly found himself on the front lines in Korea, is well suited to tell the story of his experiences. The tale he tells is a first-person narrative of the experiences of a young Marine sent to war at the age of 21.

For more than a year and a half, Al dispatched letters nearly every day to

---

[*]Hampton Sides, "Remembering the Forgotten War," *The New York Times*, November 12, 2018, A23.

his bride Joanne, from September 1950 to April 1952. As a young man serving on the front lines in Korea, he observed and experienced the worst that war can bring, and he wrote about these experiences beautifully and eloquently with the skill of a professional writer at the beginning of his career. His writing talent would bring him a raft of awards, including three shared Pulitzer Prizes for journalism, a National Ernie Pyle Award, the National Headliner Award for the best column in the United States, and a lifetime achievement award from the California Chicano News Media Association. He also received an Emmy nomination for a television series. In these letters, Martinez invites the reader in as he tells stories with immediacy and literary power. Already a man of deep feeling and great heart, he writes in a voice that will continue to mature as he becomes one of the most trusted and beloved writers in journalism. His letters serve eloquently to bring to life this neglected piece of history both for readers who are familiar with the war and for those who come anew to the story of the conflict.

Al and Joanne, both aged 21, had been married just over a year when he departed and were barely launched on their life together when they had to endure the loneliness of living apart as well as a crushing anxiety for Al's safety in the heat of battle. As befits the work of a nascent writer, Al's letters are eloquent, sensitive, evocative expressions of the terror of combat, the inner thoughts of one facing death when his life is just beginning, and the compassion he feels for his fellow Marines and soldiers and for the people of war-torn Korea. These letters possess exceptional grace, narrative flow, emotional power, and depth of understanding. Vivid, memorable accounts of the lived experience, they are filled with the hardships, fear, friendships, and even humor of life at the front. The letters also are wonderful examples of the work of a writer just beginning to hone his craft and find his voice; in them one can see the emerging professional writer whose columns and articles would touch and inform legions of readers over several decades.

In war literature, there are memoirs and collections of letters that cover virtually every war, including for the Korean conflict. For all such publications, the first-person accounts of the soldiers, sailors and Marines are essential in documenting their experiences. Even though there can be commonalities in these accounts, there are nonetheless distinctions among them that give value to all these efforts. As military historian Elizabeth D. Samet has pointed out, "despite war's universals, ... no one's war ever looks quite like anyone else's."* Theirs are authentic voices that present events central to the historical record. As for Al, with his keen eye, his literary instinct for the makings of a good story, and his ability to probe more deeply into the human experience, his letters often rise above the more prosaic writings of ordinary service people. Moreover, the corpus of Al's letters forms a dramatic arc that tells the story of one Marine's war with a beginning, a middle, and an end. His is an authentic, eloquent, literary

---

*Elizabeth D. Samet, "Introduction," in Samet, ed., *World War II Memoirs: The Pacific Theater* (New York: The Library of America, 2011), xx.

voice that deserves to be made available and that will reward readers of all backgrounds.

The three chapters of this book cover the distinct stages of Al's Marine service: Chapter One encompasses Al's induction and months in Marine boot camp, where he learned to function as a Marine and where he endured tough, rigorous training at the hands of his drill instructors; Chapter Two covers his months on the front lines in Korea, living in a foxhole, going out on patrol, fighting an often-unseen enemy, and experiencing the worst that war can offer; and Chapter Three describes his time in his regimental Public Information Office, serving as a combat correspondent and writer and editor of his regiment's newsletter, the *Ridgerunner*. Each chapter begins with a short introduction, to set the context and provide identifications where needed, but not to repeat the contents of Al's letters. The letters stand on their own as clearly written, complete accounts, best told in Al's own eloquent words.

In all three phases of his Marine Corps service, Al displays his unique voice as a budding professional writer. Where other Marines and soldiers dispatched important letters home that described their own lived experiences, Al, with his literary talent, went further, probing more deeply into people and situations, keenly observing more than those around him did and recording these observations with depth and insight. All war memoirs, accounts and collections of correspondence are important as documents that record historical events and the experiences of those who participated in them, and Al's letters hold special status given his literary abilities. He intended to publish his letters in time, and he clearly writes with this in mind. It is fascinating to watch the emerging professional at work honing his craft and perfecting his writing, and this development can be seen in the series of letters from Korea, as his letters become more polished, particularly after his transfer to PIO. A number of letters are quite self-consciously "literary," and, as one reads them, one can feel that Al is writing for a larger audience than just his wife, although Joanne is definitely present as his primary reader, clearly the one he cares most about in the immediate moment.

Unfortunately, just nine of Joanne's letters to Al have survived, mostly because Al could not preserve them when he moved frequently among a series of foxholes and, later, tents in a command post that often relocated in response to rapidly changing battle lines. The nine letters from Joanne deal only with logistics of travel and accommodations for her visits to Al during his training in San Diego and at Camp Pendleton and have not been included in this volume.

The pen and ink drawings Al sometimes included in his letters compose a wonderful visual resource that helps us to understand what the Marines and soldiers experienced in Korea. In addition to his graceful talent as a writer, Al was a dab hand at creating a visual record, often humorous, of his experiences. Some of his best art efforts are reproduced in this volume.

The Al Martinez Papers and Exhibition, The Huntington Library

As a long-time featured columnist for the *Los Angeles Times*, Al Martinez held great interest for The Huntington Library. The archive of his papers fits perfectly with other collections of original material also held by the library, including the records of the *Times* History Center and the papers of *Times* editorial cartoonist Paul Conrad and columnist Jack Smith. The Huntington, as a research institution in the Los Angeles area, has long collected material documenting the history of Los Angeles and California, so collections related to the *Times* mesh perfectly with the holdings. Al Martinez donated his papers to The Huntington Library in 2006. The collection consists of about 1,000 items, including literary manuscripts of his columns, essays, screenplays and other publications, along with tear sheets for his columns. Some of his reporter's notebooks are present, and a generous selection of ephemera encompasses posters, book cover art, photographs, and other material. One of the great strengths of the archive is the series of letters written home to his wife Joanne from the battle front in Korea.

In 2012, I curated a major exhibition on Martinez, surveying his life and career with a generous selection of items from his archive on view. Inspired by the nearly poetic qualities of his prose, I called the exhibition "Al Martinez: Bard of L.A." Tickled to be dubbed a bard, Al spun a newspaper column from his new title, revealing that, despite such a distinguished honorific, the "Bardess" (Joanne) still made him take out the trash and the "Bard Dog" bared his canines at Al in snarling menace.

Letter Selection, Editing and Transcribing Practices, Notes, and Illustrations

This edition includes 107 letters selected from the entire body of 370 pieces of correspondence. The selections made represent an effort to cover fully the variety of topics in Al's letters and to omit letters that repeat content covered in others or that are lesser versions of similar letters. Every letter in the volume is presented in its entirety. No text has been deleted or censored in any way. The letters are transcribed exactly as written, including typographical and spelling errors. When any part of a word needs to be added to a misspelled word, it is added within square brackets, e.g., bullet[s]. When any part needs to be removed from a misspelled word, the word is left as-is and "*sic*" is added following the word, in square brackets, e.g., scrupples [*sic*]. Spelling and grammatical errors are left intact but followed by the correction enclosed in square brackets. Al consistently spelled the word "night" as "nite," and this spelling is retained with no correction. Similarly, Al's spellings of "tho" and "thru" are retained with no correction where he used them as abbreviations for "though" and "through." In the transcribed letters, I have used an ampersand whenever Al used a cursive plus sign rather than writing out "and." Ellipses when present are Al's, with one exception: the ellipses in the title of Chapter Three are supplied by the editor. Al often ended his letters with xxxes, i.e., kisses, for Joanne. Following the birth of their daughter Cinthia, Al began signing his letters with capital kisses (XXXes) for Joanne and lower-case kisses (xxxes) for Cinthia. In all cases, I counted the xxxes and transcribed the exact number present.

The specific call number for each letter appears at the end of the letter. The call number has the form of a sequential, three-digit numeral following the prefix "MZ" derived from Martinez's surname, e.g., MZ 619. Each call number denotes just one letter, even when the letter was written over a period of several days, and it can be used to refer to that letter for any purpose, including requesting a copy from The Huntington Library.

Notes are provided for each letter, when there is a need to identify people, places, or events, or to provide further information on a letter's content. These notes are placed at the foot of each letter for the reader's ease of reference. The names and terms in the notes, along with other identifications, as well as expansions of abbreviations, also appear in a glossary at the end of the volume, again for quick and easy reference.

The images include photographs, pages from Al's letters, original drawings by Al Martinez and by Bob Richardson, enclosures from the letters, and a map of Korea. The map was created by Nathan Lu; the 2011 photograph of Al and Joanne Martinez is the work of John Sullivan, the chief photographer of The Huntington Library; and the rest of the images come from the archive of Al's papers held at The Huntington Library. Several of Al's drawings that appear in this book are from letters that are not included. He often added drawings when he had little to write about, and some of these letters did not make it into this book because their content was not as strong as that of other letters. Hence, as the captions will show, some of the drawings reproduced here are from letters that have been omitted.

Pejorative and Racist Language

During the Korean War and again in Vietnam, servicemen often used pejorative terms when referring to the people they were fighting. Al and his buddies were no different. They referred to the Chinese as Chinks and to the Koreans, as well as the Vietnamese and Chinese, as Gooks and slant-eyes. (During World War II, servicemen referred pejoratively to Germans as Krauts, Jerries, Boche, Heinies, and Huns [*Boche* and *Huns* were also used in World War I] and to Japanese as Japs, Nips, and monkeys.) To us now, this is, rightly, a regrettable practice of heaping scorn and contempt on races, nationalities, and ethnic groups not our own. Looking back, however, we need to recognize that the soldiers and Marines, who tended to be very young and who were thrown into dangerous battle with the real possibility of being killed or grievously wounded, needed to vent. They needed an outlet for the pent-up stress, fear, and anger they felt in their extremely dangerous situation. It was natural to aim their hostility toward the enemy, who were, after all, trying to kill them. Name-calling and employing demeaning and derisive descriptors for the enemy were ways of coping and of reassuring themselves that they might well prevail. To call the opponents by insulting names is to diminish and dehumanize them and, thus, perhaps to feel superior and more in control in chaotic scenes of killing and destruction.

We cannot know how all the servicemen felt toward the enemy, and there were assuredly those who would naturally feel contempt for the members of another race and who probably would have used the pejorative terms when referring to them even outside the environment of war. But these terms for the enemy were used, as well, by those who harbored no prejudice toward members of other racial groups and who stopped using these terms once their part in the war had ended. Al Martinez, specifically, was a humane, compassionate, big-hearted person who responded positively to all those he met, no matter their ethnic or racial background. The evidence for this lies in his writings, especially the columns he published for more than twenty years in the *Los Angeles Times*.

From the time Al was a young man, serving in Korea, his letters also show his humanity toward Koreans. In several letters, he writes of the adults and the children he encounters, noting with great compassion the suffering they are experiencing because of the tragic effects of the war. Noting the exuberance of his buddies about a devastating rout of the enemy, in a letter dated February 15, 1952, he writes, "I just keep thinking that those poor devils, Chinese or whatever they are, are dying up there and it doesn't make me feel good no matter whose side they're on. I can't be happy because I haven't been indoctrinated enough to the point where I can forget that they are human beings."

It is true that Al also writes with some degree of disgust about the filth of Korea and of how dirty the population was. However, as with the use of pejorative names for the people, the denigration of the people and country was a way servicemen could try to deal with the misery, fear, and danger that surrounded them. Moreover, Al's descriptions of the dirt, filth and primitive conditions he saw in Korea usually tended to carry with them a sense of his indignation that any people should have to experience those conditions.

As we look back at the behavior and words of those called to serve on the front lines, we need to cast our eyes with a spirit of tolerance toward the servicemen and the dire situations in which they found themselves. In doing so, perhaps we can look with understanding and empathy at words and attitudes that today we find to be appalling. It is wrong to think of, and refer to, people in other groups pejoratively, but we need to look at past events with consideration, not to excuse inappropriate behavior but to understand the forces behind that behavior.

In order not to sanitize or soften Al's letters, and to ensure that his exact words appear in the published letters, I have elected not to use substitute terms but to reproduce Al's strong language, including pejorative words, even though such usage makes us uncomfortable today. It is our responsibility to look at the past accurately and dispassionately, without attempting to deny or rewrite the facts and events of history.

Al Martinez and Ethnicity in the Marines

In the early 1950s, when Al Martinez served on active duty in the Marines, racism was a significant factor in American life and in the military, directed primarily at African Americans. In 1941, President Franklin Roosevelt signed an executive order prohibiting discrimination as it established the Fair Employment Practice Committee, but the military branches simply continued their racist practices. A year later, Roosevelt met with civil rights leaders who demanded full integration, but he failed to follow up with enforcement. In 1948, President Truman signed an executive order that called for the desegregation of the military. These efforts were intended largely to benefit African Americans, but Hispanics also suffered from racism. As the Zoot Suit Riots in the summer of 1943 show, white Americans were capable of discriminating against Hispanics as well as against African Americans.

When Al entered active duty, it might have been expected that he would experience racism in the Marine Corps. However, if he did encounter any, he did not write about it in his letters. None of the 370 total letters he wrote home contains even a hint that he experienced any racism. In fact, Al notes the significance of the friendships he forms in the Corps. Soon after arriving at boot camp, he writes to Joanne about the nicknames bestowed upon him, a clear sign of acceptance and fitting in: "I have a new nickname out here: Marty. One D.I. calls me Martinez, the other Martinee, and the fellows Marty. I'm gaining quite a collection of pseudonyms, among other things" (letter of October 23, 1950). Later, after he has been plucked from the front lines to join the PIO, he writes again of the friendships he has with the fellows: "When I told the men of Fox Co. goodbye & good luck—Jenkins, Nunn, the lieut.—and came off the line I felt happy & sad in one emotional tension. I'm not fool enough to be sad to leave the assault front, even though at one time I felt differently. But it wasn't the way I wanted combat to end for me. When I came off the lines I wanted all my buddies, all the fighting men in Korea to come with me. Jenkins, Nunn & all the old men left in the squad & myself were tied together by life & death. Jenk & I especially. We felt as long as one of us was alive & unwounded, we'd both be. And when one got it, we both would. We kept each other alive & safe, sharing the same happinesses [sic] and fears, living for the day when we'd have to fight no longer. Now, the bond is broken, and my wish has come true, my prayers are answered. But I don't feel right about it. There's a lot of good men left up there on the hill, and I don't want to see any of them hurt. We formed comradeships that was [sic] more than the shallow stateside variety; these were deep, sincere, where one hinged his life on their value & was willing to give it to maintain that value" (letter of October 15, 1951).

Al and his buddies gave one another comradeship and devotion, with no apparent thought of ethnicity or race but with total commitment to the special friendship that only going to war together can bring.

Introduction:
A Hole in History Three Years Wide*

> These things [i.e., his combat experiences] are real, so real and so moving that it takes the subtlest type of writing to portray them to make them sound real and not made up, I don't know if I'm the man for that job right now or not. But I know damn well I'm going to try and get that down until I am the man who can tell that story. I'm going to make it sound so real—the soft toughness of men looking after one another, the gruff comfort one gives a wounded Marine—that those who read it are going to live through 12 months of Korea right with me. (letter of February 17, 1952)

The war that broke out between North and South Korea in 1950 was in many respects simply a continuation of battles and hostilities that had most recently seen Japan occupy the Korean Peninsula. Invasions by hostile countries had long brutalized the Korean population, belying the nation's original name, Chosun, meaning the Land of the Morning Calm. This time, the conflict pitted North Korea, backed by the Soviet Union, against South Korea, aided by the United States and its UN allies.

When North Korean troops attacked South Korean forces in June 1950, to launch active hostilities between the two, the United States scrambled to assemble enough military power, in both manpower and materiel, to help South Korea defend itself. Part of this mobilization involved calling up reserves, including the Marine reserve unit in which Al Martinez served.

The letters in this volume form a narrative arc, documenting three phases of Al's military life: they are written from boot camp, from the battle front in Korea, and from the vantage point of a regimental writer and combat correspondent in the war zone. All the letters are written to Al's bride Joanne. They had been married for just over a year when Al was called up from the Marine Corps reserves to active duty, anticipating that he might be dispatched to Korea.

Al's letters treat every aspect of a Marine's daily life, from the exhaustion of boot camp, to the brutality of the war zone, to the exultation of being relieved from front-line duty. The terror of battle, the stressful boredom of long hours

---

*"A Hole in History …": Al Martinez, "All the Lonely People," Manuscript (MZ 4) in Martinez Papers, Box 1, The Huntington Library (May 21, 1996).

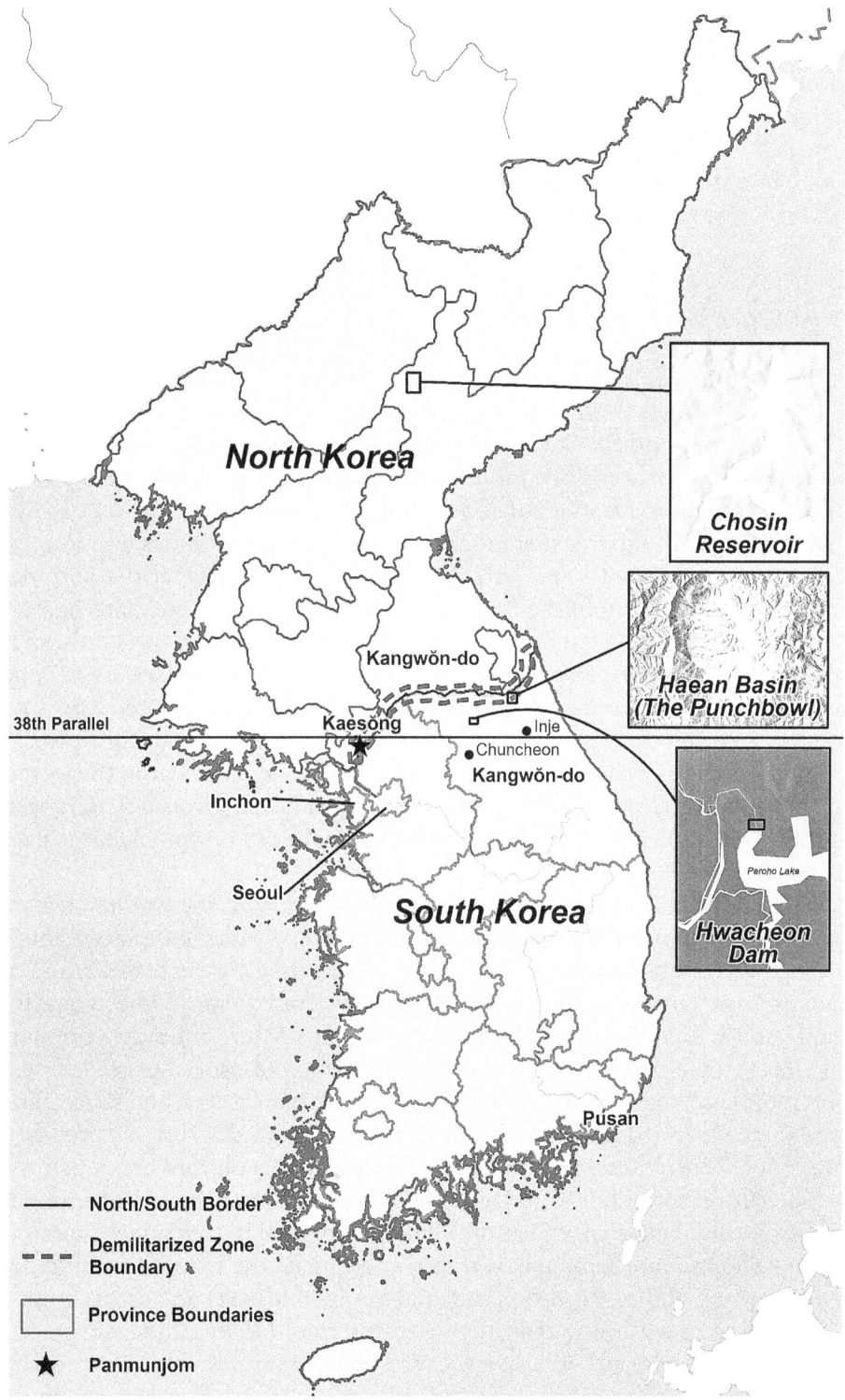

Map of Korea created by Nathan Lu, Pitzer College, and Fellow, Robert Redford Conservancy, 2023.

waiting in a foxhole, the grief for fellow Marines lost in battle, the love and lustful longing Al feels for Joanne, the simple joys of joking and teasing his buddies, the satisfaction of complaining about officers, the sharing of news from home, the heaping of scorn on the endlessly unproductive peace talks, the unexpected beauty of a moonlit night—these subjects and more fill Al's letters and afford the reader a full look into the heart and soul of a young man caught up in a world conflict over which he has no control and whose capricious events threaten his very existence.

The Korean War (1950–1953)

The Korean War was the first military conflict of the Cold War, and it carries a significance at odds with its relative obscurity in people's historical memories. The United States and the Soviet Union, the two world superpowers, faced off in opposition over the spread of communism. Japan took control of Korea following the Russo-Japanese War and ruled over it until the end of World War II. When the war ended with Japan's surrender in 1945, the United States and the Soviet Union gained control of Korea, dividing the land arbitrarily at the 38th parallel. The Soviet Union established a communist regime in the northern half of the nation, and the United States set up a military government in the southern half. War between the two broke out on June 25, 1950, when the North Korean People's Army invaded South Korea. While the Soviet Union and the United States never fought one another directly, their support of the two Koreas made for a proxy war between the superpowers. The Korean War was, in fact, not a war in the formal or official sense. The United States never declared war, and it was officially termed a "conflict" or "police action," although for the sake of convenience it is usually referred to as the Korean War.

When Al Martinez arrived in Korea on April 2, 1951, the war had been raging for more than nine months. As he and his fellow Marine replacements disembarked in Pusan, two legendary conflicts had already occurred. The Battle of Inchon began on September 15, 1950, and involved an amphibious landing at Inchon harbor. The plan, urged by General Douglas MacArthur, the commander of all UN forces, against all odds and opposed by his advisors, succeeded despite the extreme challenges of the harbor, landscape, fortifications, and tides. The UN troops then advanced on Seoul and reclaimed it from the North Koreans. The Battle of the Chosin Reservoir, in the northeastern part of the Korean peninsula, took place from November 27 to December 13, 1950. The Chinese had entered the war, and a brutal battle ensued at the Chosin, in which the extremely harsh winter plunged temperatures well below zero and caused the troops to endure frostbite, frozen food and medical supplies, and inoperable arms and armaments. The UN forces had to withdraw after they were surrounded by Chinese troops. The withdrawal, or "breakout," was spearheaded by the Marines, who, along with elements of the Army, fought fiercely and valiantly to protect the troops in withdrawal, saving many lives. These forces, revered for their bravery in the face of overwhelming odds, became known as "the Chosin Few."

By about July 1951, the war lapsed into a stalemate in which the front lines remained largely stationary while the two armies guarded their terrain and sent out patrols to scout for possible enemy incursions. Bloody campaigns continued, including the Battle of the Punchbowl and the Battle of Heartbreak Ridge. The troops were in just as much peril as they had been in the first year of the war, but little territory changed hands and the troops felt the futility of their situation. Al and his fellow troops experienced the danger and misery of the front lines as they were stuck in foxholes on one line of defense after another and as they tramped with trepidation on seemingly endless patrols to no visible purpose. They saw and lived these woes and failures, summed up by Al, who enumerated the inadequate armaments and other materiel, insufficient manpower, inept military leadership, poor strategy, and lack of proper commitment, concluding, "So, in the long run the U.S. is loosing [sic] a battle. Why? Because it is a battle which can never be won the way it goes. We have com[m]itted our troops in Korea & can't find an honourable [sic] [way] out. We are expending our magnificent strength on a peninsula!" (letter of October 13, 1951).

Peace talks took place throughout the war, at Kaesong and Panmunjom, but they were endlessly unproductive and, inevitably, they became the butt of bitter jokes among the servicemen. A peace treaty was never signed. Instead, on July 27, 1953, an armistice was signed, followed by the establishment of a Demilitarized Zone (DMZ) between North and South Korea, roughly along the 38th parallel.

The Korean War grew out of the conclusion of the Second World War, and, as a battleground about the spread of communism, it served as a precursor to the war in Vietnam. Its inconclusive ending also presaged Vietnam. Both wars contrasted dramatically with the decisive conclusion of the world war. As James Brady observed, "Because it began along an artificial frontier dividing a single nation effectively into Soviet and American zones, ... Korea might be thought of as the last campaign of World War II; because of the vague way it ended in 1953, as the opening battle for Vietnam."*

The Korean conflict occupied a gray area between the two wars in another way, as well. Situated in time between them, the Korean War bore elements of both. World War II inspired a fair degree of unity, patriotism, and commitment to a common cause among Americans, and this has only increased in our collective memory. Elizabeth Samet has pointed out the fallacy of looking too blindly at the past war, noting that "the goodness, idealism, and unanimity we today reflexively associate with World War II were not as readily apparent to Americans at the time."† But Americans by and large entered the war effort with a feeling of patriotism and loyalty. The war in Vietnam stood at the opposite end of the spectrum, engendering discord, protests, and intractable polarization within the American populace. With the Korean War, as in Vietnam later, it was difficult for Americans to see the purpose or virtue of engaging in battle on foreign soil when

---

*James Brady, *The Coldest War: A Memoir of Korea* (New York: Thomas Dunne, St. Martin's Griffin, 1990), 1.
 †Elizabeth D. Samet, *Looking for the Good War: American Amnesia and the Violent Pursuit of Happiness* (New York: Farrar, Straus and Giroux, 2021), 4.

there were no clear-cut issues and no obvious clash of good vs. evil. In a world newly mired in a cold war, it was hard to perceive the point of embarking on a war in distant lands. For the Korean conflict, many Americans suffered from disillusionment, disgust, war fatigue, cynicism, a general sense that war was a terrible waste of human life, and a deep reluctance to embark on another conflagration coming so soon on the heels of the world war. Al Martinez sums this up in his letter of November 5, 1950: "The will to fight in the Marine Corps is not as it once was. We are not the old breed, the troops of regulars who make war a profession. We are the reserves, the college kids and the old men, the dreamers and the builders—not the fighters. We don't want war; we don't want to die." Again, in his letter of December 5, 1951, he writes, "Somebody's … got to understand why a man is no longer so willing to die for a 4th of July speech."

Al Martinez—Early Years and Life in Korea

A child of Oakland, Al Martinez (1929–2015) grew up in hardship, in a family bound by poverty. He attended San Francisco State College for three years, editing and writing for the school paper, the *Golden Gater*. On July 30, 1949, Al married fellow student Joanne Cinelli. At San Francisco State, he served in the Marine reserves before being called up as a rifleman when the Korean conflict broke out in 1950. He traveled to Camp Pendleton, not knowing what his fate would be but suspecting that he might be sent to fight in Korea.

Al Martinez arrived in Korea on April 2, 1951, so he did not participate in the Inchon landing (he arrived at the Marine induction center on September 22, 1950, seven days after the Inchon landing) or in the battle and withdrawal from the Chosin Reservoir. After battling at Inchon and Chosin, the 7th Regiment, to which Al was assigned, participated in the Punchbowl region of east-central Korea and along the western front. The troops were seldom informed where they were being deployed, and Al and his buddies would simply be ordered to pack up and move, then dig in again. They came under fire, went on patrol, and guarded the line, but they usually had no idea precisely where they were. During his months on the front lines, Al participated in the battles of the Punchbowl, with its conflicts on Bloody Ridge and Heartbreak Ridge. Whether on patrol or fighting from a foxhole, he was involved in brutal combat, experiencing and witnessing all the savagery and death that war can bring.

For about six months (April to October 1951), Al was assigned to the infantry on the front lines with the Marine 1st Division (Fox Company, 2nd Battalion, 7th Regiment, or, in military shorthand, Fox 2/7). Al was then transferred to the regimental Public Information Office (PIO) where he served for about six months (October 1951 to April 1952). He functioned as a combat correspondent and he wrote, edited and printed the regimental newsletter, the *Ridgerunner*.

Beginning with boot camp and continuing throughout his year in Korea, Al wrote in his letters about every aspect of Marine Corps life. During his training at Camp Pendleton, he wrote about the waste, boredom, endless drills, and stupidity of many of the orders given, as well as the often pointless and irrational toughness of the drill instructors. But with his writer's insight into human behavior, he also saw the reason and logic even in the apparently cruel actions of his superiors. Moreover, he felt a deep pride in being a Marine and internalized the special esprit that characterized the Marine Corps. In Korea, Al wrote of the terror, danger, fatigue, boredom, and humor of life at the front.

Al wrote of the unique camaraderie that comrades in arms develop. Their buddies held a particular place for soldiers and Marines, and this was unlike any friendship outside of war. Even as he knew that he would almost certainly never see his Marine buddies again once their war was over, nonetheless he felt this special kinship and knew that nothing could ever equal or replace it. This held true even when he knew almost nothing about some of his buddies, as will be evident in some of his letters in this volume.

Beyond life in the military and at the front, Al wrote of matters great and small. A frequent topic was, of course, his love for Joanne and how much he missed her. Once their daughter Cinthia was born, Al mentioned her often as he savored photographs of her, imagined what she might be doing, and envisioned what her future could be. He replied to Joanne's accounts of their friends and family at home and would remark that, having received no letter that day, he had nothing to write about since he couldn't respond to her notes. (Wordsmith that he was, he nonetheless always managed to find fuel for his long letters.)

The Subjects of Al's Letters

The Importance of Memory

Al's letters carry the theme of memory and the need to remember the war, its effects and the people mired in it. He wrote of his desire to burn the war and his experiences into his mind so he would never forget, and he wanted to have his letters published so that all who read them would remember, to recognize the sacrifices made, to honor the fallen, and to try to ensure that nations would never go to war again. In his later essays and columns, as in his letters, Al wrote about the war and about the urgent need to remember, for the sake of humanity.

Korean War

For Al and his buddies, the conflict in Korea at its most basic was merely the setting in which they performed their required duty. Few of them would have chosen to fight or to be absent from home for so long, and, if asked, few of them would have agreed that battling communism was an important priority. However, they were placed in the situation and had to perform their assigned jobs.

Al self-censored his letters to Joanne, softening his battle stories and omitting some information in an effort to spare her the worst of the details so she would not worry more than necessary. His letters nonetheless include plenty of vivid accounts of his battle experiences. In one instance, he mistakenly mailed her a letter intended for one of his college friends and, when he learned this, he assured her that he had overstated the brutality and danger in order to impress the friend. How much Joanne believed this is open to speculation, but it seems likely that she could easily see through Al's effort to alleviate her worries.

As a young, budding professional writer, Al saw the opportunity that was presented to him, and he set out to observe, participate in, and capture as much of the action and atmosphere as he could, both in his letters home to Joanne and in the diary he kept, sending excerpts to her when he could. He asked Joanne to save all his letters and he intended to publish them after he returned home. He knew that his observations and experiences would record and bear witness to significant events on the world stage, and he felt and hoped that he would be a writer who could express and interpret these events for those who lived through them and for those who came after. As he wrote to Joanne on December 5, 1951 (not included in this book): "There'll be more [stories] coming. The story of a war as I've seen it when I carried an M-1 over the hills. A story about guys like Pvt. Joe Citera, like the Stricklands, like Pete Mamaril, like so many who have died or been hurt in mind and body because they were committed to the protection of democracy. Somehow to me, the fact of their death isn't the important thing. It's how they died, the circumstances which led to their death, what they thought, why they died, how their buddies felt, what they encompassed. Somebody's got to understand why this war in Korea (when a man spends nine months here) is far worse than all of World War II."

Peace Talks

Not surprisingly, the ongoing peace talks held first in Kaesong and later in Panmunjom commanded the attention of the servicemen in Korea. Rumors, which were as endless as the talks themselves, swirled among the soldiers and Marines, lifting or depressing their spirits repeatedly as the months dragged on and as the men were still stuck in the war zone. Al did his best not to let himself be whipsawed between hope and despair as the rumors chased each other among the troops, but it was tough when, like his buddies, Al just wanted to hear of the end of hostilities so he could go home. Even as he listened to rumors, Al was able to capture the essence of the peace talks in all their tragic but ironic humor, as in this letter to Joanne, dated November 4, 1951 (not included in this book): "And when they finally decide on a peace agreement to end the Korean war, they will probably spend 4 months dickering about what kind of ink to use to sign it with—red or blue. Naturally, the Chinese will want red. So they will break off the meeting while the poor infantry takes it up the shaft, until two months later. Then the Chinese will slyly suggest that they are willing to accept feelers to think about talking about a plan which will make them think about talking about a meeting to draw up plans for another meeting, so on and so forth. Then in a blaze of pomp, the two sides will meet again for another four months until they get deadlocked again for four months, then the whole damn thing starts in again. By that time I will either take out citizenship papers in Korea or expect my daughter to replace me over here in a new push-button war."

Family and Friends

Al relied on Joanne's letters from home to provide him with people and events he could comment on, so his letters are replete with references to people who cannot now be identified. Joanne could recall a few of these individuals, but most remain anonymous. Joanne herself, and later, Cinthia, were very frequent topics for Al, and he reiterated his love for Joanne, even as he teased her and replied to the stories of her and Cinthia's daily lives. He made valiant efforts to sustain something of a conversation with her via the letters, but it was difficult due to the generally long lag-time in their correspondence reaching one another and given the vagaries of mail pickup and delivery in a war zone.

State of the World

"It's a new year, darling, a fine, clean, new year despite all. We have much to look ahead to and nothing can swerve our determination in planning. When our job is done here, and the prospect of a better life for our children is ahead, then we can die and not regret it. But until then, we have a definite purpose in life. Had the generations before us done a better job, then we could have spent our life time [sic] really living an enjoyable life. But as it stands, we have to correct their mistakes. And though we have to fret a little, when you stop to think that it may keep our pretty little Cinthy happy in years to come, it's worth the effort" (letter of December 25, 1951).

Al was essentially an optimist and, despite moments of depression about the war and the world at large, he held on to his hope for a better world. His and Joanne's daughter Cinthia was a significant source for his optimism. But he also had larger hopes that a better world could be crafted, despite the flawed, venal politicians, if humanity could find a way to work for the betterment of everyone. Seeing and experiencing some of the worst that humans could inflict upon themselves when warring against the "other," he held onto hope that humanity would learn to go forward with greater wisdom, tolerance, and human empathy.

Drawings

Notably, Al's letters are set apart from other published war letters by the presence of his pen-and-ink drawings, some of which are included in this volume. Possessed of a certain native ability, he drew himself, his buddies, and scenes of military and Korean life. Most of the drawings are humorous, especially the self-portraits. Al grew a mustache in Korea (although he spelled the word every way possible except correctly), and several drawings feature his new crop of upper-lip fuzz, which he hopes Joanne will like. Other drawings poke fun at the military brass; at the replacements who arrive, green and untried on the field of battle; and at the vagaries of life in battle-worn Korea.

Humor

Al derived much relief from his innate sense of humor that seemingly no hardship or tragedy could stop for very long. The humor he found in his situation and with his buddies made its way into his letters home, along with the ongoing personal jokes that he shared with Joanne. An example of the latter is Al's occasional invocation of a phrase that must have been a slip of the tongue during their courting days—referring to her "ruby teeth and pearly white lips." Referring to another shared joke from their life of enforced economies, Al occasionally teased Joanne by mentioning a diet of "rice, noodles and beans." One of the best examples of Al's creation of humor from the misery of war is his poem "The Fly," one of whose verses reads:

> At work or play, at meal or sleep
> No matter what pleas I beseach [sic]
> They flit and land then buzz away
> Always, bastards, out of reach.

Al frequently remarks to Joanne that their senses of fun and humor will carry them through the lean or tough times, and this was assuredly an accurate assessment. As Al remarked to me, he continued to have nightmares from the war even into his 80s, so his ability to derive humor from the battle environment demonstrates a remarkable resilience.

The War and His Writing

Even as he saw the humor in many of his everyday situations, Al never lost sight of the tragedy of war, and he knew not only that he wanted to write this story but also that he would be able to write it well and effectively. He could tell that he was growing as a writer, just as he was maturing as a young man: "I'm coming of age as a writer, Joanne. My humor is real, my diction colorful or serious without being elaborate or frilly. I've experienced life, and now for the first time I'm telling a story which every violent sense in my body has reacted to. It was as though I just closed my eyes & remembered—not 'imagined'—and my pen acted accordingly" (letter of August 20, 1951).

Al felt that his writing ability would enable him to capture what he saw and did in Korea. His passion about war's tragedy led to his belief that war must never be undertaken again: "If there ever was a purpose in a man writing, besides love of it, I have it. I want to open the sleepy eyes of America to war at its brutalist [sic] that patriotism & a false nationalism has drugged. I can't leave out the war humor or the beauty of courage & self sacrifice I've seen, either. But they'll see as plainly as I have what a direct mortar hit does to a man & why the Marines called one hill Hamburger hill; and what it feels like to loose [sic] all human inhibitions & cry like a baby from fear; what it's like to meet the morning light with a headache because you've been staring into the blackness all nite. Sure, they'll laugh with some of the characters just as I have. But if I'm at all the writer I claim to be, they'll be dumbfounded & sick when the guy they laughed with is lying screaming & writhing with a face torn away. Usually, I'm a 'pretty' writer painting a happy-ending picture. But it's neccessary [*sic*] now to be realistic, sometimes brutal, so Cinthy will have a future & so our future sons will have something to look forward to. With the help of God & more effort than I've ever put forth before I hope I can be indirectly responsible at least for the prevelance [*sic*] of discretion at least in the absence of reason" (letter of June 18, 1951).

The letters in this volume constitute Al Martinez's cry to the peoples of the world to heed the imperative and cease going to war.

One

Come 4 A.M.—Reveille!*

> The following quotes is [sic] my inauguration into the USMC: "You're going to have a rough time here you S__T birds!" "You're a f__ken Marine now and you'll take a lot of f__ken S__T! I want no grab assing, understand? Understand?! Answer, goddamnit!" (Here a feeble "yes sir?") (letter of September 23, 1950)

> I saw a pretty sight tonite. Just before chow we were standing at ease & our D.I. called us to attention & faced us to the flag. The bugler sounded "retreat" and the flag came down. As far as the eye could see men were at attention, some saluting. Cars were stopped on the streets, doors open[,] men facing to the flag. The sun set behind it. It was really pretty. Not a person moved. It was quiet. (letter of September 28, 1950)

Along with many young men who were summoned to serve in their country's military engagement in Korea, Al was suddenly wrested from home and dispatched to basic training. In the first letter he wrote to Joanne, aboard the train headed from San Francisco to San Diego and Marine boot camp, he strikes successive tones of anticipation, trepidation and introspection and a fair amount of bravado. These and more emotions would be his companions throughout the rigors of his training for the infantry. As a peaceable young man given to writing stories of basic humanity, Al found the Marine Corps in many ways an alien environment. However, he prevailed, adjusted to the life and even excelled in many of the classes and drills that taught him and his buddies everything from Marine Corps history and traditions to marching, map reading, shooting, weapon assembling, and more.

Al had conflicting reactions to the Marines. He was appalled by the martinets among the officers and drill instructors, with their petty imposition of punishment and their occasional cruelty. Yet he appreciated the discipline they instilled in the boots and recognized that he was growing increasingly confident as a result. He believed that war was wrong, that it was a terrible waste of young life to send men whose lives were just beginning halfway around the world to fight and possibly perish in battle, yet he was increasingly proud of serving in the Marine Corps. He could grouse just as loudly as any of his fellow boots when they

---

*"Come 4 a.m. …": Letter of September 23, 1950.

felt they were treated unfairly or meanly, but he was usually able to see the other side of the matter.

The depths of Al's perceptions set him apart from many of his comrades, enabling him to see beneath the surface of issues and situations in the Corps and to understand the motivations and points of view of others even when they behaved in upsetting or seemingly irrational ways. Mention has been made of the Korean War's transitional place roughly midway between World War II, exemplified by the patriotic loyalty of the American people, and the Vietnam War, notable for the troubled, widespread opposition that bedeviled the American population. Al's Marine Corps training experience revealed the Korean War's position on the edge between the world war and Vietnam. Al's fellow boots, on the one hand, carried the flag for their patriotic duty and, on the other, resisted the call to arms. In his letters, Al describes recruits going AWOL, sometimes in significant numbers, and he writes about some who suffered psychological breakdowns in the face of intense training with firearms. In all such accounts, Al displays deep perception of the people involved, both trainees and drill instructors, and he recognizes the forces being exerted upon them. Thus, he writes not so much in judgment as in empathy.

◆ ◆ ◆

en route to San Diego
9/22/50

My darling—

The Marine Corps doesn't have me yet, but they're only about 8 hours away from it. We're just outside of San Luis Obispo now; the sun is warm on the windows. Don* and I just finished lunch of Club Sandwiches and milk.

The riding is kind of rough now, so I suppose this letter will look like hell. But, it's readable, and that's what counts. However, the trip has been fairly nice up to now; but I can't say I really enjoy it. I could, perhaps, were the nose of the train pointing the other way, but under the circumstances … oh well.

There were so many things I wanted to say to you at the depot. But the words died in my throat and instead I just wanted to cry. I suppose you could tell that very easily. The things I wanted to say to you, darling, were some of the things I tried to say when I came home from Treasure Island†; you remember when I was talking about the scared little kids in levis, bright sport shirts, long hair, etc., and how old I felt beside them?

Looking at those kids at T.I. (while sitting for 4 hours) I began weighing their value with the magnitude of the job assigned them: that of bearing the colors of the modern crusaders and marching across a country unknown. I thought about a lot of things at T.I.: I thought about the kids who would live and who would die to save the values in which they believed. I thought of them on the

---

*Probably Don Weiland.
†Treasure Island is an island in the San Francisco Bay. A naval station operated there from 1942 to 1997, serving as a processing center for Navy personnel.

fields of Korea and in the mountains of China; in the ice of Russia and the heat of the South Pacific. I tried hard to visualize them killing a man and I couldn't. And the very realization of that fact makes it all the harder to conceive how Americans could be the greatest country of fighting men in the world. But after watching those kids at T.I.—well, I knew. They have the added impetus of fighting for something in which they believe; they have something to protect and return to. They are not professional soldiers, they are civilians. War is not their game, for they hate it.

Those were some of the things I wanted to tell you at the depot and didn't. Those, and also that my days with you have been the happiest in my life. We've lived a full married life in 14 months; the tears and the happiness, the hopes and the fears—and I am better for them. The next few years to come—uncertain as they are—will pass quickly, and you and I can get started again. Oh, sure, I'll be a little different: a little more mature, older, more intent. But mine is a spirit that nothing can break, because I have the faculty of laughing the hardest when I am feeling the wors[t]. I can bury my worries in the recesses of my mind and make the most of what I have. No, darling, nothing can break the spirit of a writer, because writers see all these things in their minds and their imaginations.

So you see, fadoodle-eee-hop, you have nothing to worry about. Just keep your chin up, behave yourself (at the table, of kerse), and don't fret.

Martinez is in the Marine Corps, and Heaven help the Russians! Hold back the tears, baby, I'll be back.

> I love you with
> All my heart & soul—
> And will so forever:
> I love you.... Al

P.S. I'll write as soon as I can. By the way—did you find out what "BUNG" is? I love you, darling!
Love & xxxxxx[USMC insignia] (How'd that get there?)
   Xxx's, Al
[stick figure] Me

MZ 461

> Sept. 23, 1950
> San Diego

Dearest Joanne (my wife)

Well, darling, we're here* and this is how it happened. Last nite we walked up to the main gate about midnight, met a hard-faced PFC and began marching across a wide field. In the middle of the field he stopped us. The following quotes is [sic] my inauguration into the USMC:

"You're going to have a rough time here you S__T birds!" "You're a f__ken

---

*Al has arrived at the Marine Recruit Depot in San Diego, where he will remain until boot camp.

Marine now and you'll take a lot of f__ken S__T! I want no grab assing, understand? Understand?! Answer, goddamnit!" (Here a feeble 'yes sir?')

He then proceeded to tell us what a bunch of f__ken S__T holes we were for joining the f__ken Corps. He told us to forget everything, our names, our homes, our civilian backgrounds! "You're Marines!" he screamed! "And you'll be good ones or you'll stop a bullet!"

Then he said a strange thing: "I don't know why some grab-assing b___tard had to start this f__ken war for! Just so they could sell a few million dollars worth of goods I guess!" His voice almost broke. "I know some of you have wives & kids, and it's tough! It doesn't make a god__mn bit of difference to me being here. I don't have a f__ken thing!"

It was odd the way he spoke, hard & bitter, with command and even some emotion. I'd say he was 23 years old, thin & wiry, but with a face made square and hard by the Marine Corps. I thought he wanted to tell us to keep our chins up, but he was afraid. It was obvious he was nervous. The fellow struck me as odd. A very odd person.

Anyhow, we got to sleep (on the floor) at 2 A.M. after having a p[o]ncho & 2 sheets thrown in our faces. The floor was hard, but it wasn't too bad—we weren't there long enough to mind it. Come 4 A.M.—Reville! [sic] All out! Hit the deck you f__ken S__Y birds! The Marine vocabulary is very limited, I guess you notice!

At 4 A.M. they abused us more. We had to dump our suitcases on the deck and they proceeded to have us throw-away [sic]: all glass objects & liquids (my hair oil, shaving cream); all pills (my aspirins); all pictures of nude women (that sweet little drawing of yours); all reading matter (my Golden Gater* & some comic books)—and that's all there was to it; oh yes,—and all food!

Then we sat & they swore at us. Then we ran to fall in, then we waited. Then we walked quickly to the mess hall & waited more. Then we took our places and—and guess what—waited! For breakfast we had stew, toast[,] coffee & an apple. For lunch, roast beef, salad, mash potatoes, water, bread, jelly, peas. It was good "chow-down" as these f__ken s__t birds would say.

Well, that's all for now. I still don't know the address, but will write as soon as I get it. I love you and miss you so much—so very much. I have your picture to keep me going, and that's all.

> I love you with all
> my heart, soul & life!
> your f__ken s__t bird,
>   Al

xxxxxx times xxxx for you
I love you   Al

MZ 462

---

*The *Golden Gater* (also known as the *Gater*) was the campus newspaper at San Francisco State College. Al wrote for and edited the paper.

24 Sept 50 (Sun.)
San Diego

Dearest Joanne—

It's Sunday, and I still am not attached to any platoon, company, etc. So I have no return address. There are recruits coming in every hour, and the place is one of confusion and crowdedness. Every once in awhile [*sic*] the D.I. (drill instructor) forgets us and wants to know what the hell we're doing where he told us to be or where the hell we're going when he told us to go. That's the Marine Corps.

Last night we were assigned bunks, so I had a good night's sleep. You know that the clocks were turned back last nite, so everyone theoretically had an extra hour's sleep. Us? The Marine Corps got around that by simply getting us up an hour earlier! God bless them.

After chow this morning, we found an angel! A P.F.C. called us out to march to the Post Theater—clean up detail, it was, which consists of picking up all the crap. Well, this P.F.C. (I'll call him God) gave us hell all the way over. When we got there he said "smoking lamp lit."* No one moved. "Go ahead, fellows," he smiled, "smoke." There was a flurry of cigarette getting and I had my first cigarette in about 36 hours! Then he let us buy Sunday papers! As if wonders would never cease, he then proceeded to read us the football and baseball scores! He was talking and laughing with the guys, asking them the states they were from, etc. He let us smoke while we picked up papers around the Post Theater. The first good guy we have seen here, everyone agrees: The name "God" is justifiable.

Just a little while ago (in the barracks here) a three-star general walked in accompanied by a D.I. The call to attention snapped the air and everyone rolled of[f] their bunks (where they weren't supposed to be, including me) to the floor. The general laughed and said to relax. Funny, but those damn PFC D.I,'s make you jump, and the officers tell you to relax. Goddamn funny Marine business!

Last nite in the head, a boot who's been here about two weeks was asking me about the war. I told him my opinion. He (and Walter Winchell)† are under the impression that the Reserves would be released by Easter. I gave him my opinion; I told him about the Manchurian Reds; about the Commies; about the A-bomb. I guess I disillusioned him a great deal, because he tried to talk me into going AWOL with him. I was tempted, but desisted when thinking of me in front of the firing squad.

I brought up the above example as a way of pointing out the wide-spread distaste here at boot camp. The men don't want to fight; they don't want to be here; they dislike the Marine Corps and everything about it. It may be just the boot camp indoctrination of hate; or maybe just the fear of it all, I don't know. The morale is low, the men are beaten. I suppose it's all a part of the master plan.

Tomorrow we take a thorough physical. The men are all con[n]iving ways to get rejected. The fellow on the bunk next to me has a damn good reason! Just

---

*Marines and other military personnel could not smoke unless granted permission by someone of a more senior rank. The phrase used was "the smoking lamp is lit."
†Walter Winchell (1897–1972) was a well-known American newspaperman and radio figure.

before he came to camp he had an attack of ap[p]endoctomy. They didn't operate, because it went away. Lately he's been complaining of pains in his side and a dull soreness. Last nite he vomitted [*sic*] blood & there was blood in his stool. I've tried to get the guy to go to sickbay or to tell someone about it, but he refuses. If his ap[p]endi[x] bust, there'll be one less guy for me to talk to you about.

While taking a shower last nite, one of the fellows was whistling. A D.I. caught him and he marched for 3 hours after taps. Another Texan pop-off gave a D.I. some guff. He marched after taps. Of all the guys in this barracks (about 30) there are about 4 wise-acres. Comes the day of reckoning, and these characters will be marching and drilling till they drop. Me? I keep my mouth shut and my eyes and ears open!

The guys in this barrack are from all parts of the U.S. About 25 out of the 30 have the long Southern drawl, and once in awhile [*sic*] I find myself saying y'all. This has got to stop. There are kids here who couldn't be more than 16 years old. Some of them, I know, are only 16. They're the quiet one[s] with wide eyes, who are scared and out of place; when we talk about our wives, they stand by themselves. They're inexperienced, and have nothing to tell about; guys like me just make up things as they go along. I've talked to some of the fellows (the young ones) and tried to draw them in with some success. So have some of the other older guys. They'll fall in after a while.

Yes, honey, this is really an odd place. The fellows (even the ones who have been her[e] 7 weeks) are all friendly, misery loving company. The D.I.'s hate everyone, except for God. There are all sizes and shapes of men in this potpourri of protoplasm. And among these beardless, bearded old and young fellows, march I. It is, if nothing else, an adventure in human experience and the study of man and his uncertainty, his fear.

I'll keep you up on all the dope. Until then—I love you, darling. Keep loving me always ...

I love you—Al

P.S. I get my hair <u>shaved</u> <u>off</u> tomorrow; oh, my curly hair! And I think boot camp is 8 weeks. I love you, darling; hope to see you as soon as possible!—Al

The return ad[d]ress isn't right; I'll send you my right one as soon as I get it; hold your letters till then.

I love you
Al

MZ 464

25 Sept. 50 (Monday)
San Diego

Dearest Joanne—

It's about 0730 (7:30 a.m.) now and so far I have shaved, eaten, swabbed the barracks, swabbed the D.I.'s office and fixed my bunk in the inimitable Marine Corps fashion. Took me two days to learn how to do it.

Last nite the D.I. found someone lying on his bunk before he was supposed to; all hell broke loose. He threw the guy on the floor, threw all his gear all over the deck, threw his mattress down and proceeded to jab the guy in the stomach. Then he ranted and raved, calling us everything under the sun and more.

Right now, darling, it[']s 1:15 p.m. and I have <u>never</u> been more tired in my life! I have been (along with the rest) through a physical—the most strenuous affair I've had yet. Fat guys fail[e]d because of hernia; muscle-bound grunts couldn't see; me? "A perfect specimen!" they say, and little skinny old me rolls on.

The physical started by filling out blanks. Then they handed us a bottle. "Use it!" a medic said! Just like that. One guy was there all morning. Poor bug[g]er's probably still there. Anyhow, we went on to a (ugh) blood test. Remember that last one I took in July, 1949? Well, the same fear came over me this time. Then when they couldn't find the guy's vein in front of me and he was crying with pain, I began to worry. However, everything came out fine there. Next we had shots. There, the fellow in front of me had the needle break in his arm. The medic swore because the solution spilled on his hands. Then he turned to the guy and sarcastically said, "You can pull that out if you want to."

When it came my turn to be shot, the medic was smelling his hands and still swearing. He looked at me, "Smells like Tiajuana [sic] pussy, don't it?" he asked, shoving his hands under my nose. "Yes, sir!" I snapped like a goddamn liar. Of course, actually I didn't know! I've never smelled Tiajuana [sic] pussy!

After that we had a chest x-Ry, a dental examination and a talk with the (ahem) psychiatrist. I have to have two teeth pulled—don't know when. All the psychiatrist asked me was: "Are you healthy, boy? Can you do a good day's work? You've had 3 years of college, boy? Fine! Beat it, boy!" And that sonuva D.I. calls himself a psychiatrist! Ha!

After my talk with Dr. Kildare,* I had to stand in the sun, at attention, stripped to the waist for 2 hours. We all did. Don't ask me why, just another form of D.I. torture.

Then we had a thorough physical and that was all! After chow they let us come to our barracks to sit on the floor and here I am now. I haven't had a cigarette all day today.

But I'm eating good, feeling healthy and missing you like hell. Every night I draw out your picture, look at it, think of all we've done together—then I love you ever so much.

Write soon.

I love you with
all my heart—
Al

P.S. Withdraw me from college, huh, dear? Gee I love you & miss you.

I love you, darling. At night I lie awake about a half-hour just thinking of

---

*Dr. James Kildare was a fictional physician created in the 1930s by Max Brand, a writer whose real name was Frederick Faust. Several motion pictures and television series featuring the character have been made.

you. The Cliff House,* W.A. Balinger's,† our apartment, and everything we know together seems closer when the lights are [out]. Then when taps fill[s] the night air, and the silence settles like a soft cloud on the camp, I want to cry I miss you so much. I reach out to touch you sometimes—and fall asleep with my arm in empty space & my heart full of you.

I love you
Al

MZ 465

25 Sept. 50 (Mon)
San Diego

My darling—

I've been away from home before in my life, and I've been homesick, heartsick and lonely before. I've been at places away from home and left them on impulse without the slightest provocation, simply because I was homesick. There have been many cases where I've done that. But tonight, darling, tonight I'm so lonesome for you and so sick at heart that I have to press my lips together and sit quietly to keep from crying. It's that bad.

A little while ago I was standing in the doorway looking at the frozen sky and at the orange moon and wondering if you could see the same thing and feeling better when realizing that you could. I also looked at the lights of San Diego, and I wished with all my heart that it were San Francisco. And I did something that I haven't done for 10 years, Joanne—I prayed. I prayed to have this whole world mess cleaned up; to have you safe; to be with you. Then I felt a little ashamed because it took fear to bring on prayer.

And it is fear, darling. Fear of the future; a fear so terrible and so gnawing that it fast grows unbearable. Yes, darling, I am just the little boy you've often seen me as. But when it comes right down to it, all men are little boys, and the only thing that keeps them from crying is another fear—convention.

26 Sept. 50
TUESDAY

Good morning, darling. It's about 7 a.m. so I suppose you're just getting up now. Me? I've been up since 5 A.M.—but awake almost all night.

There's an airfield about 1 mile from here and the planes roar about 50 feet over the barracks every 20 minutes; not little planes—flight transports, bombers, 4 motor jobs, etc. Consequenteley [sic] I was awake half the night. That wasn't the only reason, however. I guess you can tell by the first page of this letter that I felt pretty lonely. Well, I still do, goddaamnit!

Daylight, however, makes things look better. It's the night that <u>really</u> gets me.

---

*Cliff House is a building on the cliffs north of Ocean Beach, San Francisco. It is part of the Golden Gate National Recreation Area. Since 1863, it has featured restaurants with ocean views.
†This is unidentified.

I found out today that boots* can have visitors on Sat. & Sun. from 1100 to 2100 (11 a.m.–9 p.m.). But we'll talk about that later. I also found out that boot camp is 8 weeks. Eight weeks, that is, after you get on schedule. Some guys have been here three weeks and have just gotten on schedule, which means 11 total weeks. We'll probably be here for another week before we go on schedule—then it will be 8 weeks of: 3 weeks right here, phase "A"; three weeks on the range, phase "B"; one week mess duty; one week of brushing up and graduation. Then a 10-day leave, and I'll be kissing my baby again.

We haven't filled out an allotment blank yet, but we will. That's all for now, darling. I'll write you again tonight. Write to me every day! I love you—Al

26 Sept. 50
(afternoon)

Well, sweetheart, if you saw me now you would get one of the biggest shocks of your life! I am bald. Completely and unadaulteratedly bald. This morning we we[nt] under the barber. They [sic] butchers chuckled as our hair hit the deck. "Girls aren't going for those wavey [sic] locks anymore, brother!" he said. And exactly 6 minutes later I was standing at attention outside with the sun beating down on my peach-like dome. When we got back to the barracks we looked at each other and laughed like hell! What a sorry looking bunch of ass holes we are! Oh, well.

I saw Don† this morning for the first time in 1½ days. He hasn't been butchered yet, so he looked at me and sque[a]led. Don is in the 38th plt., 2nd RecTrn Bn.

They issued us sweat shirts and some other gear this morning. We'll get our uniforms tomorrow. By the way, if I don't answer your letters it's because I'm not getting the mail. I'll keep writing, anyway, however. And you do the same.

If anyone tells you Marines are soft, tell him to go to hell. Then when I come back I'll knock the living dung out of him. Any Marine who's gone through boot is rough! I'll write tommorrow [sic].

I love you very much—
love me always!
Al

P.S. I eat like a pig, smoke very little, shower every nite, and shave every morning! How about that! And when I say I love you—it's not just the writer. It's plain Al, speaking more truthfully than he ever has before. You'll have a more considerate husband when I get back, darling. I've learned much thru loneliness.

I love you with all
My heart—
Al (your husband)
[drawing of a face, with stubble for hair]
Me! No kidding

---

*A boot is a newcomer to the Marine Corps. The term carries both positive and negative connotations. It can also denote any Marine new to either a rank or to a billet and is used by infantry Marines to describe a Marine who has not been in combat.
†Don Weiland, presumably.

                                    ugly, but loveable—&
                                         loving you
                               What's my name?—I don't know
                                    Your fadoodleeehoping
                                             Al
I love you   I love you
SEND SOME STAMPS

MZ 466

                                        26 Sept 1950
Dearest Joanne,

I've got a little time before lights out, so I'll write a few detached episodes here in accordance with the combined diary-short story I'm writing.

At chow we have to stand up at attention on either side of the table, facing one another. We were at attention about an hour before that and hungrier than hell. So I begin to look at the guys accross [sic] the table. Where were their eyes? On the food, natch! It looked so damn funny to see 30 guys all at attention looking longingly at their food that I started to laugh. "Wipe that smile off your face, boy!" I did.

Then there's a D.I. who checks you to see if you shaved. He gets down underneath you and looks up under your chin. Then he sticks his nose up against yours and feels your face. "Did you shave this morning, boy?" he'll ask. If the answer is no—er, no, sir—you dry shave for a week.

The guy that panics is the D.I. with the long s[o]uthern dra-a-a-awl. He calls "left flank" so you can hardly understand him, and if one guy goes right he stops him and drawls, "Wha-a-t the f-u-u-cks a matter b-o-o-o-y. I said le-a-a-ft, not r-a-a-a-ht!"

If they catch you chewing gum you were [sic] it on your nose for 2 days.

"Don't give me none of your happy horseshit," is a favorite D.I. saying. "You'll be knee deep in shit to a tall indian," is another.

"I knew refrigerators from the appetite to the asshole" is our D.I.'s saying.

"Am ah ugly, boy?" a D.I. will ask. Tempted as you are you reply, "No sir!" "Thank you, boy," he'll say.

I'll write you more tomorrow. Goodnight, my darling. Sleep well and dream of me.—I love you.

                                        27 Sept. 1950
                                        Wednesday
                                        10:53 a.m.
Good morning, dear!

I had a good night's sleep last nite except for a few disturbing moments when I woke and thought of you and wished I were lying next to you. Reville [sic] isn't until 5 A.M., but I find myself awaking at 4 and wondering what you're dreaming about for an hour. Then I climb out of the sack, shave and Gung ho!* for another day.

After morning chow (which was a nameless heap of crap over toast) we took 2½ hours of classification tests. One was vocabulary, two was mathematics, three was mathematical reasoning and four was patterns. I don't really know how I did. There are quite a few college men here and if I did any good competitively at all it was on the vocabulary test. 120 is the score you have to make for OCS. If I do get the 120, I <u>may</u> apply for it. However, the way things look it'll mean a three-year hitch in the Corps after the duration. What do you think?

I wrote about 4 extra letters last nite: one to my mother, one to Frank,† one to school & two post cards [to] Emily and Mary. The guys are beginning to kid the hell out of me. "Boy, the pussy he must have on the string." they say. I don't try to explain. I just keep writing.

You've been acclaimed by popular vote the prettiest wife any of us have. We pulled out pictures last nite and compared them. You won out of about 10 wives! Your prize is a big kiss from me and a good … but we'll go into that (literally) when I see you.

You might be interested to know that I haven't had a cup of coffee since I've been here. Yes, they have it in the morning, but I've been drinking milk. Also, I'm getting quite tan on my face & my bald head. Ha!

Well, darling, that's all for now. I'll probably write you again tonight, time permitting. I still haven't received a letter from you but I hope to get one Thursday. Don't be afraid to cry on my shoulder, darling. Tell me about Ann, W.A. and all the rest. I'll give 'em hell when I get back.

Write to me often and be honest with me on everything, health, emotions, etc. Now don't get your cute little dander up—yes, I trust you, I just want to catch the atmosphere of civilian life.

Take care of yourself, dear. Don't walk the streets at night, keep in touch with my family and think of me. I'll always think of you—and love you.

                            Your Ever-loving—
                            Al

PVT. Alfred Martinez, 1056679
PIT. #$37, USMCRD   in case you lost my address
2nd Rec.Trng.Bn.
San Diego, 40, Calif.
      I love you very, very much
          Al
Send me some stamps—Ah'm running mahty low!
      I love you, Al
[drawing of lips]   Kiss?

MZ 467

---

*"Gung ho" is a phrase that describes people or groups possessing zealous military enthusiasm. It is from a Chinese term meaning to work together. John R. Elting, et al., *A Dictionary of Soldier Talk* (New York: Charles Scribner's Sons, 1984).

†Frank Galo.

(Thurs) 28 Sept 1950
About 11:30 a.m.

Dearest Joanne,

Well, here it is Thursday, and still no mail from anyone. The guys that came here with me haven't received any either, however, so I don't feel so bad. The mail is usually delayed one day when it hits the camp. I figure I ought to get some tomorrow—or Saturday at the latest. If not—it's out to the Chapl[a]in or over the hill!

Speaking of AWOL, some A-hole tried to get out last nite. So how did he do it? Why, he packs his bag, puts on his civ[v]ies and starts to walk away in broad daylight. They're still trying to decide what to do with him—psycho ward or the brig! Honest!

This morning someone saw the headlines of a paper that said "Korea Surrenders!" At least he says he saw it. Latter [sic] it changed to "Reds Want Surrender." I still don't know what the hell the deal is. Also, the rumors were flying that the reserves would have only 4 weeks of bootcamp! Gad, how the scuttlebut[t] scuttles! For instance, a D.I. hit some boot in the stomach the other day. I followed the story. By the time it had hit the last man, the story was that the boot had been brutally beaten, sexually seduced and worked until he died of a heart attack! And they all wondered why I laughed.

One thing I know is not a rumor. Five guys have cracked up in the last two days. Three of them I saw. They were from the platoon right across from us. Poor guys just couldn't take it. Two of them were out completely, one was out—mentally, on his feet physically. I, personally, don't think the training is that rough. But, of course, some of these goddamn D.I.'s can really break you. Fortunately, we've got a good one: a little short, fat guy (a sergeant) who makes us work, but who tells us jokes and treats us like human beings.

Last nite he let us listen to the Louis-Charles heavy weight fight.* Poor old Joe L. I thought sure he'd take Charles, but his age (36) just couldn't take it. We all bet on the different rounds the fight would end. It cost each of us 50 cents. I had round 2 and lost after 8 minutes. But, fortunately, the fight went all the way, nobody had the 15th round, so we all got our four-bitses [sic] back! We heard about 4 beer commercials too, and the general reply to the radio question, "How would you like a tall glass of Schlitz?" was "Up your ass!" And I do believe they meant it!

This morning we took 2½ hours more of tests, this time on radio-communications. The first one was a record thing that made the sound of a code—I (..), N (._) and T (__). We had to mark what they were. When they started coming fast you could hardly distinguish them, and if you could you hardly had time to mark them. I think I did okay, however. The second test lasted 1½ hours, and consisted of math (algebra, geom., etc.), science (chem, physics), electricity (ohms, watts, shit) and shop (metal, coils, motors, etc.). I probably flunked that

---

*On September 27, 1950, Ezzard Charles beat the favored Joe Louis in the fifteenth round of a heavyweight boxing match.

test more miserably than I ever did any before in my life. But it doesn't mean anything—it was a Radio Technical test, and only a man who has had experience could have passed it, except for the math.

Last nite while standing at attention in front of mess hall, a sergeant was having his platoon salute. Well, they had all just gotten 6 shots & were in no mood to salute. He kept them doing it, and good naturedly. Then he'd ask, "Do your arms hurt?" They'd chorus back "Yes, sir!" Then he'd say, "Would you like to go to show tonight?" The platoon would chorus, "Yes, sir!" "Do you think you deserve it?" he'd ask. To which, "No, sir!" was the unanimous reply. When we started laughing, our D.I. shouted, "Wipe those shit smiles off your face and stomp 'em!" We jumped up and down on the "shit smiles" for 5 minutes. Then the D.I. would go to a fellow, and pathetically murmur, "Did it die hard, boy?" "Yes, sir," the boot replied. The D.I. patted him on the back. "Too bad, boy."

Before I forget, baby, if you don't get a letter for a day or so after this one it's because I only have one stamp left & that one's for <u>this</u> letter. But if you have sent me some in the meantime and I receive them by tomorrow, disregard this!

That's all for now. I'll write more on to this during the day. Don't work too hard—and love me very hard!

I love you—
Al

love for you   xxxxxx's for
                                             you

3:30 p.m.
Same day

Gee, it was good talking to you, darling. To hear your voice after a thousand years was Heaven—it has been a thousand years hasn't it? I hadn't figured on calling you, because I never thought I'd have the time. But this afternoon we got interviewed for classification and were waiting around on the lawn for the rest of the guys—and the idea hit me!

I walked to a phone booth about 50' away. I didn't know how long it would take to get you, but I tried. I asked the operator to hurry. Then about three minutes later I heard your voice. My heart was pounding—really pounding—like a bass drum! My eyes were watery and my voice chocked [sic]. Then I wanted to laugh and cry I was so happy. I guess I sounded kind of silly to you over the phone,

When I talked to you, I got the impression that you weren't too happy to hear from me. I don't know what I expected, but when I hung up I was worried. Is anything the matter, darling? Do you miss me, honey? Do you love me?

I hope you've gotten my letters by tomorrow! I've been writing like a mad fiend! I guess the Marine Corps holds the mail for a day. I don't know what I'll do after this, cuz I don't have any stamps. But I'll figure something out.

Keep writing to me, darling, and keep loving me. If you ever stop—bury me deep.

Oh, yes—we go on schedule Oct. 8. Which means my 8 weeks starts then. It also means that I'll have about ½ hour a day to shower, write letters, clean my rifle, etc. But, again, I'll cross that bridge when! That's all for now, dear. I'll write again tonight.

> I love you—
> love me, please!
> Al

SGT: "I'll give you 10,000 ex-lax, boy!"
BOOT: "But I'll die, sir!"
SGT: "You'll shit!"

> (joke) [arrow pointing up]   I love you—Al
>   xxxxxxx's

> Same day (nite)

I saw a pretty sight tonite. Just before chow we were standing at ease & our D.I. called us to attention & faced us to the flag. The bugler sounded "retreat" and the flag came down. As far as the eye could see men were at attention, some saluting. Cars were stopped on the streets, doors open[,] men facing to the flag. The sun set behind it. It was really pretty. Not a person moved. It was quiet.

That's all I can write for now, dear. I go on guard duty for 4 hours in a little while. What do I guard? Why, the young sons of the U.S. Marines, Ma'm!

Goodnight, darling. Dream of me. I'll dream of you—count on it.

> I love you—
> Al

(P.S.—Send my mail air mail; it'll get here a day sooner—Love, Al.)

> xxxxxx's
>   for my honey, bun!

MZ 469

> 30 Sept 1950
> about 10 a.m.

Dearest Joanne—

We just had a talk by our D.I. on the M-1 rifle, one of the sweetest weapons around. Just feeling it and aiming it was a thrill, even though I have fired one before. The talk he gave was inspiring and rah-rah, but you could see the man had pride in his rifle. He talked to us in our barracks while we sat around and smoked. He closed with a phrase which packs a prophetically true power: "The deadliest weapon in the world is a Marine and his M-1."

He also told us what happened to a guy who called his weapon a gun. The poor boot had to walk around for 2 days with one hand on his penis, the other on his rifle, chanting, "this is my rifle, this is my gun, one is for shooting, the other for fun." Then he had to e[n]tertain the men at night with a bucket on his head singing "The Shit Bird Song." He wouldn't tell us what it was, but I bet it's a lulu!

I found out from the D.I. today that no man leaves boot camp without being able to swim 50 yards. But, he added, they have expert instructors who teach you. There are about 5 guys in the barracks so far who are in the same boat I'm in—non swimmers—so I don't feel so bad. But we have to dive off a 30' board with full pack, and I'm not looking forward to that escapade. Oh, misery, misery, mumble and moan!

Yesterday some boot got caught marching out of step. To which our D.I. said, "Boy, if you don't get in step they'll be taking you over to sickbay for an operation—digging my boot out of your ass!" What a rough one he sounds like. But he has told us repeatedly that he's never hit one of his men, and he never will. That I believe, because he's a man of character.

I just found something out today that had never occurred to me before. These letters I write are all mailed one day later. You see, mail goes out here once a day, at 8 a.m. I write the letters the preceeding [sic] day, so they're dated one day earlier. Naturally, I could never write and have one mailed the same day, cuz I'd have to write it before 8 A.M., and that's impossible. Clear?

Yesterday was graduation day for about 300 boots, and man (or girl) was it sharp! They were Marines: marching, talking, moving. The Marine Corps band was there in full dress, and the flags slapped in the breeze. It was truly [sic] a wonderful sight. I hope you'll be able to see it when I'm set to leave.

Two weeks from now we go through gas mask drill. It consists of testing a gas mask, i.e., taking it off in a chamber loaded with live gas. "Just to get the feel of it," our D.I. says. The funny part of it is, we stay in until we sing the first verse of the Marines Hymn! "You guys that don't know it better learn it f__ken fast," our D.I. growls, "or they'll be carrying you out!" Thank heaven I know it!

There's a kid in our outfit who reminds our D.I. of Napoleon. So when the kid is at attention, the D.I. pushes his nose against the kid's, and the conversation runs something like this: D.I.—"How are you, Napoleon?" Boot—"Fine, sir." "Have you inspected your troops?" "Yes, sir." "How's the queen?" "Fine, sir." "A pretty good screwing?" "Yes, sir," and they go on like that. You don't dare crack a smile, cuz if you do you're dead.

Here's another conversation when one guy got caught looking around while at attention: D.I.—"Nice looking place, ain't it boy?" Boot: "Yes, sir." "Figuring on buying it, boy?" "No, sir." "Then keep your Goddamn EYES STRAIGHT AHEAD!" Wow!

I sure hope I receive a letter from you today, or the guys'll start telling me you don't love me—kidding, of course. And that I can't take from anyone, not even kidding. They're liable to start making cracks about lovers, and free ass, and I'm liable to rack the bastards. This letter won't go out until Monday, so if you don't get it early, that's why.

Write often—and soon.

    I love you—(with all my heart)
      Al

Keep it warm for me, honey   xxxxxx for you

1 October 1950
About 10:30 a.m.

My darling wife—

Happy October First to you, dearest! Here it is Sunday again: the sun is shining, birds are singing and D.I.'s are cou[n]ting cadence. But it really is a beautiful day down here: starting to get too warm

Guess where I went this morning? Church—the protestant church. There were close to 1000 men there. The sermon was by a Rear Admiral of the Navy. It was well spoken. Altogether, the service was beautiful. And through it all I thought of you. I thought of Joanne of the smiling face and the bright eyes; Joanne of the blonde hair and the impish look. When I sang at church, I sang for you. And when I prayed—I prayed for you.

After morning chow I took a couple pictures, then we got permission to buy the Sunday paper—The L.A. times and the L.A. Examiner. We were sitting around on the deck reading when the D.I. walked in and said, "Okay you guys, you can lay out on your sacks." When one in the Marine Corps (especially boots) is allowed to lay on one's sack, it is the privilege of all privileges. When permission was given we all immediately proceeded to crap out on our bunks. At church, I'll bet 10 to 1 that there were prayers for our D.I.!

I've been reading the American Weekly section of the L.A. Examiner. It's just like the S.F. Examiner—but no Herb Caen.* I read it for awhile [sic], but the story of divorces and broken loves got the best of me, so I dropped it. Then I liked [i.e., looked] at the Sports Page—no S.F. State score. I'm dying to know how Verducci's† mandates did. I'm hoping to get a letter mañana.

Yesterday a full-fledged, honest-to-gosh major walked in. You never saw so many guys snap to attention so quickly in your life! The major wanted to know who had at least one year in the organized Reserves –I had two. He took our names, etc. The scuttlebutt is that our training will be cut to 4 weeks. This may mean a home station; it may mean Korea. I don't know, so don't worry about it.

Stop the presses! Roll back the rugs! Sweep the poop deck, and semper Fi! Five letters today! All to me! 5! 5! 5! 5! 5! Three from you, 1 from Frank and 1 from mother. Hallelujah! You can't imagine, darling, how much your letters mean to me! Bitch all you want! Complain about invoices! Type so I have to strain to read the damn things! But, darling, keep those letters coming. I feel like a king now, and <u>nothing</u> can break my spirit! Just to see your wonderful spelling errors, your grammatical abortions & your cute signature thunders a life through me I have never known. It made me want to cry I was so happy!

Sorry to hear you're still having our old trouble of money, but that will be taken care of in due time. I should get at least <u>part</u> of my pay ($10 or so) soon, and I'll send it chop-chop!

---

*Herb Caen (1916–1997) was a long-time, legendary daily columnist for the *San Francisco Chronicle* whose columns treated local affairs, political and social reporting and a generous sprinkling of puns.
†Joseph Verducci was the San Francisco State football coach and athletic director in the 1950s and early 1960s.

Really, darling, it was Heaven to hear from everyone—'specially you. And, say, what do you mean you don't <u>think</u> there is anyone in the world you'd rather talk to than me! You know <u>damn well</u> there isn't! Good Heavens, girl—<u>I</u> know!

Seriously speaking as I close this letter, I want to say the same old thing I have been saying: take care of yourself, darling, and save yourself for me; keep your chin up and keep loving me. Because in me you have a man who is only in love with you—fiercely. For I am a man who "works hard, cries hard—and <u>loves</u> hard."

Keep those bosoms bosomy—for me. My lips are getting sweeter all the time.

I love you—
Al

P.S. xxxxxxxxxxxxxxx's
   for you. I love you.

MZ 473

2 Oct. 1950

Dearest Joanne,

Well, here it is Monday again. Hot, hot Monday. You started another week of work and I started another week of—I don't know what. All day today we have been working like hell; it's 4:35 now. I am so god-damn dirty, my slacks are filthy[,] my hands and face are greasy. I am a mess.

We <u>should</u>—should, mind you—get our uniforms tomorrow. But we were suppossed [*sic*] to get them Friday. So I'm not expecting anything until I get it. To put it bluntly, the Marine Corps is all fucked up! But it's not entirely their fault. There are 10,000 men at a camp originally designed to house 1500. Quite a crowd, I'd say.

Well, yesterday we engaged in homicidal tackle. They called it football—Marine football. It was the bloodiest sport I have ever seen; no padding, no nothing! Just our street clothes on a dirt-green field. I'm not kidding when I say bloody either. One guy is in a San Diego hospital with a broken collar bone; another knocked three vertebrae out of place; one has been out with a concussion since yesterday at 2 p.m. The other side (plts 36 & 38) outweighed us about 30 lbs a man (80 to me). And they had 2 platoons to draw from. We have ¾ of a platoon. Yet, the game ended 12–12. What volunteer murder! Me! Too small. They couldn't find or catch me! Nyahh!

We had a coke this morning as an unexpected pleasure. This was after we had worked our asses until we could hardly stand. As we drank I pulled the oldest toast in the world and even made our foul-faced D.I. laughed [*sic*]. I simply said, "Here's to the kisses I've snatched and vica [*sic*] versa." I had 'em in the aisles! Shortly after, they put me cleaning out the heads! I've cleaned out so many of those shit holes I'm beginning to feel like Hearst!*

---

*William Randolph Hearst (1863–1951) founded the largest newspaper chain in the United States. His papers emphasized sensationalism and led to the term "yellow journalism" to describe this approach.

Tonight we have 28 new men coming into our platoon, which means we defin[i]t[e]ly go on schedule Monday. Then in 8 weeks—hot dog! I hope they're good guys.

If you could only see me now, honey, you'd laugh like hell. Although my hair is longer, I'm still bald. I'm dirty, bald, tanned, and miserable looking. Above the mirrors in the head they have a sign asking, "Is your appearance a credit to the Corps?!" What a diabolic[al] laugh I get out of that!

This morning I got one letter from Dolores and one from Toni (and it's not "TONY" honey.) Toni gave out the same old B.S. Dolores said, "gee, I never knew you could be missed so much." It made me feel good. She wrote a very nice letter. The only set back to the whole thing was I didn't get a letter from my poopsy-poopsy. Whassamatter, sugar, tired of writing already? If I don't get one tomorrow, I take French [sic] leave to S.F.! But I may get one tonight. If so, all is forgiven. If not—grrrr, Ah'm rough!

About the cookies, sweetheart—no. We cannot have <u>anything</u> to eat sent to us. All packages have to be open[ed] in front of the D.I. I'd get one; the boys in the front office would get the rest.

That's all for now, darling. Write soon—<u>please</u>. I miss you a lot, and letters always make me feel good. I love you, dearest. Keep loving me.—always.

All my heart & soul,
Al

P.S. Thanks for all those x's. Here's one for you   X

MZ 474

3 Oct 1950
Tuesday

Dearest Joanne—

Believe it or not this is the first time today I have been able to sit back and relax. As soon as we got up we had to swab the decks. The consequences of that was [sic]: we didn't get 'em clean enough, so no smoking <u>all day</u>! Then we had to draw our uniforms—a 100 lb. seabag full of shit that took all morning. The guys that handed out the gear must have hated everyone; they were shitten'! One thing I can say is that every piece of clothes fits, and that which doesn't they insist on altering. What a snappy looking thing I'll be.

Well, come noontime and we relax for chow. What happens? Someone discovers I can type and I spend the whole afternoon in a sgt/major's office full of NCO's. I was nervous, but everyone was real swell to me. (P.S.—I even had 5 cigarettes; don't tell anyone. Shhh …)

That has been my day. It doesn't sound like much but when you start breaking it down—man, it's crazy. It has been confusion and chaos. Oh well—at least we got our uniforms.

Boy, the mail is really coming in. Today I got 4 more letters—bringing the total to 15 or more. One was from you (the most important), one from Mrs. Dramsfield (I wrote her), one from Galo and one from Jean Lesser. All the letters were reall[y] nice. I saved yours for last, and it's a damn good thing I did. You folded one page the wrong way and the resultant confusion from yours trully [sic] was terrific. From Travis to a diagram of a belt buckle is quite a jump. First of all I thought the drawing was a pussy. I almost got a salt peter hard-on until I read that it was a buckle. Oh, how I long for it—no, not the buckle.

Galo is M.E. of the Gater now. I'm glad to see he got it. Lesser was writing a column for one week until it got dumped. Bonnie is writing one now. Frankly, I think they're both lousy writers. I'll take File 13* any day!

About OCS, I don't know yet. All these tests we've been taking will tell the tale. Nothing will be done about it anyhow until after boot camp. I think I can qualify if I want to, but I'm still sceptical [sic]. I'd cho[o]se P.I.O.† if I had a choice.

That's all for tonight, dear. I still have to straighten out all my gear & shine my shoes. I know my letters are getting shorter, but time is getting sparce [sic]. During the regular 8 weeks (starting Oct. 8) the guys tell me I'll be lucky to write one letter a week. Don't let that stop you, however. I'll get off a letter as often as I can to you. And you know, just as sure as I miss you, that you're in my thoughts all day—every day.

Think of me & love me. The days are going faster now, and 8 weeks won't be too long. Bear with me, darling, and soon we'll be together. Keep eating those "big" 10-cent pieces of liver. And when I get back I'll give you a 12" piece of—you'll see.

I love you with all my heart.

        Goodnight dearest—
          Al

Xxxxxxxxxxxxx's for your [drawing of a heart]
        I love you, I love you[,] I love you—Al.

MZ 476

                5 Oct. 1950
                Thursday

Dearest Joanne—

It's about 11:30 a.m. now and we've done a lot this morning. The platoon drew its 782 gear –M-1 rifles, ammunition belts, knap sacks, haversacks, first Aid kit, bayonet, field mess gear and panchos [sic]. After that we marched in the hot, hot sun for 3 hours. We went through all our column & flanking movements. It looked pretty good except for a few of the new guys. It'll take time.

The fog hung over the camp this morning at 5 a.m. (shades of S.F.!). I thought it might be cooler. But at 6:30 it was hotter than hell—such as now.

All around me now the guys are cleaning and examining their weapons; you can hear the click of the bolts slamming shut. The bayonet is a deadly looking thing—2½" of steel blade with a 2½" handle—5" in all. I've got a good rifle

---

*File 13 was the name of Al's column in the *Golden Gater*, the campus newspaper at San Francisco State.
†PIO is the Public Information Office.

(#2488829). It's been cleaned before, and the wood shines. It's really a sweet weapon. And because it is sweet, it's my Joanne. And it will protect me.

One of the reasons I'm starting this letter early is so I can get a couple more off today to some of the kids & my family, explaining much. What with cleaning Joanne, shining my shoes, etc., I'm going to be a busy gawdamn geyrene [sic]!* It makes me tired thinking of it.

I wrote a letter for some kid yesterday who can't read or write, so he's letting me hang on to his pen all the time. He was supposed [sic] to get a discharge, but the USMC decided to teach them (20 of them) how to read & write. This kid's wife is 5 mo.'s pregnant and she's been sick lately. I caught him crying a couple times. Poor guy is worried as hell, and they won't even let him see the chaplain. In such a case, I'd go AWOL and spend 60 days in the fucken brig!

After noon chow ...

Hi again, darling! I just read your letter where you bitched about money. Go right ahead, dear. I don't think I've ever tried to deny you the chance to complain. And I don't intend to. I—of all people—know what it's like to get something off my chest. Don't be afraid to tell me your troubles. Me? Don't worry—I'll complain if I have something to complain about, and when you start getting all the later letters I've written you'll see what I mean. There is nothing I'm holding back. I know—you're intelligent enough to take anything I have to say.

Trust you? Darling, I trust you with all my heart. Love engenders trust; and I love you a great deal. It's just that I have a worrying mind—even though you think I don't worry about anything. I have faith in you, tho, darling—my doubt is just my own inadequacy and my own fear. The thoughts of faithlessness are an expression of despair. But don't worry, hon—everything will work itself out—for the Best.

I see we still have financial worries. If you can hang on for about a month I'll start sending some $ and that will ease the situation. About coming down here—you know how I feel about that. I'd love it. But don't do it unless you feel in your own mind that it would be financially feasible. I'm gaining a lot of patience, and can wait for 8 weeks if the need be. So don't worry about hurting my feelings if you can't make it. But if you can—don't hesitate. Make sure, however, it's on a Sunday only. That's when I have about 11 hours free. Any other day I'd only be able to see you about 2 hours—if at all.

That's all for now, dear, your note on swimming was encouraging. And if J. Martinez can do it, then A. Martinez can do it! I can do anything! Don't worry.

I love you with all my heart ...
Con Toda me Amor—
xxxx's   Al
P.S. Give yourself a kiss on the bosom and a feel for me! Lord how I miss it!
[drawing of a heart, with "Al & Jo" inside]
I love you, I love you, I love you

MZ 478

---

*Geyrene is Al's spelling of gyrene, slang for a U.S. Marine. The word may have originated by combining "GI" for "government issue" and "Marine."

6 Oct 1950
Friday

Dearest Joanne—

We got a mimeographed communique on the war news today—news I suppose you already know. South Korea has crossed 100 miles over the 38th parrallel [*sic*]; MacArthur* is awaiting word to send U.S. troops across; the Manchurian reds & commie reenforcements [*sic*] are marching. Our D.I. summed it up this way: "It looks like you guys are going to fight a war after all."

Maybe I shouldn't be bringing this up: But you said you could take anything, Joanne. Makes you feel funny in the stomach, doesn't it, darling. That's the way it made me feel, scared—damn scared.

Here's what I think: I think these "skirmishes" will continue; I think a full-scale war will break out in 2 years; I think I will be part of it only too soon; I think I will be in the infantry. It sounds rotten, doesn't it? Well it is. Particularly the last one. They need foot-soldiers, not P.I.O. men; not writers; not officers; it all looks dull and discouraging and the fellows in the barracks feel like hell about the whole situation.

I'm afraid, honey, terribly afraid. I don't want to go overseas in combat. I don't want to go anywhere. When I come home on leave, I'm going to have one hell of a time convincing myself I should return to camp. I'm not afraid to admit it. I will do anything to keep from fighting—<u>anything</u>.

Now that I've driven you to a point of distraction, I want to tell you not to worry. And that's what I mean. I've managed to defend and protect myself for a long time now—and I can continue doing it now. If I have to go, I'll go—despite what I say. And, which is more important, I'll be back in one piece—warm and alive. I'm not dying for <u>anyone</u>! The Marine Corps inclusive. I'm no hero.

All day today we've been on work details. Tonight they're going to let us see a football rally on the base—I don't know why we can't see the game! Yesterday 6 of us worked in the base bakery. The Sgt/major over there gorged us on donuts & ice cream. We were so greatful [*sic*] we could have kissed him. Not one man had dry eyes there. Seldom it is when they treat you human at boot camp!

I got a letter from Galo, Mother & Dolores this morning, but none from you. If I don't get one tonight I'm going to worry that you don't love me anymore. I expect one letter a day <u>every</u> day; 2 on Mondays.

Haven't got much more time now, dear, so I'll close. Again I want to say, don't worry—<u>please</u>. I know I'm not helping matters any but I'm just moody. You know how I write in circles.

Take care of yourself, honey. My morale depends on you. I'm a crazy bastard; I've never swam [*sic*] before in my life, but if anything goes wrong I'll swim the goddamn coast to S.F.! I'm fearless!

---

*Douglas MacArthur (1850–1964) was a five-star general in the U.S. Army and had a distinguished career as superintendent of the U.S. Military Academy at West Point and as a combat veteran of both world wars. During World War II he served as commander of the U.S. Army Forces in the Far East, and he officially accepted Japan's surrender on September 2, 1945. He effectively became the ruler of Japan from 1945 to 1951. Initially placed in charge of the United Nations' troops in the Korean War, he was later removed by President Harry Truman in April 1951.

I love you, honey. Kiss your pillow for me tonight. Then dream of me (P.S.—I made you last night in my dreams—wet dreams, tsk tsk.)

You ought to see me—gained 10 lbs—honest!

All my heart—
Al

xxxxxxxxxxxx's for you
    [drawing of heart with arrow and "Al & Jo"]   <u>Forever & ever</u>
I love you with all my life
[verso]
I love you
send me some cheap stationery, huh, kid. I'm out. Tell my ma to send it—air mail stuff. Thanks.
I love you muy mucho
    [heart drawing] Al
[written in margin: "I love you"]

MZ 479

8 Oct. 1950

Enclosure: clipping, "A thought for the day: Don't worry so much now as to whether you believe in God or not. So try to live that God may believe in YOU. SEE YOU IN CHURCH!"

Dearest Joanne—

    Well, this is one Sunday I didn't think I'd be able to write to you! This has been a rough day. Allow me to tell you about it.

    Yesterday afternoon we got another D.I.—we've got three altogether. This guy is Corporal Cook—absolutely the <u>roughest</u>, saltiest* geyrene [sic] I have seen in all my life. Last nite (since he didn't know us) he took us to the post theatre. I made the fatle [sic] mistake of leaving a pair of dirty dungerees [sic] on my bunk. After the show he was roaring mad. He called <u>me</u> & some other kid everything under the sun. I had to stand watch at 4 a.m. this morning. Then the two [of] us had to scrub the D.I.'s office with a tooth brush! So help me! I have heard of men doing that, but that is the first time <u>I</u> have ever done it! Also, he kept the smoking lamp out all day 'till now (8 p.m.). Then he refused all day to let us write letters. Now he insists that we write home and tell our people he hasn't kicked the hell out of us.

    Just a few minutes ago he came in and with a shined shoe in his hand he asked who thought he had a better shine on his shoes than the shoe he held in his hand. One person volunteered. "Okay" he said in his gravel voice, "you go in to the other D.I. on your knees, make a right face on your knees and tell him, 'sir, I think I have a better shine on my shoes than yours and I think yours look like hell, sir.'" You see, the shoe belongs to the other D.I. We all had a good laugh after a violent

---

*In Marine slang, "salt" describes a Marine or sailor who has had considerable experience and is tough as a result. The term could also be used ironically to denote new Marines who wanted to appear more tough and experienced than they were, and it could be used to describe a Marine whose uniform was visibly old, worn and distressed by age and use.

argument between the other D.I. and the shoe shiner. Then the gravel-voiced D.I. said, "that was your fun for today—that was your grab-ass, or, as the French say it, "grahb-assé."

All day today he was p.o.'d* because the Sgt/major wouldn't let him march us on Sunday. He had threatened to march us 'till we dropped. So he made up for it by giving us all our facing movements for about 2 hours in our barracks. Man, was I beat after that! Usually on Sundays we get to lie one our sacks—but not today. Usually we each get to buy a paper. Today the squad leaders bought 2, and we had to take turns. Didn't make any difference anyhow; we didn't have time to read them.

So that's our new corporal. A funny guy, but one I'm sure will make Marines out of us. He's all discipline. When he says attention, he means snap! When he says march, he means strut! When he talks he barks. But the men jump and they snap to. Our platoon is right on the ball. You can bet your last buck that the 37th platoon will be the honor platoon of boot camp. We have the 3 top D.I.'s in the outfit.

Well, I see Cal† is still going strong. Also, I see where our N.Y. Yankees won the A.L. pennant. And I also see where the Oakland Oaks‡ have cinched the P.C.L. pennant. I tried to find the score of the S.F. State game. No dice. But I'm willing to bet they won. Sounds like Verducci is going great guns!

How was your weekend, darling? I guess you & Dolores went to the show. Speaking of shows, the picture we saw last nite was "The Next Voice You Here [sic] ..."§ It was a religious picture about the voice of God coming over the radio. The voice told man to learn to love, etc. The main characters were Mr. & Mrs. Smith, Americans. It was an unusual picture—not a great one, but a good one. The message it carried told more than the plot. I wish you could see it. Watch for [it], and try to catch it if you can.

This morning I went to church again—protestant. The sermon was about choosing a wife, and it had 5000 Marines laughing in sincerity. The minister was really good. He spoke straight from the shoulder, and didn't miss a trick. I'm really beginning to enjoy church moreso [sic] than I ever have. The protestant sermons are so much more realistic. During the "silent meditation" I prayed a great deal for you, darling. The Reverend did too. He prayed for the people at home and for peace and for the lives of the Marines. And it's a funny thing, darling, but I prayed for you more than I've ever prayed for anyone before. And I prayed sincerely, without fear or shame. And I caught myself praying for everyone else. You know, dear, I actually think I'm growing up. My selfishness is leaving me.

Something else I thought about today in church was how much I loved you. You mean more to me than I do. That's a funny statement, I know, but it means

---

*Al uses "p.o.'d" to mean "pissed off." He also used "p.o.'s" to say that something pisses him off.
†The University of California, Berkeley.
‡The Oakland Oaks were a minor league baseball team in the Pacific Coast League from 1903 to 1955.
§*The Next Voice You Hear*, a film made in 1950 starring James Whitmore and Nancy Davis. She later married Ronald Reagan and was the First Lady of California (1967–1975) and of the United States (1981–1983). A voice claiming to be God interrupts all radio programming for six days. The script was adapted from a short story by George Sumner Albee.

something. When I think of going to war, I sometimes think of tragedy. But when I think of death or injury to myself, I no longer think of the dissolution of my person. I think of the affect [sic] it will have on you. I no longer think of danger to myself; I think of the happiness of my wife. And I say to myself, "A. Allan—you're getting to be a man." And it makes me feel kind of proud.

I want to apologize for yesterday's letter. It was a caustic, vitriolic piece of sarcasm that I shouldn't have written. You know me, tho, honey—impulsive, quick to imagine, and too quick to let my imagination run away with me. You have to read those letters and evaluate them by the writer—emotional, high-strung, etc. Read them with a great deal of patience and understanding, dear. Consider that I am pretty damn disgusted with the whole world situation, and am apt to indirectly express that feeling in many ways. Just believe in me and love me, darling. That's what counts. I'm an educated man, and being such I am all too aware of the mistakes of our present generation. So much ignorance around me tries my patience. The irony of education fighting a war created by ignorance is often too much for me to bear. But it's the virtue of that same education that makes me able to realize it—such as now. So bear with me, hon—and know that I have all the faith and love in you in the world. I can only ask you one thing: be patient with me in a world where patience means so much.

Tomorrow we go on schedule, so I may not be able to write again until next Sunday. But don't worry about me. If anything happens rest assured you'll know about it. But nothing is likely to happen. So keep writing to me once a day, and keep loving me all day every day. And every once in awhile [sic] tell me about it extra specially nice, cuz it makes me feel good.

The next 8 weeks are going to be the toughest in my life. But, after all, I'm Al Martinez—and I haven't met anything yet I couldn't lick! We'll go swimming together when I get back …

I love you with
All my heart—

P.S. get those pills—promise me! Eat well, sleep well, paint some & <u>love me</u>. Keep thinking of me darling!

  xxxxx's—Al

MZ 481

13 Oct. 1950
Thursday—

Hi Sweetheart!

After that letter I wrote yesterday I just had to find time to send this one off for fear of scaring 10 year's growth out of you. Yes, I'm much better today (almost perfect), I didn't go to sickbay and I'm still alive. That damn cold really had me going yesterday; today, however, my step came back, my voice came back, my coughing has almost ceased, and, generally speaking, I'm damn near back to normal. Also my knee has sopped [sic] hurting. Gung ho!

I got a big kick out of your letter today, darling. It was perfectly sweet. What made me laugh was the mistakes you made. For instance "Vivian get[s] $1.98 a month, & I get $1.60 a month." Dear, you don't get $1.60—you get $160. (Note the decimal point.[)] You almost cheated yourself out of $158.40! We can't have that!

I finally made out an allotment for you today. It meant an hour of standing in line, but I got the damn thing filed. All we can do is wait now.

We went to the show Tuesday nite & saw "Holiday Rhythm" & "Prisoners In [sic] Petticoats."* The first picture was an almost all-girl musical with the sexiest-looking women I have ever seen. I'll bet half of the barracks had wet dreams last nite! The second picture was absolutely the lousiest damn picture I have ever seen! It was psuedo[sic]-psychological, poorly cast & generally rotten! Lord preserve me if I ever have to see a show like that again!

The training here continues to get rougher with the passing days. We have about 2 one-hour classes in the morning & 2 at night; then we march and have rifle drill the rest of the time. The classes I don't mind; we've had 'em on the M-1 rifle, first Aid, Marine Corps discipline, tradition, history, courtesy, and rank & insignia. But the marching! Oh, the marching! My shoulders hurt from the M-1, and my legs & feet feel as though they're going to fall off. But I'm not alone. Believe me, darling, there is no tougher training than the Corps offers. "Ours is not to question why; ours is but to do or die." That well may have been the purpose of the USMC.

Funny what contempt the Marines hold for the Army, particularly in looks & in discipline & courtesy. "You look like a fucken Army man!" a D.I. will often say to an unke[m]pt Boot. He means it too. And frankly I can see why. The Corps is proud of the appearance and the training of its men. Do they shoot you for not tying a shoelace? No. But they can court martial you for sitting down on your guard post, looking contemptibly at a D.I. or an officer or having rust on your rifle. The first two are punishible [sic] by death, believe it or not.

That's all for now, darling. Lights go out soon & I'm beat. Take care of yourself & love me. Things will be better when I come home; I'll be a man—and I guess it's about time.

I love you, sweetheart, and will forever and ever.

   Goodnight, darling
   Con toda mi amor—
    Al
xxxxxx & a big hug for you.

P.S.—I love you.

MZ 484

Holiday Rhythm, a 1950 film starring Mary Beth Hughes and David Street. It tells the story of a young executive who hits his head, passes out and dreams of the show he is trying to convince an airline to sponsor. Also in 1950, *Prisoners in Petticoats* starred Valentine Perkins as a naïve young pianist who becomes unwittingly involved with a gang of mobsters.

20 Oct 1950
Friday

Dearest Joanne—

Well, this has been quite a day! Since you don't know anything about it, allow me to infringe upon your knowledge and tell you about it.

This morning (all morning) we had inspection with rifles for the first time. We were inspected by the captain himself! It was the first time afield that we had such a deal and we were all nervous as hell. When he came to me, I snapped to, threw my bolt open and waited. "Give me the definition of a map!" he snaps. Of all the goddamn things, I had to get that! We had studied everything but that. Anyhow, quick as a flash, I comes [sic] back with a flashy definition filled with geographical contours and scales. He looked kind of surprised and very pleased. After the inspection the D.I. asked me what I said and I told him. I think my three years [of] college are beginning to show.

All afternoon we had a parade in honor of the commander of the post, Major General W.T. Clement.* Our platoon marched in it for the first time. We marched with full colors, band and <u>all</u> regimental officers. The parade was good, and I personally enjoyed marching to music. But it lasted 3½ hours, and we carried rifles—that gets kind of rough after the first hour. But it was fun. Makes a man feel a little more like a Marine.

After that we took in some clothes we washed out yesterday. I'm improving on that end. Then we marched awhile [sic] after evening chow, took a test and here I am. Incidentally, the test was on first aid. [K]no[w] what I got? 100% So out of three tests and a possible 300 points, I have 297. I'm top man in the whole platoon now. One fellow, I think I told you, was ahead of me by one point on one test. But I lost him on the other two by pulling an even 200. Not bad for a newspaperman, eh, hon?

You asked me what I'm learning here. Well, I can field strip an M-1 rifle and a carabine in 2 minutes and 45 seconds—and I mean take them completely apart. I can name <u>every</u> part of both weapon[s]—no matter how small. I can tell you the functioning, description and characteristics of both weapons in detail. I can fix both weapons, and unjam them. I can recite the Marine Corps history since 1775 blindfolded. I can administer first aid with efficiency. I can handle the bayonet. I can follow orders. I am learning to swim. I know interior guarding. I know military courtesy and discipline: and I can now wash a pair of dungarees better than any man in the outfit! And clean heads? By God, I can scrub 'em till they glimmer!

Seriously, darling, I'm learning a great deal at boot camp. All that I've mentioned and quite a few other things that I do unconsciously. I'm also building myself up and gaining a more mature perspective on life and its ill-heeded advantages. In short, I'm becoming a man—older, tougher, self-disciplined, alert.

I can see very clearly the Marine Corps method of teaching.

---

*William T. Clement (1894–1955) served with distinction in the Marines during World War II. In September 1949, he became commander of the Marine Corps Recruit Depot in San Diego. He retired in 1952 and passed away in 1955.

I'm pretty sure you can have visitors at Camp Mathews, so I'll be able to see you after all! It's about 15 miles from this camp. You'll have to find out how to get here from Southern Pacific. So I hope to see you November 10th. Camp Mathews is the rifle range where we stay for three weeks beginning next Sunday. So I'll be seeing you soon.

Know what just happened? Some guy called his rifle his gun. So now he's going in front of each man with his penis in one hand, rifle in the other, showing all the men which is his rifle and which is his gun. I was the first man he showed, and I almost split a gut trying to keep from laughing. If I had've cracked a smile, 68 men would have been looking on the piece of property reserved for you!

It's getting close to lights out now, dear, so I'll begin to close. The platoon has been doing pretty well lately, so the D.I.'s have been easing up some. The physical rigor is still tough however. I'd like you to come to our graduation about Dec. 1. It's really an impressive ceremony. After that I get a 48 hours pass over the weekend. We can spend that together and do a little love making in bed! Ah, just to spread those beautiful legs of yours and feel, and kiss and rub and push … saltpeter, hell!

That's all for now, dear. I'll write you again over the weekend. Be good and don't worry about anything. I'm in top shape for <u>everything</u>! And, baby, I do mean everything!

Keep writing those nice letters and say hello to all my folks & friends. I'll be seeing you soon, sweety. Take care of yourself. I love you very, very much in many, many ways—

> Your Own True Love—
> With <u>all</u> my love—
> Al

P.S. What the hell's the idea of writing to Don? That old flame rising? Gawd, woman, how desperate can you get? Just hang on!

[drawing of heart, w/arrow, and "Al + Jo," all surrounded by stars]

> I love you, darling—
> xxxxxxxxxxxx's for
> you & a big hug & kiss.
>
> Con Toda mi Amor—
> Al

MZ 491

> 21 (?) Oct 1950
> Saturday

Dearest Joanne—

Well, the order was given "everyone write letters for 30 minutes!" and by Christ, everyone is writing letters. Such is the power of a command. Speaking of commands, we were having a lecture the other day on military discipline, when suddenly the instructor shouted "tenshun!" 500 men snapped to their feet in one movement. "That," said the instructor, "is military discipline." No point could have been proven more clearly. It really was odd. None of the men questioned. All snapped to attention quickly. Quite a sight.

Today a battalion of swabees* [*sic*] were parading on the field. They had been in quite awhile [*sic*], and looked lousy. Then a platoon of two-week boots got out there. They made the Navy look like a bunch of 2-year olds. It just serves to manifest the difference in training, discipline and reaction to commands. That's why the Marine Corps is what it is—and the Navy isn't.

Gee, I didn't get an anniversary greeting from nobody today. Why, honey? I've been here one month today and nobody even 'membered. Cryin' out loud.

Guess what? We go to a football game tomorrow—in San Diego. It's on our schedule for 7 p.m. We got our uniforms back today from alterations, so we can go. My trousers are a little too long, but I can take care of that after boot camp. The football game is at Aztec Stadium† and will be between the Marine Corps and the Navy. The score ought to be about 100 to 0—Marine Corps, of course. I'll write you all about it.

Tonight at chow I went back three times for food. Honestly, I'm eating like a pig. I don't know how much I weigh, but I'm gaining!

About coming home, we graduate about Dec. 1. After that we get a 48[-]hour leave then return here for orders. When we get our orders to where we report, we get a 10 day delay en route which counts as a leave. It may take a week, it may take a month, it may take 2 days. No one knows. Whatever the case, I'm going to try to be home for Xmas. If I have to go back before Xmas, I'll probably get a leave anyhow. In that case, you can come to me for the holidays! How does that sound, darling?

You seem to be having quite a time with Blaine & George. That's good. They're both nice people with good sense and a lot of consideration. Which [*sic*] is important, too, is that they like you very much. Just watch that skinny little George. He gets too playful sometimes. I'll wrap him up if he gets too wise. I'm rough.

From your letters it sounds like you're having the same type of professional life now as ever before. You asked me about my day. Here is one average day: 5 a.m.—rev[e]il[l]e; 5:06–5:24, calisthenics; 5:30–6:30, cleaning the barracks; 6:30–7:30, chow; 7:30–8:30, class; 8:30–9:30, class; 9:30–11:30, drill; 11:30–12:30, class; 12:30–1:30, chow; 1:30–all afternoon, classes, drill, swimming, etc.; 6:30, chow; 7:30–8, drill; 8–9, rifle cleaning, talks, bull sessions, shoe shining, showers; 9:30, sack time. Of course, the days vary, but everything is still on schedule. Everything is done double time. We have set a record for falling out. It takes us 20 seconds to get from our barracks (no matter what we're doing) to the street ready to march and, man, that's moving! The favorite word in the Marine Corps is "Move out, Mac!": and we move!

Well, darling, 30 minutes is almost up, so I'll start to close. Don't mind my

---

*"Swabees" is Al's misspelling for "swabbies," meaning Navy personnel.
†Aztec Stadium was home to the San Diego State University Aztec football team.

griping in letters when I do. I don't mind yours. That's what husbands and wives are for. And we're suited to each other.

Today a fella was smiling. "Are you happy, boy?" a D.I. asked. "Yes, sir," was the unwary answer. "We'll have to do something about that!" Of course he was kidding.

That's all for now, dearest. Keep your chin up & keep writing. I live for mail call—and for the day that I can be kissing you.

   I love you with all my heart—
    Al
xxxxxxx's for you & a big hug & lots of love.
   Your husband, Al

MZ 492

         23 Oct 1950
         Sunday—

My darling—

Well, another beautiful day has begun and almost ended in this beautiful resort in Southern Calif … bull crap! The day has ended, that's about all I can say, and my feet are tired.

Honey—before I go any further, you still love me don't you? And you'll love me lots when I come home won't you? I had a bad dream last nite about you not loving me anymore [*sic*] when I come home. I woke up this morning feeling all bad. Write me and tell me how much you love me, huh, please?

The football game last nite was stinken [*sic*]. The Marines won 29–0, but they did it by sheer force of power. They made less boners than the Navy. The game was at Balboa Park in San Diego. About 10,000 people were there—2/3 Marines, and the other ⅓ swabbees [*sic*] & civilians. We got home at midnight and had to get up at 5 a.m.—no fun. The game for us was stiff and military. Everybody ate pop corn and stuff but us. We sat together and asked permission when we had to piss. All in all, it wasn't very spiriting. The one high spot was on the bus when we all sang to the tune of Inky Dinky Parley Voo: "6 more weeks of sand & grass, parley voo; 6 more weeks of sand & grass, then the D.I. can kiss my ass, Inky dinky parley voo!" We have poetic souls.

Well, it's set, darling. I'll be expecting to see you at Camp Mat[t]hews.* Sunday, Nov. 10, about 11 a.m. I found out that we can have visitors there. So hurry on down, honey. When you call this Sunday I won't be here. They may switch the call to Mat[t]hews, but I doubt it. So I won't be able to talk to you. However, I'll be seeing you soon, so it's not so bad.

I have a new nickname out here: Marty. One D.I. calls me Martinéz, the other Martinee and the fellows Marty. I'm gaining quite a collection of pseudonyms, among other things.

---

*Camp Matthews, named for Calvin V. Matthews, was the Marine Corps rifle range in La Jolla, near San Diego, used for marksmanship training for boots like Al. It served as a Marine Corps base from 1917 to 1964.

When you see my folks tell them I'm awfully sorry I haven't written. But I honestly just don't have the time. Even on Sundays now we're busy ironing, cleaning rifles, studying, shining shoes, etc. Tell Frank that too and anyone else you might see. I'd love to write to all of them, but can't. You come first with me.

You asked me about my teeth some time ago. Well, they're going to pull two of them—and replace them. I don't know when, but they are. They have excellent dentists here. What's good about it is that the corps is under obligation to replace every tooth they pull. Also, I'll have some filled. Surprisingly enough, my teeth are in good condition, the dentist says, except for those two they're pulling.

This morning we had rifle inspection, and the D.I. was in a foul mood. He shook hell out of 2 guys & kicked 2 more in the shins. When he came to me I was nervous as hell, but I passed.

We've been having classes on the Browning Automatic rifle and the carabine. The BAR is a tough weapon to learn—intricate as hell. The carabine is a lot like the M-1. The BAR is one of the Corp's deadliest weapons—fires 550 armor-piercing bullets in <u>one</u> minute! Keeps a man busy.

Our softball game Sunday was fun. I played left field (much to my discontent). I made two spectacular catches then erased the glory by bob[b]ling one. I pop[p]ed up in my one time at bat. Oh, well—I'm a lover, not an athlete.

That's al[l] for now, sugar. I didn't get a letter from you today, but am excusing it cuz I got 2 Saturday. The mail is all screwed up around here. But you just keep writing. I want you to tell me you love me lots of times. Hokay.

Got to shower & hit the sack now, darling. Think of me all the time and take real good care of yourself. I pray for you every night but don't tell anyone. That's just for us. I love you, Joanne—when you're feeling bad or blue just remember that. "Say to yourself, 'he loves me'—and you'll always be right."

  Goodnight Darling
   I love you (with all my heart)
    Al

[heart, w/"Al + Jo" written in it, and arrow piercing it, and "ALWAYS" written to the right]

xxxxxx's for you & a big hug & lots of love from a husband who cherishes his wife—I love you—Al

[on verso]

I'm missing you, that's all I say
I'm missing you, my dear;
I'm missing you with all my heart …
I wish that you were here!
  "I wanna go home with you …"
    I love you—
      Al

[drawing of lips, with "here's a kiss from me to you." written alongside]

MZ 494

27 Oct 1950
Saturday nite

My darling wife—

We have 25 minutes to write letters, so I'll start this and continue it when I can. To put it mildly, the shit has really hit the fan. Our D.I. has really threatened murder because we sluffed off on our inspection. "The last three weeks have been easy," he's said. "But from now on—watch out!" He meant it too. One man (Brunn) has already been run up to the commanding officer for having one spot of rust on his rifle. The D.I. has a whole list of names of men he's going to 'get' when we're away from the brass out on the range. No, I'm not on that shit list.

Thus far, I've managed to keep my nose clean and stay out of trouble, remaining on top of the platoon in almost every phase. I've been lucky in discovering it pays to co-operate. Some of the men haven't discovered it yet, and they're paying. I hope they discover the value in understanding soon. They're my buddies; I don't want any of them to discover it the hard way in combat.

Yesterday we had bayonet practice. We practiced thrusting, blocking, slashing, guarding and parrying—all the offensive & defensive methods of hand to hand [sic] combat. It's hard and frightening work, learning how to kick your 10" blade out of a man's belly. But it's reas[s]uring to know that bayonet warfare is on its way out. I personally want no part of it. I'll shoot a man if I have to.

Lately we've had classes in map ready [sic], compass, the .45 pistol, camo[u]flage, cover, concealment & combat principles. It's surprising how many classes boot camp has. They _force_ you to know something about everything. A Marine can do anything, I am rapidly believing. History is bearing me out.

As you probably have already guessed, the ball point pen is empty. I'm using pencil again. Tomorrow we _have_ to go to another goddamn football game again. So if you call me in the afternoon I probably won't be here. Seems like we're having a hell of a time getting together. But we will. We will.

That's about all for now, darling. I love you, dear. Have a good night's sleep and dream of me. Goodnight, dearest. I love you with all my heart.... Al

28 Oct 1950
Saturday 11 a.m.

Sweetheart—

It's a great day today! We just got official word on our inspection. Out of the whole battalion our platoon _won it_! We got the highest score out of 10 platoons! Also, we took marching honors in the parade yesterday and got compliments from the lieut.col. Also, today we took a test on the Browning Automatic rifle, and our platoon took high average with 94.6. Yes, I got 100! Makes 397 out of 400 for me—still top man of the outfit!

So you see, darling, platoon 37 is _really_ on the ball. This afternoon we go to the football game, and things will be different. Our D.I.'s are prouder than hell. We can buy _anything_ we want at the game: candy, hot dogs, pop corn, _anything_!

This is unusual as hell! And the smoking lamp is continually lit. We are really clicking, so this means free sailing until the next time we sluff off.

The D.I. was looking at the test chart on the wall when he came across my top score. He got a surprised, pleased smile on his face & looked at me. "Pretty good, Martinee," he said. But he was thinking alot [sic] more. Proud of me, honey?

The news from abroad doesn't sound too good from the scattered bits of information we get here. We here [sic] that the Chinese commies are on the march. I suppose this is the precipitate for World War III. We hear, too, that all reserves are supposed to be realesed [sic] after thorough combat training—about 6 mo.'s. Well, I'm not going to get my hopes up there either. No, I'm not a pessimist. I'm educated.

Last nite myself and a comparitively [sic] "ignorant" person were standing on the platform outside our door looking at the moon. "It's too bad," he said seriously, "that the whole world couldn't realize that the moon is for everyone…" That statement, from a supposed uneducated person, summed up perfectly all the ramblings and the theories and the hopes of the educated—of the intelligent. It said perfectly what each man tries to say and what free men with wives and homes think. It's too bad the world doesn't realize that the moon and life is for everyone. I wish Stalin would take a good, long look at that moon…. I honestly wish he would!

We just had our one mail call today, and I didn't get any letters. I guess it's the same fouled-up mail deal. Monday I probably won't get any either because all the mail has to be forwarded to Camp Mathews. I should get mail about Tuesday or Wednesday though—I hope.

This pen I'm using is borrowed property, before I forget. Just thought I'd tell you.

Personally, I'm feeling in tip top condition now. I'm gaining weight and becoming physically hard. I even look healthy. My face is clear and tan. Emotionally, I still have my ups and downs, the main factor being missing you. I get blue and feel bad at something you unintentionally say. And I let my imagination run away with me. But, as I've said before, I'm growing up rapidly. Never again will I be afraid to look for a job or talk to anyone or do things a man should do. To the world I'm a man. But to you—probably as it should be—I'm still a little boy. I need you very much, and depend on you in many ways. You're my wife and my friend. Let's keep it that way forever.

So much for now darling. Love me always and keep in mind how much I love you. If you believe and act on that basis there is nothing—absolutely nothing—that will keep us for [i.e., from] the most wonderful life imaginable. As you once wrote in poetry—"…Two kids at earnest play." I'll love you forever. Charming?

All my heart & love—
Your husband
Al

xxxxxx times 50,000 kisses for you & a big hug.

MZ 497

> 29 Oct 1950
> Sunday

Dearest Joanne—

Well, at 4 a.m. we were up, at 4:30 we had all our gear packed and 4 hours later we arrived at Camp Mat[t]hews. It's really a hole. We live in 6-men tents and eat out of mess gear. The place is dirty and business-like, infested with rattle snakes and coyotes. Not a pleasant place. We have no locker boxes here so we have to live out of our sea bags—everything all crumpled up. Already I don't like the place.

About 15 minutes ago I was a casualty. I was cleaning my rifle when the bolt slammed shut on the social finger of my left hand. It scared me for a minute because it bled like hell. But I stopped the bleeding, found a band aid and pinned on my purple heart. I am now a salty geyrene [sic]. I have what is known as an M-1 finger.

The football game yesterday was really good. We ate candy and everything else, and everyone made cracks at the female yell leader. She was a sexy wench, and wiggled in a way to attract the oddest yells. It made me want to be sleeping with you. But I want to be sleeping with you anyhow.

This [sic] 3 weeks is supposed to be the toughest of boot camp according to our D.I. We fire everything. Which is worse, we have to dive off a 20-foot board. That scares hell out of me. But I guess I'll live through it.

That's all for now, darling. Write as often as possible. I'm beginning to feel awfully blue again. I love you.

> All my heart & love—
> Al

(Be sure to send me some stamps)

MZ 498

> 31 Oct 1950
> Monday nite

My darling—

Happy Hallowe'en, sweetheart! Sure wish I could give you a big kiss, but this will have to do: X! I don't know how comprehensible this letter will be—I'm writing by, of all things, lamplight! Out of 12 tents we have, 2 don't have electricity. Naturally, I got one. It gives out about as much light as my eyes on a passionate nite.

Talking to you yesterday ranks with one of the sweetest thrills since we met. It was so wonderful, and I wanted to say so much! I sang all the way back to the tent. My morale is boosted 10000 %. Darling, hearing you say you loved me brought back the tingle of our first kiss and the warmness of our nights together. And hearing you cry because you were happy to hear my voice proved to me beyond a doubt that I really have nothing to worry about. All in all, Joanne, there is little I can say that would truthfully explain to you the content, warm feeling I had after I spoke to you. It was wonderful.

Today for eight (8) hours we spent the time 'snapping in' with rifles.. That is, getting into the various firing positions for the range. I never knew that there were so many more muscles in my body that could ache so much at the same time. The whole platoon is in agony.

The positions to us are so awkward and seemingly impossible. The sitting position is the worse [sic]. No kidding, hon, this has been the toughest day yet as far as physical endeavor is concerned. I am literally beat!

Last night was colder than hell. I wore a sweatshirt and had on 2 blankets and my poncho, and I was still cold. During the day it's hotter than blazes. You can't win.

That's all for now, dear. Got to shave & get set to hit the sack. 4 a.m. comes early. I got 2 letters from you today, so the mail is coming through. Just keep using the same address. Believe it or not, that "address" took 24 hours to write. The pencil part was done yesterday. This ink part is done today, Nov. 1, 7:30 p.m.

Just as I was finishing this letter yesterday, it was announced that I was a responsible man and was therefore going to be tent commander. A tent commander is the man in charge of a tent, and has his men carry out the orders of the D.I. His (tent comm.) orders are as valid as those of the D.I., and disobedience of those orders could result in a summary court martial. The tent I am commanding houses the "shit birds" of the platoon. They are the helpless, the stupid, the clowns and the stubborn. I don't know why he put me in charge of it, but his last words were "Now let's see what kind of a leader you are, Martinez!" And that was that.

Since that time I've really had those guys jumping. Only one has given me serious trouble—a tall stubborn Texan—a redhead. But he's rapidly being whipped into shape. "You know, ass hole," I told him yesterday, "I'd just love like hell to send you up." He's been conforming. The thing that pleases me is before I took over there were constant complaints about dirty rifles[,] messy bunks, messy tent, etc. Since I took over there have been _no_ complaints. So I'm doing allright [sic].

It seems as though you're fairly determined to see your folks down here. That's okay—if you'd rather spend the extra time with them than me (makes you feel low, huh?) Seriously, hon, it's fine. But I want you to promise me that if Tony makes one fake or phoney [sic] move _at all_—you'll tell me. Promise me that. And if he does—I'll take care of chubby in a Gung ho fashion. Also—_No_! Do not _drive_! That's all.

Last nite (yes, last nite) we went swimming from 8 to 9 p.m. in an outdoor pool in 40° weather. It was so goddamn cold I nearly went nuts! The water was icy! Talk about discouraging! I didn't do a damn thing, and stayed out of the water as much as I could. It was horrible.

The training here is getting rougher than we've ever had it. All my muscles are tight and sore. I'm a wreck. But the positions are coming easier, and my aim is steadier. Tomorrow we fire the .22 rifle, for familiarization. After that it's the M-1, carabine, .45 pistol, BAR and hand grenades.

That's all for tonight, darling—again. Love me always and thanks for the stamps and refill on my pen. I love ya loads & loads. I'll be looking forward to seeing you. Give your pillow a big kiss & make believe it's me. On second thought don't—there are some things the pillow will never be able to do.

Go ahead,

> Love your sweetheart—
> > Your husband—
> > > Al

xxxxxxxx's & hug

[drawing of heart, w/ "Al + Jo" written inside, and pierced by an arrow]

MZ 499

> Nov. 5, 1950
> Sunday

Dear diary—

Four weeks from today boot camp will be over. I've been in training 6 weeks now—6 <u>long</u> weeks. Sometimes it seems longer—a hundred years maybe. Sometimes it seems like I never knew a girl named Joanne—that she's just something I dreamed of. But we won't go into that now.

Yesterday we fired the .45 automatic pistol, a cold, flat-nosed fire-spitting weapon, one of the most dangerous of the Marine Corps. I looked hard at the bullet, as big as a man's thumb, rounded and hard. The gun itself jumps like a crazy man when the trigger is squeezed, and the hole it tears in the target makes one fear what it could do to the soft protoplasm of man. They say that a man hit by the .45 at 50 yards would be flipped over backwards. Looking at firing that cold, emotionless piece of steel, I wouldn't doubt it.

Last night there were 17 rifles dirty. So after evening chow we fell out with rifles to march in the "boondocks"—the thick, chocking [sic] dust that you sink into when you try to walk in it—much less march. The morale was at an all-time low. The men were bitter because they felt they were being treated unjustly. They were tired from a long, <u>hard </u>day of work; they were rebellious. The potential honor platoon we had seemed lost.

We marched for awhile [sic] in the dust, then stopped. The D.I. looked at us. "Okay, men," he challenged, "shoot. Just what the hell's the matter with this platoon?" One would surmise that not much would be said to a superior officer, tearing down his method of training. But much was said. The men said how they felt, why the spirit was low, why the platoon had hit the bottom rung. The words flew thick for an hour. But when it was over, there was a new feeling. Gung ho had no longer connotated a pseudo-salty boot. Gung ho rang true to its Chinese translation—work together. When we marched back to the tents, it was platoon 37 snapping to again—the damn[e]dest bunch of men you ever saw in your life.

Yesterday no mail came through for our platoon. Seems there was a foul-up somewhere. It's impossible that 68 men <u>all</u> didn't receive mail the same day. Naturally, I was disappointed I didn't get any mail from Joanne. But if it means that much more Monday—I guess it's worth the wait.

There is little doubt in my mind now that I will see combat before a year.

World War III is on its way, no matter how one tries to rationalize. Last nite a few of us fellows talked about it. "It's unjust!" one exclaimed. And I could hear Joanne say, "It's not fair, honey, it's just not fair." No matter what way it is put, the feeling runs high against organized murder. The will to fight in the Marine Corps is not as it once was. We are not the old breed, the troops of regulars who make war a profession. We are the reserves, the college kids and the old men, the dreamers and the builders—not the fighters. We don't want war; we don't want to die …

The way things sound now I'll be home for either Xmas or New Years, and maybe both. The Marine Corps is supposed to guarantee you at least one of the holidays home as long as your [sic] stateside. I don't know how this will work out with my 10-day bootleave [sic]. But I do feel certain I'll be home for Xmas. My second Xmas with Joanne…. It doesn't seem too long ago that we spent our first together: our Xmas tree, typewriter, cigarette lighter … it wasn't so awfully long ago. It will be even more fun this year. Joanne and I know and understand each other so much better. We're so much closer, and our love is so much deeper. This Christmas will mean much to both of us—I'm sure it will.

Well, it's 2 hours later now, but this diary would never know it. We just watched some boxing: 37 against 36—out of 10 fights we took 9. We have a fighting platoon. Hell no I didn't fight! I'm a lover, not a killer!

I guess I ought to start closing this day. We have to start cleaning rifles now for 3 hours—we start firing next week. Even Sundays aren't free. But that's the way it goes.

Let's see—how would I close this were I writing to Joanne. It's hard merely to say 'I love you' all the time, because it doesn't really say as much as I want to say. I want to say I love her, miss her and want to be with her more than anything else in the world. I want my wife not to worry about me, because I'll be alright and nothing can keep me from returning to her. I want to reassure her that I don't intend to get hurt. I just love her an awful lot. I love her with all my heart & life.

     I'll love her always—
     Al

(P.S.—Keep care of yourself, darling—I love you.) xxxxx's—Al

MZ 501

     7 Nov. 1950
     Tuesday 6:05 p.m.

Dearest Joanne—

I'm in the guardhouse. Not like you think though, dearest. I'm on guard duty tonight for 4 hours. My tour of duty starts at 10 p.m. and lasts 'till 2 a.m. It's not just the regular platoon watch; this is base security, watched over by M.P.'s, officers of the day, corporals of the guard, etc. The D.I. said he picked the best men to represent our platoon. I don't know about that, but I don't mind this duty at all. We ate at a great mess hall tonight—off trays, the food being separate. The M.P.'s here are real fine. We can smoke, crap out, write letters, etc. No sir, I don't mind this at all.

Tonight before we left, the shit really hit the fan. They pulled a surprise tent inspection—3 out of 11 passed. He really chewed me out. He says he has "special duty" for all of the tent leaders—I'm not looking forward to it. But those are the breaks of life.

Today we had quite an experience—we fired the Browning Automatic Rifle. It's really an amazing weapon—deadly. You can fire a full magazine of 20 rounds with one pull of the trigger in about one second. My aim was good with the BAR. I really tore hell out of the target. The only bad thing about the rifle is that it weighs 47½ pounds, and is no fun to carry around. But when you lay on your stomach and pull the trigger—power, power, power!

This coming weekend is really going to be a lulu. Friday has been declared a holiday here—the 175th birthday of the U.S. Marine Corps. We're going to march in San Diego that day. Saturday we go to a football game. Sunday is our regular crap-out day. Every man in the outfit is counting the days to Friday. I'm counting the days to when I can be with you. I want to be with you so badly—sooo badly.

Because I came on guard duty, I made special effort to be neat—I put on a pair of dungerees [sic] I washed. Notice, I neglected to say "clean" dungerees [sic]. Anyhow, it's the first time I changed for 3 weeks. The boys here were ready to break out the beer. The hat I wear, however, is the same one I put on my head is the same one I put on [sic for repeated phrase] when I first came here. Looks real salty. My dungeree [sic] pants and jacket are dirty as hell. They're the ones I use to fire with and crap around on the ground with. I change my jacket & take off my hat when I eat—sort of casual. We refer to those as our "loafer" or dinner jackets. It's a standing joke. We amuse each other that way.

This morning it was so foggy you couldn't see your hand in front of your face—no kidding. It was that way until about noon, then the sun broke through and the temperature jumped to about 80°. Quite a change in this San Diego weather. Nothing like dear old San Francisco. The more I see of the Southland the more I appreciate Herb Caen's mistress—San Francisco, the queen of them all.

Lights are going out early, dear, so I'll quit. 7:15 we sleep tonight. I love you loads—here's a big kiss. X—my darling.... Al   I love you

(send some stamps)

MZ 502

8 Nov. 1950
Wednesday

Dearest Joanne—

First of all, thanks for the wonderful lighter, darling. It's the most beautiful thing I've seen. I've always wanted a Ronson lighter, and now, thanks to you, I have one. Everyone in the platoon has admired it.

Now on to the serious business. I'm disappointed that you don't want to come down here for my graduation. It means we won't have those 2 days together on my 48[-]hour leave. And here's something it means that I haven't yet told you. An honor platoon is chosen out of each battalion; our[s] is almost certain for it. But which is more important, an honor man is chosen out of each and every platoon. He is the outstanding man, top test scores, cooperative and sharp in every military respect. So far, I am the honor man of the platoon. Now there are only two things that could keep me from the coveted position—swimming and firing. To be honor man of an honor platoon is the highest of glories in boot camp. I wanted you to be there Dec. 2 to see me parade in full dress. I wanted to be with you in privacy for 2 days anyhow. I had made big plans. But I guess they're all off.

I guess you have a good financial reason for coming down the 19th instead of the 2nd. I wish you could come down both times, but you say that is impossible. Honestly, darling, I did so want you to come down for graduation. I can send you $20 next week from part payment on my check. Please, please, honey try to come down for graduation. I probably won't be honorman, cuz I can't swim, but you'll be proud of me anyhow, I'm sure. Please, please try!

On the 19th I still haven't been able to find out when we're leaving back for San Diego. But the best bet would be for you to go [to] the Recruit depot and wait. We'll undoubtedly be here before noon. In fact, we may even stay here for another week for mess duty. I just honestly don't know. But I'll try again to find out.

Today was foggy, cold and miserable. So what do we do? Yeah, we go swimming. We were only in for about 20 minutes, so not much was accomplished. The instructor said to us, "I don't give a damn whether you learn to swim or not!" And he didn't.

<u>Nov. 9–6 p.m.</u>

Hi again, sweetie—

I feel in a little better mood today after a good night's sleep. I hadn't mentioned it before but I only got <u>one</u> hours['] sleep all night while I was on guard. Consequently, I was a tired, tired Marine yesterday. Considering that I was in a bad mood I think that yesterday's part of this letter is very well tempered. Don't you? But I remain firm—I <u>want</u> you to come down Dec. 2—no exceptions, including WA Bolinger. Phone me again before you come down if you can—then we can talk. Phone me anytime [sic].

Yesterday (I think it was) we threw hand grenades. Some kid got a big gash in the back of his head from the guy next to him throwing his hand around to[o] high. Fortunately, the grenade was a dummy, and all the guy did was bleed. I think he was alright. I was nervous as hell when I pulled the pin from the live grenade—wanted to get rid of it as soon as possible. Quite an experience watching the thing go off.

Listen, darling. I'm doing this on the sly, so I'll have to close. I'll right [sic] you a more complete letter today if I can. I want to stress how much I want you to be here for graduation. I want to be alone with you now (not only for sex) more than anything in the world. Please, hon, accommodate me just this once. Christ only know[s], if this war goes on we won't have too much time together for a few years. Let's make hay while the sun shines.

                              I love you, darling
                              (and that doesn't say half of it)
                                Al   xxxxxxxxxx's
                                           &
                                       A big, big hug
                                           Xx
                                       [drawing of lips]

[drawing of heart, w/ "Al + Jo" written inside]

MZ 503

                              14 Nov. 1950

Dearest Joanne—

Boy am I pissed off! Everything has happened today to make everyone say to hell with it all. First of all, rev[e]ille has been changed to 4:45—theoretically giving us 45 more minutes to sleep. So our D.I. gets pissed off & tells us we have to fix our bunks, clean our tents, roll up the tent flaps, clean the bore of our rifles & wash & be ready for chow by 5 a.m.! I don't give a damn how fast a man moves, 15 minutes just isn't enough time! So he says we'd better get up at 4 a.m. as usual—only the lights have to remain out! So we do all this in pitch black!

That's not the only thing that has p.o.'d me however. Our 2 D.I.'s have been arguing among themselves and contradicting themselves like mad. We get 2 different orders and they're both wrong! Everything has suddenly turned B.S., and the internal bickering is terrible! No, I'm not moody or psychologically gloomy—just pissed off!

Another thing that p.o.'d me was some guy[']s wife divorced him the other day, and he's been a wreck since. The poor guy loved her a lot, and she gave him the old war-time brush. Tonight the kid dropped his rifle twice, and one D.I. chewed his behind. Then he wouldn't let it go a[t] that—kept harping at him for quite awhile [sic]. It's things like that that keep me going for the day I can tell these D.I. I.Q. O.'s just what the hell I think of their gung holess [sic] spirit!

This morning it was still raining when we put on our ponchos, slung rifles and took off for the range. The rain stopped, but the mud was a foot thick on the firing line. Imagine lying & sitting in nice thick, gooey mud! Oddly enough, I did my best firing today, but that doesn't alter the fact that I was wet, muddy and indignant.

We're having a rifle inspection in the tents in about two minutes, darling, so I'll have to stop. It's 8 p.m., and one helluva time for inspection, but that's the Marine Corps for you.

Don't worry about me, dear. I'm my old normal, fiery self. I'm looking forward to giving you a couple big kisses Sunday. Love me always, darling. And don't give me the war time brush-off. I love you too much!

>Your loving Husband—
>Al
>xxxx's & lots more for you
>[drawing of heart, pierced by arrow, w/ "Al + Jo" written inside]
>[drawing of lips] for you
>I love you—Al

MZ 508

>[postmark San Diego]
>15 Nov 1950

My dearest darling—

I just got your letter, sweetheart, and it's the most wonderful thing in the world! I'm so happy for both of us I could cry. I was eating dinner when I opened the letter, and let out with a burst of "I'm a father!" Men I'd never seen before were congratulating me. When I explained the situation, the guys in the platoon were all sharing my new-found happiness. All of them are trying to think of names for him (they refuse to admit it might be a girl).

Honestly, darling, I'm so happy I'm confused. Ever since I got the letter I've been walking on air—marching out of step, not paying attention, etc. All I can think of is "I'm going to be a father!" Sometimes I even say it out loud. But everyone, including the D.I., smiles along with me. How does Nik sound as a fellow's name? or Allan? Alyn? Shit (an expression, not a name).

It's 9 p.m. now, and lights go out at 9:15, so I have to rush. I'm looking forward to seeing you Sunday so very much. We have a lot to talk about and look forward to. Take it easy always dearest, and don't lift anything or nothing. Don't worry about me at all, because I swear I'll put every ounce of intelligence & physical capacity I have taking care of myself. You be careful & love me always—just as I love you—so very, very much!

>I love you, I love you, I love you—
>xxxx Al

MZ 509

>21 Nov 50

Dearest Joanne—

Don't have much time to write, so I'll have to cut this letter to practically nothing. But I just couldn't let our two hours together go by without telling you how wonderful they—and you—were. The old thrill of a first love & a new date came back; my heart was pounding and I was as nervous as a kitten.

It was all so wonderful! I looked forward to kissing you & holding you close. I wanted so badly to rub my hands through your hair and feel your lips on my face. Darling, I can't tell you how much better I feel since I've seen you. I go to bed at nite thinking of you, and when I'm asleep I dream of you. Your image and personality are so strong & beautiful in my mind.

I guess we didn't get much settled in the way of technicalities, but we got a great deal settled as far as I'm concerned. We are the same two people, darling, so in love—and we can still holler with the old fire "The rest of the world be damned!" because neither war or loneliness or being apart or the Marine Corps can kill a love so strong & so fine. It will survive everything. I want you to listen to a record by Frankie Laine, "We'll Be together [sic] Again." Dolores has it. It expresses so beautifully what I have failed to say. When I left you Sunday I had to bite hard to choke back a lump in my throat. I kept waving at you (who the hell was that Marine who walked up to you on the steps of the guardhouse & what did he say?) but you wouldn't look back. I guess you felt as badly as I did. All in all, our Sunday was wonderful! I wouldn't trade those two hours with you for a million years of extra life. I wouldn't trade the thrill of that kiss for anything in the world.

Believe me when I say, Joanne, that seeing you makes life liveable [sic].

By the way, did you check at Oak Knoll? Also, no more laundry carrying down to the laundromat. Figure out some way to get around that. Strain is the easiest way to start a miscarriage. And we <u>don't</u> want that to happen. So use your head, hon, and don't overdo anything. Let's have a child that's strong & beautiful—and wonderful. A child just like you in <u>every respect</u>—unless it's a boy.

xxxxxxx   I love you, darling
  xxxx//   Al   I love you

MZ 510

> Wed. [i.e., Nov. 22]
> [envelope postmarked Nov. 24]

Dearest Joanne—

This letter should be full of woe & self-pity, because tonight I am tired. But instead I'm going to deep six that stuff and write a letter with a little more sense and (I hope) a lot more meaning. Because this letter is about tomorrow—Thanksgiving.

Now most people would enumerate just what they have to be thankful for—the blessings that were <u>heaped</u> upon them. But not I. No, I'm going to talk about the blessings we have brought upon ourselves—the thousands & millions of little things I hope you will remember tomorrow. Because tomorrow is the one day of the year to close your eyes, part your "pearly lips to show your ruby teeth"* and remember—and be thankful ...

How many times we swore at life and cursed all the misfortunes it offered us! Those nites—those terrible nites—that you spent sick, and I spent on the verge of collapse. Those nites of unhappiness and sorrow. We thought we had nothing to be thankful for. Realistically, maybe we didn't. But actually, now when we realize

---

*"Pearly lips and ruby teeth" was an ongoing joke for Al and Joanne, presumably harking back to a misstatement by Al while praising Joanne's attractive looks.

the purpose it served, it was all a part of the makeup of our marriage and the challenge of a young strong love. So we can be thankful.

Sure, we tossed caution to the winds a lot of times and went to the Castro* when we should have bought food. Remember our penny bank ("one for the money ...")? That didn't last long, did it? Oh, well ...

The shows were always fun, but I got kinda [sic] tired of rice[,] noodles & beans†—not to mention frozen hamburger. We had no particular physical reason to be thankful or even happy then. But we were then. Because we could laugh. And we're thankful now for those days, because they counted. And we can always look back on them and smile.

What have we to be thankful for, Joanne? It all adds up to so many things that it would be impossible to put them down. They're for you to think of when you're alone & lonely—in confused thoughts and blending dreams. They're yours to keep but not express—yours to think of, but not too clearly.

"Have a cigarette? ..."—our thankfulness began somewhere back there. Remember them, darling, because I'm helpless at writing them. Tomorrow I hope you think of all our wonderful times together, and I hope you can laugh and smile and cry at the memories.

If you can, say a little prayer for our past & future—for all three of us, and say a big prayer for yourself as I will. Because without you I would have had no past. You've been the most wonderful thing in the world to me—you know that.

And for our blessings of love, darling, we can both be thankful. As I am now.

I love you with
All my heart—
Your husband
Al
xxxxx

MZ 511

12/21/50
12:05 p.m.

My darling wife—

I guess when you get this letter at your folk's [sic] place I'll either be there with you or I won't. I'm hoping, of course, that we will be able to spend our second Xmas together. I couldn't leave such a pretty little girl without her husband on Christmas, could I? Such a pretty little girl who is loved so much. But that's all up to the Marine Corps.

The real reason for this letter is a pessimistic one. It's in case I can't be with you in person—I'll at least be there in communication and in spirit.

---

*The Castro is a neighborhood in San Francisco whose character changed over the years. It became a working-class neighborhood in the 1930s and over the next several decades into a gay community. Presumably, Al and Joanne might have strolled the streets and looked in at restaurants or clubs.

†"Rice, noodles and beans" was another recurring joke, harking back to their regular, economical diet when they had very little money.

This, using poetic license, all takes me back to our first Xmas together in 1949. It doesn't seem too long ago that I hurried home from work to see my typewriter; or that we walked the streets to buy you a lighter. Our Xmas tree was small but awfully pretty.

9:05 p.m.

It's been awhile [sic] since I finished that last paragraph, Joanne, and since then much has happened. I received my transfer orders—Replacement in the 3rd Infantry Battalion—First Marine Division. Tomorrow I leave for tent camp 2 to begin my advanced combat training. There are about 10 more of my buddies leaving—neither Don nor Hall nor Brunn is one of them. They may get their orders tomorrow, I don't know; they've been coming in since yesterday.

My orders mean almost definitely that I will be a foot soldier in whatever conflict follows this Korean thing. I asked about that Russian school, Hal tried for athletics, Don tried for the band and we all got the same answer: all reserves are infantry; it takes an act by the Commandant of the Marine Corps to change a specialty number. And that's the story, darling. No, I'm not going to stop trying, believe me. I've learned a few more of the angles in the Corps. But it all looks rather futile. One of my greatest regrets is that I've come to the parting of the ways (now, anyhow) with one of the nicest guys I've ever met: Don Weiland. I hope I see him after this whole filthy mess is over.

This isn't the kind of letter I started out to write but I wanted to tell you this so you could understand how I feel tonight and so you could hold me closer in your heart & love me. I need your love, Joanne, more than I've ever needed anything.

This Xmas will be a little different for us, darling. Much will be the same, but the fear of the future can't be erased. But Xmas, as I wrote and believed many times, is the day to humble ourselves and forget the disaster for the hope of life and the promise of happiness it whispers of. And, more important, it is the time to have faith in a power which many of us occassionally [sic] question—but which none of us with conscience could doubt.

So we'll count our blessings and forget our troubles and have faith in a God which only now can determine the course of action man will take. Oddly enough, I still have that childish, idealistic Martinez faith that tells me not to worry—that everything will turn out alright. I want you to have that faith also, darling. For your sake and for the sake of our child.

I'll be back, Joanne, I promise. So give yourself a big kiss for me. I'll see you for sure in the next 2 months. And we'll talk a long time. I may even see you for Xmas. I hope so!

'Till then darling take care of yourself and God bless you.

I love you with all my heart
Al
xxxxxxxx's & lots of love

MZ 514

3 January '51

Dearest Joanne—

Another day has passed, and some of us are still waiting. We expect to be placed in D Company today and begin training tomorrow morning. The training maximum is 11 weeks, but none of the past training groups have been here that long. We figure 4 weeks or so, but then again a draft is supposed to leave here for Japan Jan. 28. That may be us. We don't know. We never get the goddamn word—10 percenters!

Don, Brunn & Hal are all here in rifle companies! We're in the same battalion so I guess we will ship out together after all. Last night Don & I had a beer at the slopchute* and talked for quite a while. None of them got 10-day leaves. Hal, Don & some other guys flew home for New Years—and spent it in bed sick. All of them had stomach flue [sic]. Their luck has been rotten. On Xmas they got leaves Saturday; they could have gone Friday, but they had <u>one</u> class Saturday morning. They had to be back Sunday. Then they got leaves to Tuesday morning. Poor guys <u>couldn't</u> have got the full 4 days, oh no. The Marine Corps had to screw them. I've been luckier than I thought. I'll probably get the old shaft sooner or later. Oh well …

You'd be surprised, Joanne, if you could see the tremendous amount of apathy & disgust here at Pendleton of all places. Men talk openly of going AWOL, and mean it!

They plan it all out in the open. Two or three are always missing at roll call in the morning. The average has raised to 15 men a nite going over the hill. One of my good buddies has never come back from his 10 day leave. Officers practically beg their men to stay, and advise them to come and talk to the CO's if they feel like going AWOL. The situation is desperate. Everytime [sic] a newspaper circulates around the barracks the talk is the same: the fight will last forever if we fight the Chinese; that it's a needless sacrifice of our lives. Propaganda has failed to stimulate the "killing" urge. It looks like a hopeless situation. But, fortunately, there are those who hang on.

Someone said we were suppossed [sic] to get paid Friday, but no one believes it. There's a fairly good chance, however. If so, I'll call you at Mrs. Rozelles [sic].

That's all for now, darling. Take care of yourself and love me[,] honey. I love you & will always.

All my heart—
Al
xxxxx & love for you

MZ 516

Oceanside
4 January 1951
9 p.m.

My darling wife—

It's almost time for lights out, honey, but I thought I'd begin another letter while the spirit moves me. Rain (oh yes, it's raining) always inspires me. And the

---

*Slopchute is slang for a bar visited by members of the military.

loneliness of the night makes you come so much nearer. Something else inspired me tonight—we saw "Woman on Pier 13"* at the post (outdoor) theatre. It was filmed in San Francisco and I saw many of the places we lived and loved in in our Baghdad by the Bay. It made me kinda sentimental and sad. But we crabs (astrology) work better at night, no?

Whadda you know, you know, the wind is beginning to blow! Must've been that last sentence. Any minute now I expect lightning and thunder. Guess I'm getting carried away.

You know, hon, I've finally developed a searing [sic] ambition. The first thing I'm going to do is write the drama of the Marine—not the gung ho glory, but of the boots laughing at each other in the rain; of the guys lying awake at night dreaming of a cigarette when the "lamp" is out; of the jokes and of the laughs; of the love, fear and uncertainty. Joanne, I'm going to write about the individual. And I won't be restrained. I'm not going to confine myself by writing for a market. I'm going to let myself go as I never have before.

I've never had such a burning desire to write about any one thing before in my life. It's got everything I want to write about: the simple comedy and the tremendous drama; the suspense and the human appeal. I believe I can transform it into the best I have ever done. I don't exactly know what I'll do with it, but I'll have it published if I have to kiss every newspaper editor's ass in the country. I know, Joanne—it doesn't sound like me. But I'm beginning to realize a lot of things I never knew before. But I'm learning, honey, I'm learning.

Take all the letters I've written and put them in chronological order by the post mark on the envelope. Would you do that for me, darling? It'll pay off. Hones'!

Time for sleep, honey, I'll finish this tomorrow. I love you, darling. Sleep well and take real good care of yourself for me. Oh yes—I won't be able to have that card signed until Monday when we start. But I'll mail it right away. Okay darling?

Goodnight, Joanne—My darling Joanne ...

I love you—
Al

Good morning, dear! Or should I say goodnight! There's one good thing about getting up at 5 a.m.—I like to watch the moon go down. But it's 7 o'clock now and the temperature is still in the 30's. This has been the coldest night I have ever seen. All night long I froze, even though I did have on my dungeree [sic] pants, sweatshirt, socks and two blankets. Not a bit like Southern California.

Last nite we heard on the news that Truman doesn't want to bomb red China because we are not officially at war with them. My utter contempt for that man has increased by leaps and bounds. Obviously, Truman disregards our losses on the battlefields; he pays no attention to the dead and to the dying. If it is not war, then it is murder, and the United States government are accessories before & after the fact. It is first-degree premeditated murder, and someone beside our innocent

---

*The Woman on Pier 13 was a film made in 1949, starring Robert Ryan, Laraine Day, and John Agar. It told the story of a man blackmailed by the Communist Party into spying for it.

men ought to pay. If it is war then it should be handled as such, and at least a good portion of our armed might ought to be thrown in to save lives. It's a confused issue to our government. It is very plain to the Marines overseas. This is war.

1/6/51

Hi darling! It's Saturday morning and we still haven't got paid. And we won't for 2 more weeks. Meanwhile I am flat—too flat to even buy cigarettes or get a haircut. So if you can possibly afford it it [sic] (if you haven't already) please, darling, send me a few dollars (sounds like old times). I've got to get my stuff cleaned, laundered and pressed or I'll be run up like a monkey.

Just happen[ed] to think—this is a 3-day letter. Not bad, eh? Listen, hon, I'm going to finish this off so I can get the crap off my rifle. Write to me often, hon, and let me know exactly how you're doing. When I get paid I'll send you all the money I know I won't use—probably close to $100.00. So keep your chin up, darling, and keep loving me.

                  All my love—
                     Al
                  I love you with all my
                  heart—and always
                  will. I love you.
                  xxxxxxxx

MZ 518

                  Oceanside, Calif.
                  13 January 51
                  Saturday
                  9:35 p.m.

Dearest Joanne—

I'm in the sack now, and one of the fellows' radios is playing a song that brings back the most wonderfully nostalgic memory I could ever remember. The song is—you know—"Oh how we danced on the night we were wed …" The Anniversary Song. Remember that, darling? Highballs at Helen's? Our reception! The Justice of the Peace of the 7th district? It doesn't seem like so long ago. And when I think of how much I love you—it was only yesterday.

Camp Pendleton and all the fear and heartache and frustration of the future just doesn't [sic] exist when I think of our young, serious love growing into something so beautiful. We did dance on the night we were wed; and we waited and stalled. But we had to go to bed sooner or later. Just a couple of virgins sweating out that "first time." You were scared? How do you think I felt?

Gee, honey, when I stop to think of all that it makes me want to be home so badly that I feel like just leaving. Remember when I was living in Richmond and you worked for Jerry Batt's? I got the same feeling then—I had to be with you, or else I'd go nuts. So I'd pop out of nowhere and we'd baby sit or just talk and wish we had money. Now I can't just "leave" to be with you. But sometimes, sometimes

I get that irres[is]tible urge to say to hell with it, and hurry to meet you. I'm glad you're coming down next weekend …

Good morning, darling! That first page was cut rather short last nite by the guard sticking his authoritative face in and screaming "lights out!" And that was it. So we begin anew this morning. I say this morning, but actually it's 1 p.m. You see, I didn't get up until 11 a.m. Naturally I missed breakfast, but I made lunch. So now I feel relaxed and ready for what may come.

When I talked to you on the phone the second time last week I guess I was kinda grumpy, but here's why. The day before we had taken a 10[-]mile conditioning hike in the morning that last[ed] from 7–11 a.m. And that <u>same</u> nite we took a tactical 12[-]mile hike that lasted from 7:30 to 9:35 p.m. It wasn't so bad walking, even though we had combat packs, helmets (those damn things) and rifles, plus the divided carrying of the B.A.R. (50 lbs.) No, it wasn't so bad that we had to carry 75 pounds on our backs. It was the damn pace that almost killed all of us! Baker Company took that same hike after a full day's rest the day before. They left at 7 and came back at 11:15 p.m.—4 hrs & 15 minutes; they had 7 breaks and didn't go as far. We made the hike in <u>2 hrs</u> with <u>one</u> break, and we went all the way! So help me it's the truth! I have never in my life been so tired from walking (half-running) before in my life. I was so sick and sore the following days that I was unapproachable even by Brunn, Hal & Don. That was why I was kinda bitter and grouchy when I spoke to you on the phone. It was the only time in my life that I have <u>ever</u> reached the point of sheer exhaustion. But I guess it won't be the last time, heaven help me!

Twice now we have hit the combat obstacle course. An 8[-]foot wall is the first of it. The wall is made of wood and has no ropes, grips or anything. When I first went over it I didn't know whether I could make it or not, so I took a fast leap at the wall, gripped the top and hurdled over. I made the wall by 4 feet but missed the purpose. I was supposed to hug the top close. But I made it, which is more than many of the guys did. After the wall the rest was a maze of tunnels, pits, barbed wire and rope—tiring, but easy. Also we have had several classes, bayonet drill, combat fire team* maneuvers (I'm a scout) and all sorts of things.

To confirm our meeting date, be at the Hotel San Clemente, Saturday the 20th at 2 p.m. The Santa Fe train goes there from L.A. The hotel is on a side street off Highway 101 which runs through San Clemente. Wait in the lobby for me. Something may happen that I'll get the guard or something, so wait till about 4 then phone the camp—3rd Inf Trng Bn. I'm in barracks #232. Honey, do me one favor. Leave Friday night and get there in the morning. San Clemente is a rough town, and has a reputation of snarling in pretty young girls such as yourself. If you can get to the hotel about noon, that will be fine. Because I'll probably get there about then too. Liberty goes at 11:30. Rent a room when you get there and rest. We can stay there that night even if we have an apartment, okay?

Will write more later. I love you.

Al

---

*A fire team is the smallest group in a military unit, smaller than a company or platoon. A fire team might typically be comprised of four members. In later letters, Al mentions fire teams and becoming the leader of his.

Honey, the address of the hotel is 120 Avenue Del Mar; the phone number is San Clemente 404. Take a taxi to the hotel from the San Clemente station. If you don't, I don't want you carrying any heavy suitcase. So take <u>good</u> care of yourself, darling, and hurry down here. I'll be counting the days until next Saturday.

> I love you with
> all my heart –
> Al
> xxxxxx & loads of love.,
> Al

P.S. I love you …

MZ 520

> 15 January 51

Dearest Joanne—

I said to myself, "Now, Al, dammit, if you're going to write Joanne a letter make it cheerful—make it happy!" But when I sit down to write, I find that if I don't get everything off my chest to you I brood and feel like perfect hell. Oh, I suppose I could cry on some of my buddies' broad shoulders, but it's not the same as telling it to you. You understand. Yeah, maybe it is self-pity. Anyhow, here's poor Alfred's Almanac.

This morning, after a few sundry jobs in the field, we had a clothing inspection on our bunks—you know, all laid out by the inch, folded a certain way, etc. My washable clothes were clean, but the stuff that needed laundering—not so. Same with the stuff that needed dry cleaning. Everyone else was like that, however, so he chewed us all out with a passion and said we'd have another inspection at 7 p.m., thereby restricting everyone to the base. That all didn't disturb me too much; I don't go on liberty anyhow.

So this afternoon we went on a 12-mile hike. The sun was up around 80°. We had blanket rolls added to our packs. The hills were steep. We were on our way back when some kid dropped his gear and went screaming down the side of the hill—completely and hopelessly snapped. The gunner caught him then started spouting off: "What the hell's Uncle Sam supposed to do, apologize to your mothers for bearing idiots?!" The kid was laying conscious in the back of a pickup truck, and the gunner approached him with, "Why don't you scream now!" He continually rode the subject, ridiculing the kid.

I didn't know the kid personally. But I do know that he wasn't kidding. The stretch was just too much for him, and it seemed that he had to crack sooner or later. He was sensitive, homesick and maybe a little too young to think in terms of guns and war. I wish I knew.

The closer I come to a military machine, the further away from it I grow. I suppose in time they'll make a Marine out of me—hard, without scrupples [sic]. But never without a mind. Watching the lives of a bunch of nice people being chewed up is too much to pass me without leaving an impression. I can't watch someone crack without feeling my legs weaken for a minute and my stomach flip. And all the time I think of them, their families and you; and I think, there goes their future. And it seems such a shame to waste a generation that might have done something.

So you see, Joanne, this day has been rather miserable. It wasn't the gunner's fault; he had to handle it that way to keep the company from mutiny. Naturally, we failed our inspection tonight. Don't ask me why.

Now that I've got that off my chest, allow me to thank my darling wife for an enjoyable book, my shirts and one of those thoughtful little things that makes her my sweetheart—a soapdish! So thanks, hon! I've already finished the book and lent it to Brunn. It sure made me homesick for San Francisco & you. Oh, well.

The weather out here is sure odd. One day rain-storm, in fact. Next day, 80°. Next day fog. Then 30°. Then, rain again, and the unholy cycle repeats itself. But weather I can stand. Even the Marine Corps I can stand. But when this is all over, I'm going to fight like hell for a job, settle down and join nothing. And my son isn't going to join nothing. And my son's son isn't. Martinezes for generations will be disjointed. But, by God, they'll be civilians.

Well, so much for history, darling. Don't feel sorry for me. I feel too sorry for myself. However, I'm sure I'll live through it all. I'm just that kind of person who gets beaten enough to be bruised, but never broken; hungry but never starved; miserable, but never cracked-up. I'm just a normal child.

And you know, honey—sometimes it's rough being just normal! I love you ...

All My Heart—
Al
xxxx & love for you

MZ 521

16 January 51

Dearest Joanne—

I received 3 letters (4, I mean) from you today. Three were nice. One, well one, made me feel kinda' [sic] bad. But I can say truthfully, I had it coming. First of all I didn't understand why you were angry and what you meant by the sentence, "... as for what I'm thinking—I don't know." Then your very sweet letter that came this afternoon explained everything. And, darling, I'm sorry.

When I made all the plans for the weekend, I didn't mean them to sound like orders, hon. I guess I projected my own anxiety into the letter—and it came out the way it did. Baby, no one knows better than I that traveling is hard on you. Who worries about you all the time. Who has spent half of his married life saying "take care of yourself"? Honest to gosh, darling, I'm more concerned about you than I am about me! That's a fact.

So please, don't think that I'm not giving a damn about your feelings, health or anything else. You mean much too much to me to have our love intentionally violated. Understand me, darling. And I'll try to understand both of us.

It rained like the devil until about noon this morning. The afternoon?

Typically California—hotter than hell. So what did we do this morning?—shots, two of them. I walked through the line completely non-plus[s]ed. The first needle was a snap. The second—God, the second! It was "cow pox." My left arm is almost useless. But I'll live.

This afternoon we had familiarization with the M-1 rifle—you know, the various forms of firing. We did that all afternoon. It's a good thing we didn't do more. Well, the day ended—or so we thought. Then spoke the gunner: "We will have an inspection of all equipment on the bunks at 7 p.m. tonight!" The stuff hit the fan. Everybody bitched.

We left for chow at 6 p.m. They delayed us and talked. Came the mutiny. Everyone started hollering and swearing at the NCO's. Tempers became short. The men were bitter, and some moved from the ranks with clenched fists toward the non-commissioned officers. The reason for it all was that we wouldn't eat until 6:30 and we had to have our gear out on our bunks by 7—in perfection. They expect the impossible, and they got the logical reaction.

But all came out well.

Well, honey, that's all for now. I probably won't write anymore [sic], in case you do come down Saturday. If you don't feel well, don't make the trip. But if you're okay—hurry, darling—I'll be waiting with open arms. I miss you so much …

> I love you
> Al
> xxxx & all my love.
> Al

MZ 522

Two

Through Mud, Mortars and Hell*

> Fox Co. crapped out on the ridge we just took. Charlie Co. moved up beside us. We were laying there, feeling pretty good, waiting to chase the Chinese off another ridge about 100 yds. away. Then the devil stepped in. Mortars came in on us. The deadly silent explosives that whoosh before they hit. With deadly accuracy they hit into the crowd. Screams & the cry "corpsman" filled the air. They came one right after another: the whoosh & the detonation. I buried my face into the earth & prayed. (letter of June 3, 1951)

> Why war! Oh, God, why war? (letter of May 16, 1951)

On March 15, 1951, Al Martinez and his buddies in the seventh draft embarked for Korea on the U.S.S. *Thomas Jefferson*. After about two weeks at sea, the ship reached Japan before continuing to Korea. Within a few days of arriving in Korea, Al joined Fox Company, 2nd Battalion, 7th Regiment, of the 1st Marine Division on the front lines. Some of the bloodiest fighting of the war had already taken place before Al's arrival (e.g., the landing at Inchon, September 10–19, 1950, and the Battle of Chosin Reservoir, November 27–December 13, 1950), and by the time Al was posted to the front, the war had largely become a stand-off, with battle lines on both sides remaining somewhat static and featuring repeated, often pointless patrols of soldiers and Marines in search of North Korean and Chinese foxholes and artillery. Nonetheless, Al and his comrades saw plenty of intense fighting action, receiving heavy casualties at times. While on duty at the front, Al received a promotion to the rank of corporal.

Much of the time, Al and his buddies had no idea where they were on the front lines, but he took part in action in late April 1951, along the Yalu River, and he fought in the Battle for the Hwachon (or Hwacheon) Dam between April 22 and 26. He participated in "Operation Mousetrap" in May, when the 7th Marines were airlifted to an area in advance of the front lines in order to lure the Chinese troops into a space where they could be attacked by troops from both sides. In June he took part in a battle at an area called the Punchbowl. Taking place in August and September, the Battle of the Punchbowl encompassed the Battle of Bloody Ridge and the Battle

---

*"Through Mud …": Letter of June 3, 1951.

of Heartbreak Ridge. Marine forces gained control of the hills north of the Punchbowl. Hill 749 was taken by the 7th Marines. (For further information about these battles, see the glossary and the letters' notes.)

Beyond the dangers of being in the sights of the enemy, Al describes the trials and discomforts of life on the front lines. He and his buddies had to tolerate C rations for days and weeks on end, with the often-resulting diarrhea; a lack of water, sometimes for two or three days at a time; perpetual dirtiness; brutal cold with no proper warm garments; and a crushing boredom relieved only by action against the enemy.

Al Martinez was patriotic but he also saw that the "police action" in Korea was a waste of young men's lives for a cause that was far from being just. His peaceable nature rebelled at the senseless loss of human life caused by the war. "Everytime [sic] I see a Marine lying with a shelter half over his face I want to cry & scream to the politicians back home that this is their war—and these are the men who are paying. It all can be prevented, I don't care what they say. I don't wish combat on anyone, but I wish everyone in the U.S. could see with their own eyes a war which is gloryfied [sic] & so badly misinterpreted by propoganda [sic]—newspapers inclusive. I wish they could see the complete waste of human lives on the front lines" (letter of June 18, 1951).

Despite his revulsion at seeing young men cut down in battle, Al was very proud of being a Marine, and this comes through clearly in his letters. Along with showing pride in his buddies and unit, he reacts to the army with a Marine's contempt for the army personnel, or "doggies," although he is scrupulous in giving soldiers appropriate credit when he feels they merit it. He also comments on the Marines' lack of equipment and supplies in contrast to the abundance enjoyed by the army units. This applied to everything—food, uniforms, proper gear, and arms and ammunition.

Al Martinez, 1951 (The Huntington Library, UDID 324236).

As noted previously, Al's letters to Joanne are self-censored, i.e., he refrained from telling her about the most brutal battle action he experienced, in order not to cause her more worry than necessary. He alludes to this in one letter: "You were right about my not telling you a lot of the things that happen here. Sometimes it's not very nice to tell—especially to a girl about to be a mother. I don't even write most of the gory stuff in my diary—just human interest things. But I needn't worry about forgetting them—I never will. As for telling you about things that we're going to do—darling, if I could do that I'd be the most valuable man in the Corps. I don't even know what I'm doing when I do it, much less before I do it. So don't worry about that" (letter of May 14, 1951).

Like all military personnel serving in Korea, and as discussed in the Introduction, Al watched for news from the Kaesong and Panmunjom peace talks with great interest, riding the crest of hope and tumbling to the trough of despair depending on the reports he heard. Even though he wrote to Joanne that he was not swayed by either the positive or the negative news, he was affected by it and his moods are readily apparent in his letters. For Al and his buddies, everything, including their very lives, depended on the outcome of the peace talks. Success in the negotiations could mean going home soon, while failure meant continued deployment in the war zone, always with the possibility of the escalation or expansion of the conflict.

Like his buddies, Al used pejorative terms (Gooks, Chinks, slant eyes) to refer to both Korean and Chinese people. As noted in the Preface, these words must be understood in the context of the time and situation. While such terms are racist and appalling to us today, they were in general use at the time in Korea and, later in Vietnam, by the troops who were demeaning and demonizing the enemy, as soldiers do in every war. It is likely that at least a few of the servicemen in Korea saw nothing wrong with these words and might well have continued to use them later, but for many, including Al, the use of the terms reflects only the danger and stress of living in daily peril of their lives, along with their conforming, with their buddies, in a common parlance.

In the midst of the fear, blood and exhaustion of battle, Al found spiritual and psychic relief in the love he felt for Joanne, in the basic human goodness of his buddies, in the innocence of the Korean children he encountered, and in the beauty of the natural world around him, such as the stars in the night sky. Most significantly, he derived the greatest joy from the anticipation and then the birth of his first child. Cinthia Louise Martinez was born on May 31, 1951. He learned of the baby's arrival on June 3 but not of her gender until June 14. In some of the letters leading up to her birth, Al refers to the unborn child as "Allan," clearly his favorite name for a boy. Also in May, Joanne sent Al a small plastic turtle as a good-luck piece. Al kept the turtle through the rest of his time in Korea and named it "Boondocker," after the Marines' name for the boots they wore. From then on, Al signed most of his letters "Al and Boondocker."

Throughout his time on the front, Al longed for the chance to write professionally, and, as the weeks went by, he referred to the possibility that he might join the regiment's Public Information Office, which would get him away from battle and enable him to fulfill his calling to be a writer.

Al managed to keep a diary while in Korea, and in several letters he quotes excerpts from it for Joanne. He intended to publish the diary but never did. The diary no longer survives, so the excerpts are important for the extra impressions of his experiences, along with his letters.

◆ ◆ ◆

30 March 1951
Kobe, Japan

Dearest Joanne—

At 2:45 p.m. the U.S.S. Jefferson docked at Kobe, Japan. Funny little bug-like animals followed us around in the water—Japanese junks. Small, brown, slant-eyed dock hounds looked curiously at us as we tied up; some wore handkerchiefs tied around their heads; others wore those odd quilt-like outfits that characterize oriental fighting units. All of them were dirty and mysterious-looking.

Kobe harbor is a masterpiece of camouflage. You can't tell it a 1000 [sic] yards out. In the bay are half-sunk remnants of the Imperial Japanese Fleet—bomb holes of another world war yawning like decayed sores in their bulkheads. Everything looks morbid and eaten away.

We got the word that we are not leaving this ship; we will stay aboard & go directly to Pusan. Tomorrow we <u>may</u> get <u>2</u> hrs. liberty—in groups of 25 with an officer in charge! How chicken shit can one outfit get! Yeah—the Navy went on liberty. They're big boys. I guess they just don't feel that the Corps has come of age.

The only thing that saved this day was 8 darling, wonderful, sweetheart letters that came 5000 miles to me right from my baby's heart! I wish I could tell you the change that came over me when I got those letters, darling! It was as though I was home again—almost. I grabbed McCall's leg & did a tip-toe tanner* around the tiny compartment. And the pictures of you were the sweetest ones yet! Especially the one where you're standing by the pony. They couldn't be sweeter! I also like my "angle" shot from the backward position. Not a bad photog, huh?

I wrote you a real long letter yesterday, but lost it. So I'm trying to remember everything & put it in this one along with all the latter [sic] developments.

I'm sure glad to hear you're feeling alright, hon. That makes me feel good just to hear it. As for me—well laying around this ship has made me fat, lazy & out of fighting trim. But I feel great, honest!

About a week ago I started growing a muschtache [sic]. It was doing fine until—you know, trim a little off the left, then off the right—then, no[,] too much off the right, a little more off the left, and—the CO told me to wash my face and, pride injured, I shaved off the last remaining hair. I've also thought of a tat[t]oo, but that 2-hr. liberty deal kind of killed that. Anyhow, it was just going to be a <u>little</u> tat[t]oo.

---

*Tip-toe tanner presumably describes a dance step, but its meaning has proven elusive in searches of dance terminology. Joanne Martinez suggested that it was probably a term that Al invented.

By the way, how's Boondocker,* itchy pup† & the family? Fine I hope. Also, how's your nookie? [these last three words printed in very small letters]. Give my love to little Allan too. Glad to hear he's up & kicking. A chip off the old block.

Oh, thanks for the $10. I'm sure you could have used it more, hon, but knowing you—I wouldn't refuse it.

later

More hot scoop. We leave Kobe sometime Sunday for Pusan. There we get our orders for the 1st, 5th or 7th Marines. From there we take an air lift to the front lines. They're trying to keep the company in the same regiment, but no one knows for sure just what's coming off. By 1600 tomorrow the ship will be combat loaded: ammo, rations, etc. As the CO says, "they're hauling our asses into combat in the Marine fashion—in one big hurry." But I'm not afraid.

No, hon, I'm really not afraid –maybe for really the first time in my life. It's not as if I were walking in a store to ask for a job, then turning away in fear. It's not as if I were shying away from competition—afraid of failure. For once in my life I've got to go through with something, and though I wish it were just a little journalistic competition, I'm glad in a way that it isn't. The Marine Corps, so to speak, is forcing my hand. Now let's see what I've really got!

Keep writing to the same address until I let you know differently. And, above all, keep writing even if it takes months for an answer to reach you. I'll write as often as I can!

Honey, I've said it before and I'll say it again: I love you more than I've ever loved anything in my life. You're everything I want and the only person whom I can love without fear of ever "losing interest." I love you, Joanne, and I'd do anything for you. Maybe there's a lot of things I haven't done, and a lot of promises I haven't kept; and a lot more ways I could prove my love. But a fact remains: I have a lot of time to prove it, and all this that's happening now makes me want to prove. It takes big things to push a point across to me, and a world war has finally done it: I love you, more than any one man could ever love his wife.

Love me always, darling.
        All My Heart—
           Al
[Sketches of three Marines]
I love you—
   Al

MZ 527

---

*Boondocker was a small toy turtle, probably made of ceramic, plastic or rubber. Later, Joanne sent it to Al and he carried it with him throughout his time in Korea. He named it Boondocker after the lace-up boots worn by Marines.

†Itchy Pup was probably a stuffed animal Joanne had. Al occasionally sent greetings to Itchy Pup.

2 April 1951
Enroute [sic] to Pusan

Dearest wifey—

In about 1 hr. & 15 minutes we should dock in the war-time, temporary harbor of Pusan (pronounced 'Pusan'), South Korea. 'Tis a moment of tension among the men of the Corps. Brunn says gravely, "Oh, yeah." Bagley takes a long drag on a cigarette and murmurs "What time does chow go?" McCall questions, "Pu-Who?" Thus is recorded a moment of drama, unparalleled in the history of the Corps.

To my immediate right a high-voiced Texan and another yokel are discussing whether or not pork chops have ribs in them. McCall is reading the "Keyhole"* out loud. The headline reads, "Raped Before Grandma's Eyes." Personally, I believe grandma bitched cuz she was jealous. To my rear, Lutke (to my rear, that is) is standing in the middle of the compartment with naught but a towel wrapped around him exclaiming how as he's taken his final douche before leaving for combat. And, of course, the Navy P.A. system is saying "Now hear this .. ." and that's all I ever hear.

Rifles are now being cleaned, packs packed, knives sharpened and pistols examined in readiness for combat. 'C' rations have been issued (6 cans of chow about the size of soup cans, plus cigarettes, etc.) and all the guys can think about is how in the hell they're going to fit them in their pack—paying no thought as to what they'd do without them. Me? I am squared away as usual. In my pack I have: 1 pair greens, 2 sets dungarees, mess gear, 6 cans of chow, 6 pair field socks, gloves & liner, a flannell [sic] shirt, poncho, a pair of air-tight pants, 4 pair shirts & shorts, 2 gung ho hats,† towel, toilet articles, rifle-cleaning gear & other incidentals which I have accumulated in the course of the journey. I am ready for anything!

I read a cute joke:

A star-struck female fan wrote to Sinclair Lewis applying for a job as private secretary saying, "…I'll do anything for you, & I do mean anything!" Lewis' wife got the letter & promptly & courteously replied "…I act as his private secretary doing everything for him, and I do mean everything!"

It has been recently learned that the 7th Marines (me) will leave Pusan aboard plane[s] for the front on April 6. That means about April 7 (roughly) I will get my first taste of combat. Already I don't like the taste.

Seems the escence [sic] of this letter is nothing imparticular [sic], so I'll continue with just that. It's fun.

Someone just poured lighter fluid on his buddies [sic] shoe & touched a match to it. It blazed awhile [sic] until someone saw it—then all hell broke loose! Right now I guess buddy is chasing buddy on the after-upper deck.

Land has been sighted, hon, so I guess I'd better close. No one knows for sure

---

*The Keyhole mentioned here was apparently a periodical but there have been numerous magazines bearing the name, so it is not possible to identify the precise publication referred to here.
†Gung ho hats are cloth caps with a visor.

whether we're going ashore tonight or tomorrow morning, but I'd better be getting set. Besides, I want to look at Korea.

Keep your chin up & don't worry. No damn Chinaman is gonna keep me from you too long!

I love You—
Al

[several Japanese language characters]—this means "no smoking" in Japanese; it was on a warehouse in Korea.

MZ 529

Pusan, Korea
April 3, 1951

Dearest Joanne—

I bitched about tent camp 2—it was filthy. I complained about Camp Mathews—muddy. Kobe was a mess. But Korea—Pusan, Korea outdoes anything I could describe in sheer degradation, filth and physical corruption; it completely baffles the imagination as to poverty and downfall. Picture is [*sic*] you can black and dirty buildings, dirt roads, open sewers, men eating from liquid garbage cans! I saw it, Joanne! The people themselves actually stink! And for vegetables they use human fertilizer. I have never seen anything like it in my life.

We left the ship about 10:30 a.m. this morning and boarded trucks for the tent camp I am now at. We road [*sic*] through the city of Pusan—if you can call it a city. There is nothing about it even comparitable [*sic*] to an American city.

Before we left the ship an army band played away, along with a Korean Navy band. A Korean welcoming committee was there[,] as was a general of the 8th Army. He gave us that "God-bless-you-boys-give-'em hell-and-keep-low" routine full of fire and pathos. His voice quivered with emotion.

In our tent (which is floored with an ancient oriental material—mud, I believe they call it) we found a Korean kid by the name of Kim. He speaks pretty good English & can read some. We have adopted him as our houseboy. He now wears a gung-ho cap and says quite clearly (pardon the language) "Chinese no fucken good!" That wasn't my idea.

We leave for the front in about 3 days. Right now I'm writing from a red cross building. Not bad! Music, books and, yes, free coffee & doughnuts.

That's all for now, darling. Love you & miss you terribly. Give my love to our family.

I love You—
Al xxxx for you & Allan

[several Korean language characters]
"NO SMOKING" in Korean.

MZ 530

Al Martinez poses with the sign for Fox Co., 2nd Battalion, 7th Regiment, that has the company motto "Hot to trot," 1951 (The Huntington Library, UDID 324237).

April 8, 1951
Korea

Dearest Joanne—

Believe it or not, I am now sitting in a fox hole atop one of the highest mountains in Korea—and getting here seemed to me one of the greatest accomplishments of my life. It was about a 4-mile trek—<u>straight up</u>! And that was with rifle, helmet, sleeping bag, pack & a lot of other crap on my back that just about killed me. I'm so out of condition that I actually crapped out coming up. Three of us had to drop out & be brought up later with a guide. I'm not ashamed, however, and no one thinks I'm a drag in any way. I climbed up when the average person would have died & when I hadn't slept for 2 days or had any chow to speak of for 2 days. And on top of that, 15 days aboard ship didn't put me in the best of shape.

But I made it after about 4 hrs. & met some of the nicest guys I've ever met. I was assigned to Fox Co., 2nd plt. The lieut. is a hell of a good head & he & the men treat me like a long lost buddy. They gave me their chow, water & cigarettes, & put me in a fox hole with one of the seasoned men. Again, I'm in the hottest, hardest-hitting co. in the Marine Corps & I love it!

They took this mountain just yesterday morning, with no casualties & only one wounded—grenade shrapnel in his behind. He refuses to leave, however. Just winces every time he sits down.

Last nite a trip flare was set off in the valley below us, & since the Gooks are dug in on the mountain right accross [sic] the valley from us, we thought it was them. We could all see them along the ridge-line. I unclicked my safety & the Bar [i.e., BAR] man was set to let a burst fly when the call "Roks!" went up. Roks* are South Koreans. Seems they had gone out on a patrol, got lost and hit by our artillery. They don't know how close they came to being completely wiped out. The Roks are loyal, but stupid.

This morning I washed for the first time in a week—cold water in the face—and went to the head for the first time in a week also. The only things I've done with faithfulness is [sic] brush my teeth & write in my diary. Shaving is something I used to do with a grumble—now I don't do it at all.

After a goodnight's [sic] sleep, I feel pretty good today. In good health & in better shape. Aside from feeling slightly cruddy, I feel fine. This company has had no casualties since it[']s been on the line, so don't worry. They take good care of their men & we're so high up the Gooks could never reach us. We're supposed to stay here & be relieved in 4 days. We all hope so.

I'm not expecting any mail from you for a month, knowing the system as I do. I hope you've been getting mine. Keep writing though.

They captured a prisoner yesterday, & here's what he had to say (interpreted): "We shoot soldier when he eat & sleep (Army). But yellow legs (Marines) no sleep, no eat. Can't shoot. Velly bad." How about that!

> I love you with all my
> heart & miss you terribly.
> Take care & [sic] yourself & Allan.
> Oodles of love & kisses
>   Al

Man am I salty! I got ribbons up the—you know!
>   love ya—
>   Al

[verso]
PFC. A. Martinez, 1056679
'F' Co., 2nd Bn., 7th Marine Regiment
1st Mar Div., c/o FPO SAN FRANCISCO, CALIF.
    my address now [arrow pointing up]
(We're about 2 miles crossed [sic] the 38th; crossed it the 5th.
P.S.—don't believe <u>anything</u> the papers say: bayonet charges, etc—a lot of horseshit!)
>   love—Al

MZ 532

>   April 10, 1951
>   Korea

Dearest Joanne—

I wonder what you're doing this morning, honey? Sitting down having a cup of coffee, talking to Mrs. Rozelle or going against my wishes (you little devil) and

---
*ROK is an acronym for Republic of Korea. Al and his fellow Marines referred to the South Korean soldiers as ROKs, pronounced "rocks."

working somewhere. I wonder what you're saying, what you're thinking. I wonder if you're thinking of me. I hope so, cuz I'm sure thinking of you.

I'm sitting in my fox hole listening to the artillery, mortars and small arms fire nearby, and looking down into a fog bank every once in awhile [sic]. Now and then a plane drones lazily overhead, kind of like a fly on a hot day in San Francisco—you know, like when you're laying in the sun & that soft buzz sounds in your ear. Except these flies are spitting napone [i.e., napalm] & 50 calibers. And it's cold here. And this isn't deah old S.F.!

Last nite was a nervous one for me when I was on watch. A trip flare was set off in the valley & I thought sure as hell the Chinks were coming. Either they chickened out or the flare went off by accident, because nothing happened. They wouldn't've caught me napping, however. I had my rifle loaded, my cartridge belt on (100 rounds) plus 3 bandaliers [sic] on my shoulders & 5 within reach—a total of about 1000 rounds of ammo plus 5 grenades. The guys all got a big kick out of it this morning, They swore I could've taken on a whole division myself. But I was jumpy last nite & didn't want to take any chances. If anyone even nudges me in my sleep I'm up, rifle in hand, safety off & hot to go! So when I get home you'd better not nudge me or I'll be on you like a tiger, hot to go! Come to think of it, that sounds pretty good to me!

We're supposed [sic] to get 2 cans of beer this morning, so I'm sitting around waiting eagerly. Even if it is colder than hell, that brew sounds pretty good. Oh, yeah—it snowed a little night before last. Not much, just enough to put patches of white on the ground. Our fox hole wasn't even touched tho: we have an elaborate shelter, what with ponchos, shelter halves, etc.* I stayed warm & dry. I'm beginning to love my sleeping bag. I don't even take off my hat when I hit the sack now.

I've written a couple letters to my folks, letting them know I'm alright. I told them I was in Pusan & now I don't know what to say. But I'll keep writing & saying a lot of nothing, as I can so easily do.

For the last 3 days we've had it easy up here: no trouble, hot chow (not like the army, however), good sleep & lots of time. Everyone is telling me how lucky I am, but I don't feel so damn fortunate myself! I joined this outfit to fight! And don't give me that you're-too-cute-to-fight routine either! I'm a killer I tell you! Yeah!

Oh, yes—I have a battle star on my Korean ribbon. Had I been here one week earlier I'd've had 2. I'm also entitled to wear that U.N. rope on my shoulder & the french [sic] rope. Also a unit citation, the presidential citation & the Asiatic Pacific ribbon—plus the reserve ribbon & good conduct. They can keep their purple hearts! I want none of it!

Well, darling, give my love to the neighbors & tell them to buy war bonds to keep the army in hot chow. Poor fellows barely have enough to keep body & sun glasses together. Until I write again, you keep care of the family & write to me. I haven't gotten any mail yet, but I expect some by Xmas. Love you loads & oodles & rice, noodles & beans! Take <u>good</u> care of yourself!

---

*A shelter half is essentially half a pup tent, used for shelter in a foxhole.

> I love you with all my heart—
> Your Husband—
> Al

[drawing of man in heavily decorated uniform]   me? Yeah, I saw a little action!

[several Korean language characters]   —Joanne in Korean—no kidding!

MZ 534

> April 11 (I think)

Dearest Joanne—

It's 2:30 now and the heat of the day is torturous. There's no shade, no breeze & no comfort from the afternoon heat. All you can do is wait it out & pray for wind. To top it off, an order has come out making us keep our shirts on. I tell you, there's no justice.

This morning about 5 of us went swimming against orders. The hole is about a mile in front of our lines, but I had to cool off somehow. I got there and dived (honest!) into about 5' of water, no fear, no nothing. I actually swam some it felt so good. It's on days like these that I believe I could become a champion swimmer. I didn't give a damn about drowning or anything else. All I wanted was to cool off. It felt wonderful. By the time we walked back to our positions, however, we were drenched with sweat again. You can't win.

You might have heard somehow that the 2nd Bn, 7th Marines has been wiped out. The Chinese have been broadcasting & printing that through various propoganda [sic] channels. Believe me, we are <u>far</u> from being wiped out. I don't know what they expected to gain by telling us that—we know damn well we're not wiped out! So don't fret if you hear that anywhere.

Do me a favor if you get time, hon: cut out about 5 of my better File 13's & send them. Send them all from the 2nd semester. Send the first one, some of my election columns & a couple of my stories (Dean Valentine,* new campus, etc.—all by-line). The guys have asked to see them, and I'm certainly one to oblige them. Make sure there are duplicates at home to all the ones you send, though. Thanks, sweetie.

Pretty quick I guess you'll be moving in with Mary. Let me know so I can start addressing you're [sic] mail there. If I don't hear, I'll start sending it there in about a week or so. Gee, hon, I don't know what else to write. I've written you so often that nothing new transpires in between letters.

Oh, yes—I have a bitch. Bugs! All kinds. Ones that fly, others that cry. Some buzz, some chirp, others just sit & look. There are furry ones & hairless ones, purple ones & black one[s]. Anytime [sic] you sit or lay, there is something crawling on you. The ants are huge & black. Mosquitoes, flies & God only knows what else spend all day tormenting us. When you kill them they let out a dying wail for their relatives & counter-attack. They march on us in a route column & attack en

---

*P.F. (Percy Friars) Valentine (b. 1884) was a dean of general education at San Francisco State College from 1945 to 1950.

masse. The flies aren't the kind you can shake off! They cling, and rub their hind legs at you. Then when they take a bite out of you, they buzz you like a Corsair.* One of us has to go—I or the slant-eyed insecticides. And I'm afraid that we'll both be here for awhile [*sic*]. They're worse than the Chinks.

That's Al [*sic*], for now, sweetheart. Take care of yourself & don't worry about me. All is well. I love you muy mucho!

>Love to you & Alan (or Andy)
>Your husband—
>Al
>xxxxxxxxxx

[drawing of a Marine's face in profile]
HOT TO GO!

MZ 535

>April 12, '51

Dearest baby—

This won't be much of a letter—just a line to let you know that all is well. We went out on a combat patrol today—about 10 miles straight up, and your husband is literally exhausted. I'm in the sack now and it'll be a wonder if I survive this letter. We didn't run into anything today; fortunately, because my fire team was the point—right up in front. The Chinks had one mountain ½ hr. before we got there, but when they spotted the platoon they left in a hurry—leaving fires burning & rice cooking. That's all for now, honey. I'm beat. I've just got to sleep.

I love you, Al

>April 13, '51
>(The Following morn)

Hi sweetie. Sorry, I petered out on you last nite, but I just couldn't take it. I was exhausted to the point of collapse. To give you an idea of how tired I was, I woke up for my 2-hr. watch at midnight and sat staring grog[g]ily into space for <u>5 solid hours</u>! At 5 a.m. I came too [*sic*] and layed [*sic*] down, having to practically be dynamited out of the sack at 8 o'clock.

More about our patrol yesterday. We left at 9 a.m. and got back about 4 p.m. (all day without chow). Our object was to seek the enemy out on the highest ridge and destroy him. The 1st plt. sat [i.e., set] up at the bottom, the 3rd plt. patrolled the valley, and our plt. went up, and up, and up. When we got there all that was left was their fox holes and a few booby traps. They really must've high-tailed it, because everything was just as if they'd stepped right out the back door for a moment. I personally looked in every fox hole around.

Because my fire team was the point, and because I think the lieut. wanted to see how much I could take, I had the hell worked out of me. Every Korean house or village we passed, our fire team had to search. Every time we crapped out, the

---

*Corsairs were the type of plane flown by Marine Corps pilots.

lieut. sent me on top of the next ridge to see what was on the other side. Then when I got back it was time to move out. But I wanted to make a good impression, so I went the lieut. one better: I carried the BAR of our fire team (47 lbs) up those damn hills for half of the way! I staggered all the way up, but they didn't hear me bitch or crap out or even ask for a break. The lieut. was obviously pleased with me, because all the way back we walked together, talked and kidded, and he told me about the plt. & the company before I joined the outfit. I'm in like Flynn* now, but I swear I did it the hard way. But it was worth it; to have the lieut. like me was one of my aims, because I think he's a fine man. And a smart one.

In a day or so our Battalion goes in to regimental reserve for a week or so, so we'll have it easy. We'll move to the rear area about 10 miles back, eat good chow, take showers, sleep on cots and have a ball! That suits me fine, cuz already I'm tired. From what I hear, though, they have inspections up the gigi!† But that's okay. I'm use[d] to that.

How's everything at home, darling? Fine I hope. I hope you're over that siege of nausea and are feeling tops. It must be getting warmer around the bay area now. It snowed again up here nite before last—quite a bit too. But, aside from being a little windy, the weather has been generally good.

I still haven't received any mail, but it should only be a week or so before I do. I've been dreaming about you every nite for the past 4 days, and they've been wonderful dreams! I love you with all my heart, darling, and all the feeling I'm capable of—and that's quite a bit. We're going to be terribly happy when I get home. My last nite with you and my time over here has taught me a lesson: I'll never purposely hurt you again. I swear it.

I love you, darling. Think of me, because I'm always thinking of you.

                              I love You—
                              Al   xxxxx and a million hugs

MZ 536

                              Pusan, Korea
                              April 14, 1951

Dearest Joanne—

Last nite from 11–1 a.m. I stood what might be called my first guard duty in a combat area. It was an eirie [sic] feeling, quiet but for that strange whistling sound the night always seems to make. It was a black night, a strange night, with all the movement and feeling one imagines when alone.

When I first went on, rifle shots sounded in the hills—one's echo rang close. "Enemy snipers," someone said casually. "They're even around here at night." I had

---

*The expression "in like Flynn" was probably based on the actor Errol Flynn, whose womanizing and drinking were legendary. To be in like Flynn means that one "has it made," i.e., has attained a goal quickly and easily. The title of the film *In Like Flint* (1967) is a play on the phrase. As a result, people often erroneously use the phrase "in like Flint," rather than the correct, original one.

†The word gigi, sometimes spelled "giggy," is a slang word for anus. The phrase "up the gigi" is a coarse phrase denoting that something occurs constantly or to excess.

to run my fingers over my M-1 in case, just in case. But there's no fear of them coming too close if they value their lives; there's a guard about every square foot of mud.

Something happened last night which has never happened to me before and which I hope will never happen again. My guard mount extended from left to right, and I toured that for about an hr. I was standing facing ahead when suddenly I found myself moving forward, without control, without feeling or rational method or reason. I moved about 15 steps before I caught myself; then I felt foolish. But for just a brief moment it was a[s] though I were detached from myself. I don't know if you can picture it or if you can get the feeling. There's probably nothing too strange about it—I was tired and might have fallen asleep on my feet, I don't know.

I just don't want it to happen again.

As I said before, I was tired last nite—but I couldn't sleep. I went to bed (on a cot, fully dressed, <u>under</u> my sleeping bag) about 9 and lay there thinking & smoking until it was time to go on guard. Then at 1 a.m. I lay for another hour, nervous, restless and slightly nauseated. I finally fell into a deep sleep and slept right through chow this morning. I think it was all just a case of nerves. This morning I feel fairly calm & composed. Must've been my period last night. Think I'll get pregnant & end those "monthly worries!" Hokay?

You know hon, it's amazing how clearly I can remember & imagine things when I let my mind go. I can picture you so clearly and imagine myself next to you in San Francisco without effort. It use[d] to be that my mind wouldn't concentrate, and I had to look at your picture to get on the right mental track. But now I've learned a power of concentration which summons picture-images without exterior help. It helps to relax me and get my mind off the present situation. It's wonderful, honestly!

The day at 10:30 a.m. is warm & still. Last night it rained some & made the ground muddier, but today is actually nice.

You ought to see the difference betw[ee]n the Army & Marine Corps over here. The doggies are even dressed better! They have fur-lined field jackets, we have the old green army rejects; they have heavy, green dungerees [*sic*] with all sort[s] of tricky pockets, etc.; we have our salty, thin army-reject (again) dungerees [*sic*]; they have fur-lined hats, we have our old gung-ho hats; they have combat boots, we have leggings. But the doggies still look at use [*sic*] with awe, and you can't mistake the unconscious swagger of a geyrene [*sic*]. What do the Gooks think about it? They don't mind the ones with the boots, but they don't like the "ones with the yellow legs," a POW says. And when we asked Kim if he knew Marines he replied, "They're the tough ones." Gung ho, Rayder!*

That's all for now, darling. Will write more tomorrow. Take care of yourself and love me lots. I love you with all my heart—but I guess that's obvious.

Love you—
Al

MZ 538

---

*Rayder. The meaning of this reference is unclear. It could denote someone named Rayder, or it might be a misspelled reference to Marine raiders.

April 15, '51

Dearest baby—

It's Sunday again, but you'd never know it in the mountains of Korea. The artillery keeps its barrage up, and awhile [sic] ago we could hear the tanks moving into firing position. Right now it's comparitively [sic] quiet, and if one had a good imagination he might imagine that it could be the day of the week designated as the sabbath ...

Today I'm almost alone here: one squad is out on patrol, 24 men went down the mountain after beer, some went down to take showers & a couple went to church. I'm doing none of the [a]forementioned.

Here's a page out of my diary to give you an example of what I'm doing: "April 9—Ran into a So. Korean patrol today. One member was a kid about 4'5" & about 8 or 9 yrs. old. Had an M-1 on his back as tall as him & the helmet he wore covered his shoulders almost. And he had seen combat!

"Some fella (Rodriguez) was sentenced from a court-martial today in the field. Mr. Stone read it with a smile: 'a $30 fine & 3 mo.'s restriction.' I don't know whether it was an abortion of justice or whether it follows that 'justice will out.' I have my doubts on both ends.

"Someone stole my 5 of spades out of my deck of naked-women cards; as long as they don't steal the 4—that's the one!

"Guarded 1st plt. chow while they were on patrol—still 6 cans missing though.

"Expecting the Chinks to attack tonight. All is in readiness for them. If something should happen, I love you very, very much, Joanne. And it gives me an odd feeling of power (which I know you'd be proud of) to realize that I'm not afraid. No, darling—I'm not afraid!"

And often in my diary I become reminiscent: "March 21 (aboard ship) ... It's raining heavily now, and the reflection of light on the wet deck reminds me of the grey overcast days of San Francisco, Richmond or Oakland ... of streetlights shining on a wet pavement on a nite that has come too early; of people rushing under awnings thru the rain.... This storm ... reminds me sorrowfully of the dampness, the greyness & the reflection of light on wet streets which is peculiarly my home."

And descriptive: "The water smashes an inky purple against the sides, then dashes back into crisp white foam & silver crystals and settles into turquoise and white patterns along the prow of the ship ..."

Human interest enters in: "April 4—Kim (our littler Korean house boy) is being fed by 6 Marines who aren't much older than he. Crackers, cheese & one man's 'C' rations are his meal. He eats them shyly and his small dirty face lights up and he says, 'PFC good man!' Marines are soft-hearted people ..."

And when we crossed the international date-line & lost one full day I wrote briefly: "Saturday, March 24. Lost. Our yesterdays. The day that never was, and never will be." And what a story that entry will tell!

Those are but a few pages from my diary, Joanne, and certainly not the best.

But it gives you an idea of what I'm doing. I'm not pulling an Ernie Pyle* & writing only about the dehydrated eggs the boys ate for breakfast; nor am I writing only of a South Pacific 'Bali Hai'†; nor am I being Hearstling & writing only of bayonet attacks up hand grenade hill. I'm writing of all of these: of a Marine fresh out of the diaper brigade in Japan (17 yr. olds) wondering if he should shave because it's Sunday when he has nothing to shave anyhow.... Of another picking leaves out of his yellowed coffee.... Of yet another looking about 16 years old, and loading a rifle like he's been doing it a hundred years.... I'm writing of a chipmunk scurrying suddenly through the leaves and bringing 40 men to a firing position, silent & listening.... Of a flare lighting up the sky & of eyes staring into the blackness it leaves when it fades. I'm writing of nite and day, of life & of just existence & of death which is the inevitable for some who must fight a war. And I'm writing of men like myself, who love & watch & think, and who laugh at their misery because it holds a plot that no other writer has been able to top.

There are no 'Bali Hai's' out here, Joanne—that's to[o] fantastic. There are just men who are dirty because they sleep on the ground, who are tired because they climb mountains & who are afraid because they might die. As simple—as <u>beautifully</u> simple as that. And I'm going to tell about it—just as simply!

I love you & miss you. Take care of yourself.
        Al

MZ 540

        April 26, '51
        Wed.

Dearest Joanne—

It's a warm day in Central Korea. The sun is soft on my shoulder, & for the first time since I hit Pusan I have nothing on but a shirt & dungaree pants. I went down to a stream this morning, bathed & washed my hair. All is quiet, and which is even more important, yesterday I got about 10 letters from you, one from Frank, one from Dolores & one from Helen & from mother [?]. As the soldier spoke, "...I am content."

Before I forget, you mentioned something about reading in the papers where the Chinese were trying to blow up the rese[r]voir & flood the Halu [i.e., Yalu] river. I was there. We were set up on Hill 53‡ over the waters & it was us they were trying to stop. They succeeded in neither flooding the river [n]or stopping us. Cut out all the clippings in the paper about the 1st Marines & I'll tell you the incidents I participated in. Gives me a thrill, you know.

Too bad about the Seals,§ but I saw this downfall coming. They've been on

---

*Ernie Pyle (1900–1945) was a famous American journalist in World War II who wrote about ordinary soldiers. Winning a Pulitzer Prize in 1944, he was killed by enemy fire in the Battle of Okinawa.

†"Bali Hai" is a song from the Rodgers and Hammerstein musical *South Pacific* (1949). Bali Hai is an island paradise, visible but always out of reach.

‡Hill 53—the identification of this has proven elusive.

§The San Francisco Seals were a minor league baseball team that played from 1903 to 1957 in the Pacific Coast League.

the skids since '49 now. I bet Lefty O'Doul* isn't manager much longer. He may buy out Fagan (the owner)† but I bet he stays out of the management picture. As for the Oaks—don't worry about our boys. They'll be near the top again this year as they have for the last 5. Same goes for the Yanks.‡ I'm betting on 'em this year too.

Yesterday I got what might be called a promotion. I am now a scout instead of an assist. BAR man. It's what I trained for at Pendleton & is what I'd rather be. Jenkins§ got fire team leader & I'm in his fire team. Also I was told that I'm next in line for that job. Not bad for a "new man" eh? What really tickled me is that LeBlanc¶ (my old fire team leader) is now assist. BAR man. He's been P.O.'ing me anyhow and it may do him some good to get that gung ho crap out of his system. He'll live longer using his head,

I read parts of two of your letters to my buddies: the parts where you mock the ignorance of some of our politicians & where you tell me to keep my chin up. They were both sincere, well-written passages, which meant a great deal to me—& my buddies.

Looking through your letters again, I see where the same old domestic worries still ...

<u>half hour later</u>

Well, the old words have sounded again: "Saddle up & stand by to move out." Where are we going? Who knows. Manchuria, reserve, Russia—I'll not even know when I get there. Will finish this later. Love ya—Al

<u>April 27</u>

Hello again, Hon—

It's tomorrow now. We're set up on a small knoll 5 miles South of where we were yesterday. Those words to "saddle up" were sounded at 12:30 p.m. yesterday. So what time did we leave? 2 a.m. this morning. More fun climbing down a mountain in pitch black. Again, our gung ho C.O. took off at a breakneck pace—naturally he carried no pack. We got to where we were going at 5 a.m., dead tired. I threw my sleeping bag on the deck, climbed in & died. We had word to be ready to move out at 6, but I slept 'till 9:30. It's 3:10 now and we're dug in. We leave here tomorrow or the next day. We keep moving South. I don't know if we're headed toward reserve or if they're taking us to another front. Someone said they're expecting a Chink push somewhere else. I don't know. No one ever tells me where the hell I'm going. They could lead me to kingdom come & I'd bitch cuz I had to walk. I have a Gook sword & a pipe now too—extra weight. The sword looks

---

*Francis Joseph "Lefty" O'Doul (1897–1969) was the manager of the San Francisco Seals following a career as a player in major league baseball.
†Paul Fagan, businessman and owner of the Seals.
‡Yanks. Presumably, Al is referring to the New York Yankees. There doesn't appear to have been a Yankees team in the Pacific Coast League in the early 1950s.
§Bert Jenkins was Al's buddy and often his foxhole mate, a 19-year-old from Kentucky. Al mentions him frequently in his letters.
¶Earl Leblanc—Al's buddy and fire team leader in boot camp, from Texas.

funny hanging out of my pack. Attracts stares. I'll probably dump it, but I hope I can hang on to it. I must present quite a sight—pack, sword & M-1—walking down the dusty roads of Korea!

A couple days ago we were on the march, moving like mad to get out of a would-be trap. We were bitching all the way, tired, sweaty, dirty—every truck that passed kicked dust in our throat. We had no water, & things were generally miserable. We stopped for a break when one of the guys passed use [sic] to catch up, & with a hapless, resigned look on his face querried [sic], "I wonder what the poor people are doing today?" Thus speaking, he limped on.

Got your letter this morning & it was the sweetest letter yet. It was a long one & told me about the fun you had at my sister's places [sic]. You'll be surprise[d] how good it makes me feel to know that you're feeling well, having fun & dreaming of me. You're always dreaming that I'm being nice to you & it kinda makes me feel like a rat realizing I wasn't when you were awake. Repent you sinners!

Jenkins is lying next to me in the foxhole reading "What's Wrong With Our Abortion Laws?" I honestly doubt if he knows what "abortion" means, but he's reading it anyhow. Good kid.

I guess it's about time for me to tell you what kind of a person war is turning me into. Much to my dramatic chagrin, I haven't changed a hell of a lot! I found 2 gray hairs in my head, & have a mushtache [sic], but aside from a little harder appearance, less weight, more dirt & more muscle—I'm physically the same. Psychologically, I still give the appearance of being carefree—"don't worry about it." But I'm more alert than I've ever been in my life. Every sense has been sharpened to an unusual degree by constant use. Which is even more important in my make-up, I still have a sense of humor; & can still laugh at myself. It makes me feel better, too, to be able to laugh off a too-near mortar shell; or a whining bullet. I've begun to realize why so much humor comes out of war—it's an old American custom.

Remember how I use[d] to be impatient with ignorance? No more. I'm not Joe College anymore [sic]. I've quit flouting education. I realize the most important part of intelligence is tolerance (don't like that word)—acceptability. My buddies aren't minds or degrees—but humans, who'd help you when you need them. Lookit [sic] me, hon—I'm growing up.

Jenkins says he hopes the baby doesn't kick too much. Quite a boy, Kentucky.

That's all now, hon. I'm feeling fine, & loving & missing you loads. I can hardly wait to get out of this hell hole. The Orient! Nuts! Next time I go to Russia where everyone is rich, yeah!

All My Love—
Al
XXXXXX
(love to Alan) (to Cynthia [sic] too)

P.S.—tell Bob he never had it so good. He doesn't know what fighting is. He was in motor transport!

April 29
(I think)

Dearest Honey—

The other letter (condition of it) is the result of: forgetting to mail it one day, 2 days of forced marching in rain, the rain itself, sleeping on it in the mud & several other adverse conditions which certainly do not add to the appearance of any written matter. However, I'm going to send it anyhow, hoping you can decipher what I've written 3 days ago. [He refers to the preceding letter, mailed in the same envelope.]

We have moved South again. The Army 24th division broke & was routed by what appears to be a huge Chinese force, estimated at 60,000. Yesterday we moved 14 miles & are now set up in a steal [*sic?*] defense on a ridge 750 KM high. All of the 1st Marine Division is on the line. We are 6 miles north of Honchon.* I suppose the defense line stretches all the way across Korea, what with ROK & Army forces. I know the Marine defensive set-up is tremendous. Even Hitler couldn't penetrate it! Much less the Chinese.

The misery of the march yesterday was added to by the rain, wet gear, wet men, mud & 2 days chow in our packs. About 6 men out of our plt. fell out & haven't shown up yet. I imagine there were about 50 in the battalion. I guess they're at the CP & will show up later. I think the main reason for their dropping out was just plain disgust. The pace was too fast, the breaks too few. Everyone was just plan P.O.'d. You should've heard the bitching! I was doing a good deal myself, but I stayed with the plt. Man am I in condition! I take these mnts. like nothing! If this keeps up I won't have any trouble climbing mountains to hunt tigers when I get home!

I got 2 more of your letters 2 days ago, & didn't have time to read them 'till yesterday. Sure makes me feel good to know my family is treating you tops & taking care of you. Just goes to show how much they think of a sweet girl. Tell them for me how much I appreciate it, because I sincerely do. I won't forget their help, & will certainly repay them as much as possible. I swear it.

The scarf I sent you had no particular significance. I bought it in Pusan & didn't have time to send a letter with it. Just a gift. I sent something to my mother at the same time, I can't remember what. Oh, yes—give my mother a big birthday kiss for me & tell her I wish her the happiest of birthdays. She's been a wonderful mother to a selfish & often narrow-minded son, & I am realizing that more & more today. Show her or read her this letter & let her know that I haven't forgotten all she's done for this individualist. I'll send her this for a birthday present because I know, being the kind of person she is, it will mean a great deal to her: my good health & a promise that I'll return to the U.S. in good health.

A Walter Winchell quotation: "If your son is in Korea, write to him. If he's

---

*Honchon—this place name eludes discovery. It might be Al's spelling of Hongcheon.

in the Marine boot camp, pray for him." Explanation: Winchell's son committed suicide at Paris Island & the old man has never forgotten it.*

As for Galo joining the Corps—I warned him. That's all I could do. The rest is for him to learn by experience. And since he is so wishy[-]washy & emotional, I hope his experience isn't too bitter.

All for now, darling. Will write again soon. Let me know all the time how you're feeling & take care of the family. All the love in the world from a husband & a father-to-be who loves you dearly ...

I love you—
Al
XXXXXXXX for you & Alan or Cindy

MZ 546

May 3, '51

Dearest Joanne—

It's an unusual day in Central Korea. It's overcast, but sometimes the sun breaks through & it's hot—then it's windy. I've been taking my sweater off & on all morning. Now I've got it off, and damned if I'll put it on again. I'll freeze first.

Last nite and early this morning I had security watch, and I have never been so impressed with nature. I had the nite watch in time to see the gray mnt. horizon turn purple & the stars—millions of them—fill the nite. This morning I watched the sun come up in a clear, fresh sky. It was really like a morn in spring: birds singing, the hills all green, the sun already warm. But a deafening mortar barrage killed that picture muy chop chop.

There really isn't a lot to tell you. So far today (it's 12:15) I've just been laying around. I cleaned my rifle, wrote to my mother, ate chow, wrote in my diary & thought of you. I'm sleepy, but can't sleep. I'm tired, but restless. It's a paradox. Thanks for the compliments on my letters & my diary. I'm really proud of my diary & I love to write you letters. Sometimes I read my diary over & get a little annoyed because I haven't really captured the spirit. But, as usual, I always feel dissapointed [sic] at everything I write, so I leave much to memory. Fortunately, I have a good memory, so I'm not really worried. I'm more confident than ever before that I can make a good story out of all this—one that will sell. I'm betting on it. I've always hollered that I needed something to write about. Now I have it, and if I miss the boat, I kiss goodbye to writing and launch myself on a salesman's career. As for "my head getting too big for my helmet"—Have you ever worn a helmet? When my head gets that big, then I start charging people to look at me.

---

*Winchell's son, Walter Jr., did indeed commit suicide, not at Parris Island, and not while in the Marines, but in the family garage on Christmas night, 1968. According to Herman Klurfeld's biography, *Winchell: His Life and Times*, Walter Jr. joined the Marines after dropping out of school. Leaving the Corps, he traveled to Africa, returning home to speak of his misery in the Marines and of his adventures in Africa. His behavior was erratic, and he began seeing a woman he identified as the daughter of a Nazi general. After their marriage, he wore a Nazi uniform in public, goosestepping and crying out "Heil Hitler!" He eventually received psychiatric treatment, but it apparently did little good, and he drifted from one low-end job to another until he took his life in 1968.

Yesterday we got a treat, if you can see it as such. Each man in the company got 1 fresh egg, 1 apple, & the equivelent [sic] of 2 slices of bread! Remember in "Battleground"* how Van Johnson treasured his egg then busted it? I fooled them all, and ate it immediately. It tasted good, but I wish I had more. Even got a pair of socks & a pair of shorts. No dungerees [sic], however. Maybe today. If not, I just go on looking salty.

Nothing more to say, hon, so I'll stop. Got 3 letters from you today. Keep writing, darling, I love it—as much as I love you, my precious wife. Lots of love to you & the baby—

xxx   Al   xxx

MZ 549

May 18, '51

Dearest Joanne—

I'm writing this letter down deep in my foxhole, comfortably ensconced on my sleeping bag, peaceful & at peace with the world. For the past 2 days we've been on the move at the usual break-neck Marine pace over hill and over dale. "Where're we going?" I asked idly yesterday. "Back to the front lines," was the reply from the gunny. "Back to the lines?—Where we've been?" "Oh," he pondered, "about 6 miles into No man's land." Had I known that that [sic], I wouldn't have slept nites, believe me! I thought we were on the lines with troops all around. There were troops all around. Chinese troops! As it was, the 7th Marines were bait for an "operation Mousetrap." We stayed out there 'till the Chinks hit, then withdrew. They followed right into the mousetrap (an ambush) and we got in the show. 105 Chinese dead, 250 captured, 240 wounded—an enemy battalion wiped out! The papers you read will probably say, "General Ridgway† [sic] & his 'U.N. forces' (get that!) succeeded ..." etc. But I'm telling you the facts! It was an all Marine show, with the 7th starring. And we never shined brighter! And they call us "U.N. forces!" Nuts!

We all thought after that we would surely go in reserve. But no. 48 days on and in front of the lines on C rations, but would they send us to a rest camp? Hell no! We replaced the 1st Marines on the line! They've been here all of 2 weeks—they're going in reserve. The 5th just got out of reserve, but they'll be going back! Damn me anyhow. We haven't even had mail for a week! I'm gonna bitch to someone. You, I guess. Don't I always.

The ridge we're on is a beauty, though, so I shouldn't complain. The foxhole-bunkers were already dug. They're about 3 feet deep, 7' long, & 2 feet wide; they have log & dirt covering on top about 4' thick, sandbags all around and

---

*The 1949 film *Battleground* starred Van Johnson, John Hodiak, and Ricardo Montalban in the World War II story of the Battle of the Bulge and the 101st Airborne Division. Al recalls a humorous episode in the film featuring Van Johnson's character and a precious fresh egg.

†Matthew B. Ridgway (1895–1903) had a distinguished career in the U.S. Army. Following service during and after World War II, he became the commander of the 8th U.S. Army in Korea. After President Truman removed General MacArthur as commander of all United Nations forces in Korea, Ridgway replaced him.

a place to fire out of. In other words, they are rain proof, bullet proof, wind proof, mortar & artillery proof & even air attack proof. This is the first time we have had sandbags or tops on our foxholes. That's not the half of it. About 100 yards to our front is barbed wire blocks & a whole area of land mines, booby traps, flares, fragmentation grenades. In front of us is a valley covered with mines, to our rear are tanks & artillery. In my foxhole are 10 hand grenades, 5 rifle grenades (I'm the only rifle grenadier in the squad), 1 white phosphorus, 2 flares, about 500 rounds of ammo & me! Why, hell, I could hold 'em off by myself! This is the most protection we've ever had! Usually[,] they throw us out in front of God & the Chinese with an M-1 & say, "Kick hell out of 'em!" Now we'll be able to hear them 10 miles off & let the tanks take care of them, maybe picking off one or 2 to keep in shape. We've got it knocked! But we'll probably move out mañana, so I'd better quit clapping my skinny little hands in glee.

For the past 2 days (while we were moving) it's been hotter than hades ("hades"—I'm repenting). Now that we're settled the sun dips behind a cloud & it looks like rain. I swear the weather is against us! I don't know, I just don't know!

Since I haven't gotten any mail lately, I don't know how things are going in S.F. but I know you're doing okay. I guess the pressure pains you wrote about would thrill you, hon, because they even thrill me. I can hardly wait to have the Red Cross notify me that I'm a daddy! Doggone—<u>me</u>, a father! It's so wonderful I can hardly believe it. I lie awake nites planning how we're going to raise our child into a fine person. We being so young ourselves, we can all have a lot of fun together. You know, hon—once I get a job & get going, I would like a dozen kids! Hell, maybe even 2 dozen—we're Martinezes! How does that sound, <u>Maw</u>? Charming? Deee-lightful! Feel energetic? I do—<u>uh, huh</u>! So much for education.

I've been seeing a lot of the guys I came over with lately in Dog & Easy Co.'s [*sic*]. I can hardly recognize them under dirt & beards; in fact, I don't even remember their names. I give them the old, "Hi, mumble-mumble, how are you?!" "Well, I'll be doggone! Mumble!" they answer. We talk for awhile [*sic*], give each other curio[u]s parting glances, then wander away muttering "Who in the hell was that?" Half of the time I talk to a guy about old times & discover I don't even know him. Funny part is, the damn fool does the same thing! Stupid, huh?

Also, it's getting so you have to be careful who you talk to. Even the officers are running out of gear, so they pick up dungeree [*sic*] jackets wherever they can. Some are second hand & have PFC stripes on them. So you're liable to be cussing out the corps to a peon & find he's a major! Oh, me …

> Love Ya, Sweetheart—
> Loads of kisses—
> Your husband & the father
> of your (our) child—
> Al
> XXXXXX

P.S. x—a little kiss for the baby—it's just a <u>little</u> boy (or girl).
P.S.—This letter is written all backward, in the true Martinez fashion. However,

the pages are numbered, so all is well. The only right thing I've ever done in my life is marry you!

                Al

[Drawing of a Marine's face in profile, captioned:] Look, Alan—daddy! Alan, come back!

MZ 560

                May 20, '51

Dearest Joanne—

    Well, things are finally looking up. Yesterday we got beer (2 cans) PX rations, mail & packages. Today we got beer (4 cans), mail, showers, clean clothes, PX rations &, after 49 days, hot chow! It's almost like Heaven, all this. I received my first package from you—shirts, shorts, hankies—and Boondocker. I knew that little sonofagun would turn into a front-line turtle. I'll take as good care of him as I possibly can, but if worse comes to worse I may have to send him home or leave him in Korea. The underwear was greatly appreciated. I gave all but one set away, seeing as how it would be extra weight if we have to move out; you have the thanks of me, a fire-team leader & an assist. BAR man. We thank you.

    The weather over here has been good & bad, off & on. Today it's good. A couple days ago it rained. Yesterday the Chinese tried to advance in bad weather, but it turned good. Artillery & air strikes & our combat patrols cut them to pieces. There are many a dead Chinaman today who will never again trust the weather.

    The other morning (3 a.m.—6 a.m.) our fire-team had a patrol in the rain & I caught a pretty bad cold-sore throat. After treatment by the corpsman, it's a lot better today. Just enough to be bothersome.

    Seems your baby shower was quite a success. To tell you the truth, I thought you knew about it all the time. No one told me it was suppossed [sic] to be a secret. The only reason I didn't mention it was because I thought it would be old stuff to you. Why doesn't someone tell me when something is suppossed [sic] to be hush-hush? Anyhow, I'm glad it was a success in every way, hon. You & Alan deserve the finest. As for making room for me in the house—I was just wondering whether the baby & I wouldn't have to get rid of you! ... Ah, no, darling—I was only kidding. But Alan will just have to sleep in the bathroom! No room! But I'm sure we'll be able to improvise some way. Be sure you thank everyone for me for the nice baby presents. Even though they weren't much, they'll do (what a heel I am).

    That Gater you sent me has caused quite a furor. There's a story in it about Truman firing MacArthur & how most of the college clan agree with the move. "Those goddamn chocolate-malt sucking pigs," was one statement. The guys over here don't see eye to eye with the collegians. The story was silly & pointless. I'm dissapointed [sic] in the Gater, Galo & the quality of writing. <u>Nothing</u> is good in it. The paper is gutless. The election results (500 votes cast as to 1200 last year) shows the Gater didn't pull the interest of the students. What they needed was a File 13. And, as concieted [sic] as I sound, nothing they have compares to what I published for a year of columnizing. If this is an example of my future competition, then I have none. And that includes Galo & everyone else.

That's all for now darling. When I find an envelope I'll mail 2 letters. Be good, stay healthy, and love me as I love you. Thanks to everyone for being so nice to you.

   Love to you & the baby
   loads & loads—
   Al & Boondocker

MZ 561

           June 3

Dearest Joanne—

I'm tired, honey. Awfully tired & weary. For about a week & a half I went without rest, without sleep, too nervous & tense to notice the strain on my physical self. But yesterday afternoon we moved to the rear & to reserve. And I became weary. Everything relaxed.

Since I last wrote you we have been a regiment in attack. It was the first for me. And the most hellish week I ever lived through. They were days & nites of more fear than I've known.

It all began when we were moving through the valley. The Chinks hit from both sides. We had casualties—not many. We went up the ridge & Fox secured one. As we started up, mortars hit in the valley and put out one 75 mm. I heard screams. We moved up on the ridge & dug in. The Gooks were dug in on the opposite ridge. That nite a white phosphorus shell landed on our hill; three men screamed in the nite. And it was all over for them.

The next morning we prepared to assault the ridge. The 3rd plt. moved into position. And I saw what proved to be the most dramatic sight in my life. We hit that hill like Marines at last, screaming & hollering as we ran up, firing from the hip. A Gook leaped from a bunker—a Marine grabbed him & through [*sic*] him down the hill. There was silence. Then a yell went up from those who watched— the Gooks were running! Someone hollered, "We got 'em by the balls, now let's squeeze!" Mr. Buckman, plt. leader of the 3rd plt. ("I shall lead the grenadiers") led the attack. A grenade hit him & knocked his helmet off. He got back on his feet & kept running. Another grenade stopped his courageous advance forever. The ridge was secured, about 154 prisoners were taken. Four marines paid for it.

Fox Co. crapped out on the ridge we just took. Charlie Co. moved up beside us. We were laying there, feeling pretty good, waiting to chase the Chinese off another ridge about 100 yds. away. Then the devil stepped in. Mortars came in on us. The deadly silent explosives that whoosh before they hit. With deadly accuracy they hit into the crowd. Screams & the cry 'corpsman' filled the air. They came one right after another: the whoosh & the detonation. I buried my face into the earth & prayed. Five men grouped around me. Another mortar landed about 10 ft. away. All 5 were wounded. 2 squads of ours were on another nose away from where mortars were landing. "They're <u>our</u> men!" someone shouted. "Let's get that fucken mortar!" 26 men fixed bayonets & charged up the hill against God only knows how many Chinese. Their only thought seemed to be that we were getting hurt, and they were going to stop it. They took that hill; the dead dropped & the wounded kept going. The mortars stopped. 2 squads had taken the hill. Without planes, without artillery. Just guts & that peculiar brand of anger than makes a man a Marine.

You asked me once why I was proud to be a Marine. That's why. Because Marines are the only men alive who can assault an objective, take it & hold it. They are the ones who care more about their buddies than their lives. They are the men who stand fast under fire & artillery while the army breaks & runs. They are the ones who will stand on their feet with mortars falling around & tend the wounded though it may mean their lives.

We were Marines that day on mortar hill [sic].* And I was damned proud of it. We were Marines all the following week when we marched in rain so hard there wasn't a dry portion on anyone's body: the men shivered in the unbearable rain & cold. There was nothing to look forward to either—no dry doggie tents or clothes, not even fires for fear of giving away our position—just the proud, cold voice of the CO ringing through the dampness at the base of a hill—"we're going up! We're going to take it!" It rang like a battle cry, and the men checked their weapons, hunched their backs & went up.

We, the Marines, have moved forward ridge by bloody ridge. Day by day, mile by mile. We've moved on when the tanks were stopped by the mud & headquarters couldn't move because of enemy artillery. The infantry moved on through mud, mortars & hell. The rain stopped all air support & the Chinese took casualties with their heavy stuff. Some turned yellow & went to the rear with fake illnesses. But no one ran.

That has been the last week or so. And it is all so easily symbolized in the salute of a tankman standing by the road as we moved by—a salute to us; another passing out cigarettes to us when ours were soggy by the rain.

I never want to experience another week like the one past. But I never want to forget it: Mr. Buckman assaulting that hill, not driving his men with a .45, but leading them with courage that cost him his life; a Marine hollering "You're not fighting doggies now!" & proving it with cold steal. Those were sleepless nights & hungry days. But when the 5th Regiment replaced us on the lines, when we marched by them, they snapped to. We were the 7th Marines! And every Chinaman that tried to stop us knows it. The dead enemy are uncountable; the prisoners the same.

Little else has happened of interest. We've moved forward quite a ways north. Lost a lot of good men. 6 left in our squad. That makes me almost senior NCO. Oh, yes—I made corporal, retroactive to April 13. Pete Mamaril & I were the only ones from the 7th draft & 2 out of about 15 in the regiment. I'm now fire team leader. Not bad, eh?

---

*Mortar Hill. Research has failed to identify a location with this designation. It is probably Al's personal name for the site of the intense action of his unit.

I've received all of your letters just recently, and they sure were nice. I'm glad you realize how much it means to me to be the father of our child. I'm glad it means the same to you, darling. We're going to be an awfully happy family—with a smarter & older husband & father.

Well, darling, not much more to say so I'll sign off. Don't worry about me, hon, despite all I've told you. That operation is over & we're in reserve. And after what I've gone through, I have no doubts that I'll be home safe & sound when my time is up in Korea. It may sound silly coming from me, but I went to church this morning and—well—God is on our side.

> I love you with
> all my heart & soul
>   Al (& Boondocker)
> Love to Alan or Cindy
> & take care of both of you
>   I love you   (don't forget)—it's
>   xxxxx   Cpl. A. Martinez now!

MZ 565

> June 3

Dearest darling—

I just heard the wonderful news from S-1 about my being a papa & I'm the proudest dad in North Korea! I still don't know whether it's a boy or girl, & I forgot when he said it was born or how much it weighed I was so excited, but I know I'm a dad & they said you & baby [are] both fine, so that's all I need to know.

I was sitting on the deck cleaning my rifle when someone clear across the field called my name. They kept calling & finally I went arunning [sic]. "Married?" he asked. I nodded. "You're a dad. Congratulations! We'll find out more for you later." All the guys were listening & I got congratulations from the company. I got ahold [sic] of a few cigars & gave them out. Since I made corporal I also had to draw money & pay for the beer.

But it's been a nice day! We may even go pay to mason* [i.e., Mason] for a month in reserve!

So congratulations to both of us, darling—and boy or girl, I bet it's a fine baby! Let's love it to pieces!

> All my heart & love & life
> forever & forever to
> you & our baby—
>   Al & Boondocker

MZ 566

---

*Mason was the location for a reserve area. The meaning of Al's phrase, "go pay to mason," is unclear.

June 4

Dearest wife & mother—(not mine, our child's)

Did he speak? Can he walk? Can he write? How big is he? (using he as a generality). I'm getting anxious as heck to know whether I've got a baby girl or a boy. Everyone I tell asks me & I just shrug. This is a heck of a predicament! They'll probably never tell me, so when you're able to write give me the sex—and the vital statistics. I feel like a father already. A very proud father! Maybe it's a good thing I didn't know you were in the hospital—I'd have really been sweating it out. But all my love was with you—you know that.

Despite the fact that it's been raining off & on since yesterday evening, everyone is in good spirits. Almost all have –

There's been an interruption. I just came back from a company formation where the CO gave us our corporal warrants. Kind of a nice ceremony. I'll send you the warrant to keep for me. Who knows, 2 more months & I may be Sgt. Martinez! I'll run the war my way yet! A chicken in every pot!

Diarrhea (a continuation from paragraph before last). I have it too. But, as everything else, I have it just badly enough to make me miserable—nothing serious.

Today we made out: 4 cans of beer, candy, cigarettes, etc. Hell of a time to get beer, but a man can't be particular in Korea. Seems we always get it on cold days & suffer on hot ones.

Already I'm bored with reserve. Not that I want to go back to the lines, mind you. I just want something to do. Restless as usual. I've even tried to borrow a typewriter somewhere, but no go. I'm a frustrated writer!

My diary is coming along great. It got wet & ran in places & is falling apart, but it's still readable. Quite interesting too. Even looks like a combat diary.

Enclosed you'll find 25 cents in military script (the type of currency we use overseas). Jenkins sends it "…to buy beer for the baby." A good lad, this Kentuckyian [sic].

Here's a rundown on my personal health: thinner, lighter, jumpier, wiser, stronger & smoke much more. But, generally speaking, I'm in good shape. Even a day of rest puts me back in good humor. So there's nothing to worry about on this end.

How about giving me all the lowdown on you, hon. Tell me all. I'll be waiting to hear from you.

All my heart & love—
Al (& Boondocker)

P.S. 2 reserves who served in the last war were sent home. The new reserve release program is underway!
P.S. Tell Bob I was only kidding about him having it easy. No one has it easy in war!

Love to Bob, Mary
& Kids—
Al

(All rates are "temporary" for 6 mo.'s—I'll keep mine.)

MZ 567

June 7

Dearest Joanne—

It's a warm beautiful morning in Korea & nature is at peace with herself. Even the distant roar of artillery is gone, & all is quiet on the oriental front. I am again in my right mind, unruffled by mortar or rifle, artillery or grenade. It's amazing what a few days rest and some unbroken sleep will do for you. I feel great now—laughing at what a few days ago I was shaking because of. I can now smile away some of the bitterness which time and rest have softened in my heart. Even the fearfulness of one horrible week is gone, and my mind refuses to recall its tragedy.

On mortar hill, for instance, I remember one humorous thing. When the first mortar came in I was lying on flat ground. When another came in only seconds later, I had dug a hole with torn & bleeding fingers & was lying in it. I doubt if <u>anyone</u> has ever dug a foxhole that fast. And once when we were sitting in the valley watching Chink artillery tearing up the ground around us, a sniper took a few shoots [*sic*] at the plt. "What was that?" someone asked. "Only a fucken sniper," came the calloused reply. And all went back to watching the shell holes, ignoring completely the 'whang' of the guided missile. Such is war.

Since this is June I suppose the usual summer routine prevails at the land of the Golden Gate:—young love blooming on warm nites and the smell of perfume and the taste of lipstick; the beaches cluttered with only weight-lifters and bosomy french [*sic*] bathing suits, exposing all with a flutter; states-side [*sic*] warriors (sailors) sporting their form-fitting blues over the cement rail at the beach by the cliffhouse –asking forbidden things of the women & the women loving it; Playland, crowded & noisy, with the mute fat woman roaring her endless, ironic laughter over the funhouse—and the guys waiting there self-consciously waiting [*sic* for word repetition] for a dress to blow up. And I suppose Market street [*sic*] is busy & humming with pretty girls in low-cut, bright summer dresses, women looking for bargains & men looking for women; Everyone going somewhere in a big hurry; and bearded, Leo the Lion Voss, cast & shorts [these two words doubtful], ambling down the middle of the sidewalk, still boasting it can lick any 10 men …

Yeah, I suppose San Francisco is much the same on this June day as any other—each person weaving his own individual tale; but one which has been told a million times. Each too concerned with himself to worry about Korea & the little war over here …

I can almost forget war back here too—on such warm, peaceful days. But then I remember that my buddies are out there on the lines living through nites & days of terror and hell—then I can't forget. It's too close.

Oh, well—I shouldn't complain. They say there are those worse off than I. Of course, I don't believe it, but who am I to argue with Aristotles [*sic*]?

The Fly

I've nothing 'gainst the insect world
There's none so tolerant as I
But, gentlemen, appeas[e]ment's failed—
I'm off to war the demon fly!

> For never a moment do I find
> When truly let I [*sic*] troubles by
> When bird and beast are both at peace—
> But never so the taunting fly
>
> With ink I make a letter to
> The folks at home who sit & sigh
> But find my efforts thwarted by
> The buzzing of an insect fly—
>
> At work or play, at meal or sleep
> No matter what pleas I beseach [*sic*]
> They flit and land then buzz away
> Always, bastards, out of reach.
>
> So, gentlemen, let's square away—
> I warn the insects to stand by—
> Museumists grab your model <u>now</u>—
> For soon he'll be extinct—the fly!

  Al Martinez

Need I say more? I love you loads & loads.
 All my heart & love to you & baby
 xxxxxxxxx Al & Boondocker xxxxxxx

MZ 570

           June 12

Dearest Joanne—

 Since the last letter I wrote we left reserve & went out on the attack again for 5 days. It was quite a surprise to all concerned. The 5th Marines couldn't take the ground assigned them, so we had to do it. Of course, it doesn't make me feel good knowing that the 7th has to do their work, but it's nice knowing I'm in a good outfit. We thought we'd go back in reserve, because we've taken more objectives than we're supposed to. But we're still going strong. We've secured the valley where we lost so many men & all the ridges surrounding that valley. We lost a great many out of our company alone. But we whipped the Chinese despite our losses, their numbers & their artillery.

 Right now we're up on a ridge awaiting orders to move on. We haven't spent more than one nite in the same place, so it's almost inevitable that we will move. This morning we went out on a combat patrol—just our platoon. We are 15 men understrengthed [*sic*], & our objectives were deep in enemy territory. Our acting plt. leader (the plt. leader was hit) said before we left, "don't waste your ammo, we may be encircled. Our numbers are puny, but if we play it cool we <u>may</u> come back." Naturally, that made us feel <u>real</u> good. However, we went out on patrol, captured 12 prisoners & came back safe & sound.

 For the past 4 days Chinese mortars have taken a heavy toll. Fox Co. is minus 1 co. commander, 1 gunny, 1 top sgt, 1 executive officer (Mr. Stone our ex-plt. leader), 2 wireman [*sic*], 9 mortar men, 1 runner & about 25 squad leaders & men. Only about 5 have been killed, the rest wounded. Pete Mamaril was hit yesterday—badly—in back of the neck & in the back. They had to give him plasma, but they seem to think he'll survive. I certainly hope so.

Out of the 7th draft, almost all the guys I know have been wounded. LeBlanc & I are the only ones left in Fox Co, aside from about 3 more. Fortunately, most have been wounded & are returning after a week or so. Others aren't so lucky.

The weather these past days has been all but fair. Rainy, cloudy & cold, cutting out our air support for the most part & making the troops miserable. Today, however, is beautiful. Warm, clear & sunshiny. Lots of heat & airplanes. And we're getting a little rest—no moving out at 0600 in the a.m. So, right now things aren't too bad. But one never knows, & there's no use of my rationalizing myself into a careless slumber. My alertness has kept me alive, & I'm not about to ease up now.

While being in the attack, I haven't received any mail. I suppose you're able to write by now, but they just haven't brought any up. Wish they would. I'm anxious to know whether I'm a mother or father! Everyone asks me & all I can do is shrug. Lutke got annoyed asking me the weight, sex, etc. & when I couldn't answer added, "are you sure it's a Martinez?" Another said, when I didn't know the sex, "haven't they figured it out yet?" I shut them both up fast.

How've you been feeling, sweetheart? By now you're probably feeling better than a week ago. Childbirth is no easy feat, I know (I guess). But with the right frame of mind & attitude it can be made easier. And I know you have both.

As for a rundown on my health, it's just that—rundown. Naw—seriously, I'm in good shape. Just don't holler "mortar" real suddenly when I get home or you're liable to be digging me out of the foundation. Also, don't go "whoosh" or I'll go right through the door. Come to think of it, I don't imagine you'll be hollering mortar or going whoosh at me anyhow. If you do, we'll both turn in! Let the good times roll!

Last nite was real clear & star-filled, and I got to thinking about your ruby teeth & white, pearly lips—remember? Then I kissed you & apologized. Poor John Robben[s]—I sure put the squeeze on him. "Now, John, you don't won't [sic] her she's narrow." So John trots in the office & says, "Joanne, you're narrow!" So now we're married, narrow one, & John is still smarting from my counter attack. Tee, hee—they have to wake up early in the morning to fool old Dad! Wot a man!

It's funny, but I start a letter real seriously gung ho talking about a regiment in attack & wind up laughing. Just goes to show you what thinking about you will do, you sweetheart! You'd charm the Chinese right out of their bunkers.

The enclosed 50¢ in military script is from Jenkins for the baby again—two bits for last time & two bits for this time. Says it's for milk, however, & not for beer. If those babies drink up all the beer on the market then there won't be any to steal from the army & that would never do! So Cindy (or Alan) will just have to settle for milk. And if the baby's like its old man, I know bitterness will prevail. Sorry, child, this is war. As Mr. Stone use[d] to say, "nothing is to[o] good for Marines in combat. And nothing is what they get!"

    Love you & the baby loads & loads!
    All my heart

Al & Boondocker
(both fit as a fiddle)
xxxxxxxx

MZ 571

June 14, '51

Dearest Joanne—

Since last I wrote you our CO went down & raised the devil with Battalion, so we got mail. They had stacks of it down there but "just didn't get around to bringing it up." Anyhow, now I know, I have a baby daughter—Cynthia [sic] Louise, 6 lbs. 13 ozs, born May 31, 1951. I know now that all is well, mother & baby doing fine. I got mail from my mother, too, & she fit in the pieces. Also, surprise, I received a letter from Galo, Lesser, little Helen, Dolores & about 5 from you. The info in a nutshell: Galo flunked his M.A. physical (teeth); Lesser is on the verge of a nervous breakdown (again); and things seem pretty much the same. I'm glad Frank isn't going in the Corps for his sake; he doesn't have the guts or emotional stability to make a Marine officer. Awful to say, but true. As for Lesser—poor girl. That's all.

Cindy sounds like the dream of 2 parents very much in love. I bet she is a little doll, & I bet already she knows it. My nose & mouth, huh? I thought my face was missing something. Your eyes? How do you get around? Yeah, I'm a clown. The way you talk about childbirth, it sounds like a snap. I'm glad they have it down to such a perfect process. It also seems like the best method to let you do things for yourself. All in all, dearest, congratulations on everything. By the way—no one even wished me happy father's day. I am a daddy, you know: ... my nose & mouth, huh? She must be a doll.

Life in Korea is much the same. We're still on the lines, but day after tomorrow we go back in reserve. The last 2 days we've taken more objectives with comparative ease. One hill gave us some trouble, but our plt. leader in a moment of compassion said, "fix bayonets & purple hearts, we're going up!" And up we went. Naturally—we took it. Oh, yes, I captured a prisoner (singular). We were checking bunkers & caves leading to our next objective. I walked over to one & looked in. "Thought I saw a Chink," I said to myself, walking away. "I did!" First of all I didn't know what to do. I looked in again & he looked out. I took a grenade off my belt. But he hadn't shot at me or anything. So I put the grenade back & levelled my M-1. "Etawa!" I shouted (come here), exploiting my limited oriental vocabulary. He came out readily, threw down his weapon & smiled. Confounded by the lack of violent action, I searched him, marched him to the skipper & that was it. The interpretor [sic] discovered that he had deserted from the Chinese army & was waiting for us. He had no thought of resisting—disgustingly enough. We sat & looked at him as he calmly smoked a cigarette I gave him. "Lucky guy," someone said. And he was—his war was over, his life would be soft. The lucky guy.

Well, darling, that's all for now. I'll write you again as soon as I can. Rest up & take care of yourself. I'm still fine despite all, so you have no worry there. Just relax & love our little Cindy all to pieces. You know how wonderful I think parenthood is, so I needn't say more. All the love in the world to you & our Cynthia [*sic*].

Love you both—
always & always …
Al & Boondocker

XXXXXXXXXXX
xxxxxxxxx—little kisses for Cindy, cuz she's just a little girl.

P.S.—If she has white, pearly lips & ruby teeth I'll never forgive myself!

<u>Al</u>

[enclosure of clipping, a short essay called "What Is a Girl?" Al has circled the title and written next to it] "I couldn't have said it better!"

MZ 572

June 18 (I think)

Dearest Joanne—

It's another one of those days around here—hot, sultry, with lots of determined flies and renegade insects, all clamouring [*sic*] for you. I've eaten all my chow, read all I can find to read, day-dreamed continuously, talked 'till I've run out of conversation,—but …

Mail! I just got 2 letters from you & the article you sent from the Post. That breaks my day considerably & gives me more to read. Gee, hon, you sure come through at the right time. Sounds like my mail is being forwarded in a shuttle run from Mary's to S.F. That's nothing. You ought to see the way it goes around here. You give it to someone to take back to Bn. & he carries it for a day until he comes back. Then he goes down again & gives it to a tankman to take to regiment. The tankman forgets it & brings it back to Bn. Bn sees it & sends it up to me again. I start the whole confusing procedure all over again. That's a bad example, but it has actually happened. Usually they take better care of your mail than they do of the troops. When we were moving ahead of Bn. in "operation mousetrap," they often couldn't get us chow & ammo, but there was always some poor little guy lugging a mail bag up the hill. And to the men who were lonely, it meant & means a great deal.

Sounds like you were having quite an arguement [*sic*] with Truman just before Cinthy was born. She'll probably grow up to be a beauracratic [*sic*] republican because of it. But that's okay with me. The way the democratic administration (Truman especially) has messed up the world situation & international policy, I'm a republican myself—at least a bi-partisan. Everytime [*sic*] I see some poor kid lying on the ground screaming corpsman it sends a chill through me that only complete humiliation of the narrow little missourian [*sic*; i.e., Truman] will satisfy. Everytime [*sic*] I see a Marine lying with a shelter half over his face I want to cry & scream to the politicians back home that this is <u>their</u> war—and these are the men who are paying. It all can be prevented, I don't care what they say. I don't wish combat on anyone, but I wish everyone in the U.S. could <u>see</u> with their own

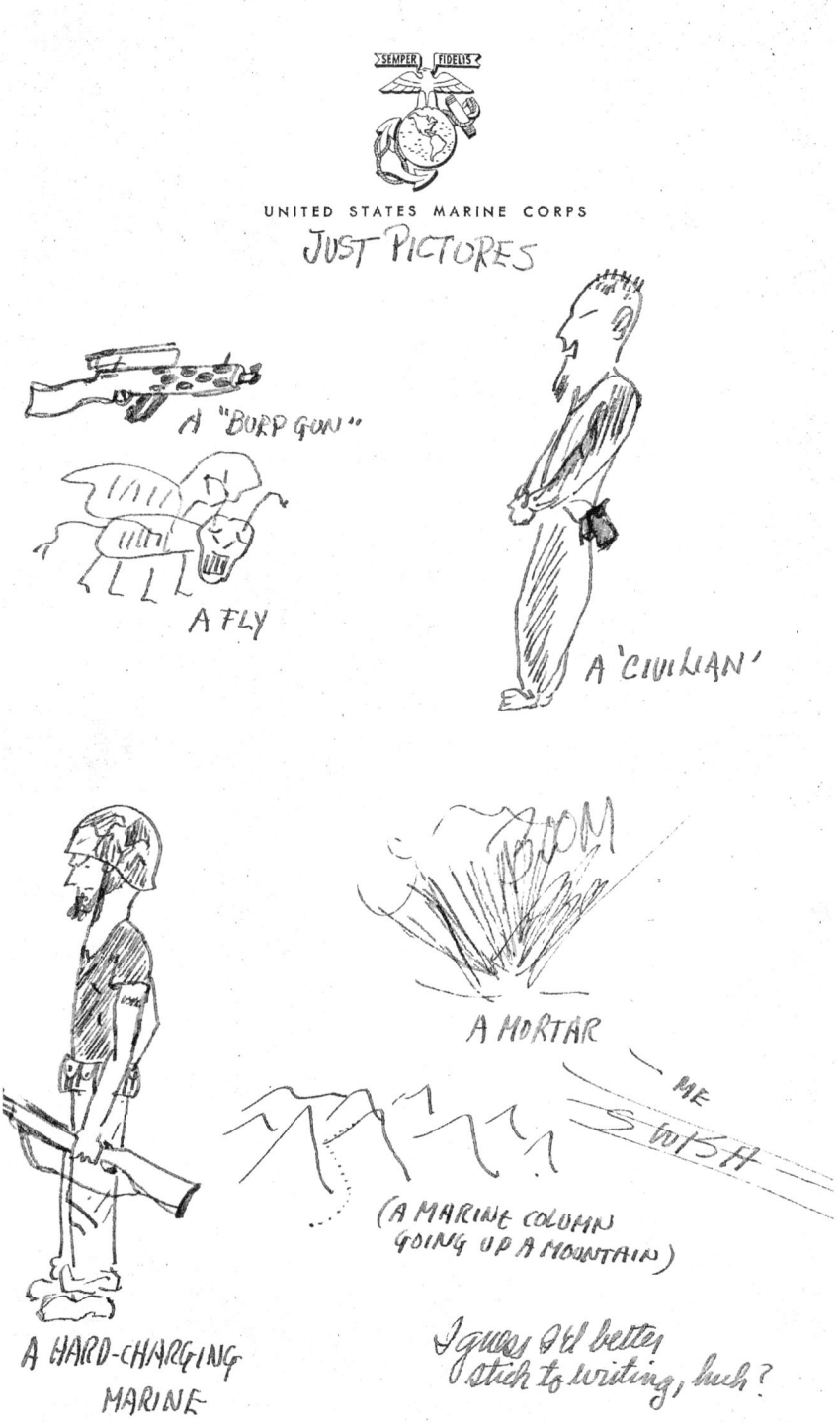

Al Martinez's drawings on the last page of his letter dated June 18, 1951 (The Huntington Library, MZ 575).

eyes a war which is gloryfied [*sic*] & so badly misinterpreted by propoganda [*sic*]—newspapers inclusive. I wish they could see the complete waste of human lives on the front lines.

If there ever was a purpose in a man writing, besides love of it, I have it. I want to open the sleepy eyes of America to war at its brutalist [*sic*] that patriotism & a false nationalism has drugged. I can't leave out the war humor or the beauty of courage & self sacrifice I've seen, either. But they'll see as plainly as I have what a direct mortar hit does to a man & why the Marines called one hill Hamburger hill; and what it feels like to loose [*sic*] all human inhibitions & cry like a baby from fear; what it's like to meet the morning light with a headache because you've been staring into the blackness all nite. Sure, they'll laugh with some of the characters just as I have. But if I'm at all the writer I claim to be, they'll be dumbfounded & sick when the guy they laughed with is lying screaming & writhing with a face torn away. Usually, I'm a "pretty" writer painting a happy-ending picture. But it's neccessary [*sic*] now to be realistic, sometimes brutal, so Cinthy will have a future & so our future sons will have something to look forward to. With the help of God & more effort than I've ever put forth before I hope I can be indirectly responsible at least for the prevelance [*sic*] of discretion at least in the absence of reason.

Getting back [to] the immediate present, something has to be done about the flies. I've killed them, cursed them, threatened them and unleashed my artistic wrath on them. I've talked to them, warning them that I am a Marine & not to be messed with; but with utter disregard to rank or outfit, they still come. I've begged them, reasoned with them & appeased them by setting out part of my rations—to no avail. They come litterally [*sic*] by the dozens per person, Joanne, & there's no way to stop them. When you try to shake them off they cling; and when you throw a fit & finally do make them fly, they buzz you once & return. I've seen a man walking with 20 flies on his back. They eat on me, reperpetuate [*sic*] their breed, use me as a toilet, rub their legs & generally use me as the local meeting place. I'll go bats if I can't do <u>something</u>! They drive me to distraction. Honey, what'll I do?

Today I was talking to some kid I went through training with. He's from S.F. & his wife had a baby girl about 5 mo.'s ago, so we have something in common. He showed me pictures of his wife & daughter & I gave him the tongue-in-cheek "how cute" routine, thinking all the time his wife was an ugly individual & not being able to tell much from the fuzzy picture of the baby although there was one cute picture. However, we had a nice talk & he had some Herb Caen colunn's [*sic*] so we made out. He probably thought I was a bore.

Darling, I'm going bald. That's a fact. My hair has receded on both sides at least ¼"! Will you still love me if I come home with no hair? I'll have a head anyhow if that's a consolation. Also, I'm loosing [*sic*] weight. My leg muscles bulge like tennis balls, then I sort of taper up to a pin head—kind of a backward Sampson [i.e., Samson].* I'm painting a rather miserable picture of myself, but I have no choice. It's not really that bad. Worse.

---

*The Biblical Samson was betrayed by Delilah, who had his hair cut off, causing him to lose all his strength.

I think I told you about this guy before, but the circumstances under which I met him again after quite awhile [*sic*] made me laugh through the mud. I was down at the CP when 3 mortars came in. I dived for the nearest hole which was occupied [*sic*] already. We were both lying face down in the mud when I heard him mutter with a despondent passion & a completely hopeless voice, "I wonder what the poor people are doing today?"

That's al[l] for now, darling. When I scrounge up an envelope somewhere I'll give this letter to someone to carry around for a few days until he brings it back then I'll mail it myself.

Love to you & our little Cin (pronounced "Sin"—how's that for a nickname?). Tell her her old man's not psycho yet—just crazy with flies.

   All my love to both of you,
   a darling pair
    Al (& Boondocker)

P.S.—Boondocker sends his love to itchy pup.
P.P.S.—So Auntie May's son Ray is going to Guam with the air force, eh? Man, he must really be having it rough! Just kidding—I love the air force. Tell May I wish him all the luck in the world & if he ever does a mission over Korea I'll be waving at him. And if the Chinese fight back I'll beat 'em off with raging editorials.

   All my heart & love
    Al
   XXXXXXX
   Xxxxxxx

[Drawings, full page]

MZ 575

      June 21

Dearest Joanne—

Since yesterday afternoon about 6 p.m. the 7th Marine regiment has been in reserve. About 7 a.m. yesterday (after a nite of ducking from artillery), we awoke, rolled our gear & waited to assault one of the thousands of Korean ridges. Dog Co. jumped off. We waited & waited—at 2 p.m. we were ordered to move out. But instead of moving up we moved down! Then with a nonchalance that was disgusting, the word came back: we're being relieved; we're going in reserve. Jenkins summed up the attitude of the battered company: "I'm so happy I could cry!" And some of us did.

We walked back about 5 miles while the Gooks threw mortars at us. Then we boarded trucks & began the bouncy, dusty ride back through the valley we had secured only a short while ago—suddenly pretty & almost peaceful. Marine & Army artillery had moved up; tents were set where artillery had once fallen on us. Some of the guys were playing baseball & volley ball [*sic*]. Trucks moved freely around. We passed the river we had waded, too anxious to get out of the open to use rocks to cross it. We passed the small, sandy hills we had clung to to avoid being seen. We passed the trees, the rocks & the streams; the burned-out houses & the standing ones. We passed a sign the 11th Marine artillery had set up: "this is the valley the 7th took"—a tribute that brought a yell up from the men. This was the valley we had taken—a different valley now. Our artillery blasted away. The men watched them silently. I wonder what they thought.

The trucks took us about ¼ of a mile from our area. We filed down the road in a column; the men unconsciously keeping an interval. There was no snap in our step: only a shuffle & a limp of weariness that fell when the tension was off. It was Fox Co.—the best Co.—coming in. But it was a tired, understrengthed [sic] company. We were proud of the job we had done, but not "thrilled." Someone pointed & said "that's where Jack was killed." And that was why. That was it. Operation Pursuit* was over.

We set up our tents & listened to the reminiscent tunes they played over a loud speaker: The Gypsy, We'll Be Together Again, Stardust, Whispering, & all the other soft ones, the dreamy ones. They brought us 4 cans of beer apiece & Jenkins & I picked up 8 more. We sat by the music & got high on beer—just high enough to become sad & homesick. I talked of you & Cinthy all nite. The nite came in slowly, softly. We watched the ascent of the moon over the ridges—one of the most beautiful I've ever seen—full & yellow. The stars became clearer as it grew darker. It is poetic justice: the violence of war must be fought in the violence of nature. But now we—the 7th Marines—are at rest, while nature gives us the full benefit of her beauty. He has given us peace.

Jenkins & I walked back to our tents about 11:30 singing the songs we had been listening to. We climbed in our sleeping bags & talked for awhile [sic]. Then his breathing deeper [sic] & a calm silence settled over the rows of tents. The last thing I remember hearing is a fire team moving up a small hill to keep the ever-valued Marine Corps watch no matter where we are. Then I too, content & drowsy, fell into a deep, calm sleep.

As for me, darling, I'm fine. I slipped & almost broke my leg yesterday but, unfortunately, failed. I know you & Cinthy are fine & I know you'll stay that way. I bet you're having a great time spoiling our daughter! When I get home I'll spoil her more.

About 3 hrs. later

You're spoiling me! 4 packages yet! Gee hon, everything in them is a representative of Heaven. The magazines are great & the canned fruit—baby, I love you more & more each package. The coockies [sic] are almost gone & the candy is going fast. Everyone I've seen has got 'next' on the magazines & pocket books, but I'm determined not to let them go 'till I've read them. The firs—I got interrupted & now I forgot what I was going to say. Anyhow, thank you, darling, again & again for doing the right thing at the right time. Your husband is now clean (I bathed & washed my clothes), shaved & happy! Honey, it's your thoughtfulness that makes me love you so <u>very much</u>.

---

*Operation Pursuit is an unidentified battle action.

I'm at your feet, my servant ...
>All my heart & love
>to you & Cinthy   XXXXXX
>Al   xxxxx

MZ 576

>June 25

Dearest baby—

Another day has bloomed strong & fine over the rugged eastern horizon, and the heat of the morning is with us already. There is hope in the air this day and all nature seems to reflect the attitude of man. Talk of peace and cease fire have lifted the spirit of the 7th Marines and added a smile to the activity. And if the talk is false, then frustration and disappointment will be present. If it is true, we will thank our God and pray that it lasts forever.

This morning for the first time since I have been in Korea, someone shouted "colors!" And to the cool, clear command of the bugle, the flag whipped & snapped her way to the top of the mast, lifted there by the salutes of her disciples. The echo of the bugle echoed and seemed to rise there for all the world to see. It was a pretty sight and one that seemed to blend the order of spit & polish to the shabbiness of the combat Marine.

Also this morning the 2nd Bn. of the 7th Marines was awarded the highest unit citation that can be given an outfit—the presidential unit citation. It marks the first time in military history that an organization as small as a battalion has earned it—usually it's given on a regimental or divisional level. But, as the top said, because we had 473 casualties out of 800 men, because we took ground that even other Marine outfits couldn't take, because we advanced against overwhelming odds & deadly enemy artillery fire, we earned it. Perhaps another Guadal Canal [sic] is written into American history. Now that it's over, I'm proud to say I was there.

Hon, this will be short as again there is little to say. But I will say I love you with all my heart & our little Cinthia the same. I'm looking forward to holding you both.

>All my love—   XXXXXX
>Al (& Boondocker)   xxxx

MZ 580

>June 27

Dearest Jo—

I wrote you one letter this morning, but I'll start this one now & finish it tomorrow. In its perfect, peculiar disconformity a sunny day has turned into a rainy evening. However, I am determined to go to the outdoor movie, be it rain or snow. Bob Hope in "The Lemon Drop Kid"* is playing, and miss it I shall not.

The Lemon Drop Kid, starring Bob Hope, Marilyn Maxwell and Lloyd Nolan, was a 1951 film about a swindler who must raise $10,000 by Christmas to repay a gangster.

Guess who is over here? Ferdinand J. Castellio [i.e., Castillo],* the kid from State who I use[d] to write up in File 13 for swimming the bay. He's the guy who invented the toy skunk and is going to give me a few thousand. He's assistant to the Chaplain or something over here & seems to have quite a racket from what the guys say. Anyhow, he's in the rear echelon. He was shocked, humiliated & bitter when he learned I wasn't a war correspondent. When I tried to explain the system to him, he still didn't get it. The guy doesn't seem to understand we don't have typewriters on the lines. He says he's going to get me a typewriter to use & is also going to get me in P.I.O. Also he says he's taking me to Church with him. Already he's given me a Catholic Digest & has said he's "…going to take care of his buddy." Must be my fatal charm.

This afternoon, the regimental Commander came around & in a discussion explained the full details & strategy of this last operation since we were in the attack. It was really quite interesting. He told us what all the other outfits were doing, why and where. He told us that we were thrust into the attack in this particular area to take the artillery & mortar fire off the KMC's [sic] (Korean Marine Corps), which we did –moreso [sic] than he expected. He kidded about our fears and said he'd never forget Fox Co. trying to cross the river with mortars falling around. Neither will I. Something else interesting he told us: on the day we went in reserve, the General had told him that if the 2nd Bn. took objective 12 before 9 a.m. we would go in reserve. Dog Co. jumped off at 6 a.m. that morning & was on 12 at 7:30. Otherwise we might still be on the lines.

All this area was called the 'Punchbowl' because of the huge valley surrounded by ridges. I won't easily forget that place.

June 28

Morning, sweetheart. It's another beautiful day, fresh & alive after the rains. The morning sun shines down on a forest which was once barren ground. And herein lies a tale:

The order came out that all men will camouflage their tents from air observation. So the men, with that peculiar corps wit, went out, chopped down trees & bushes of all varieties and set them around & over their tents. The area is now a mad conglomeration of vegetation that even Einstein couldn't cross, intermingled and growing together when I'm sure they wouldn't under natural circumstances. But with a silent humor that mercilessly mocks orders, they've built bushy arches, stone gardens & little flower boxes out of scroungy [sic] limbs & half-dead bushes. If the Chinese are observing us by air they have a before & after picture that would make the choisest [sic] of targets: in a barren rice paddy, surrounded by nothingness, a forest has shot up—and what a forest it is. I can hear the Gook pilots wink & say to each other, "now—what do you suppose that it [sic]?" There can be only one answer, darling, humorous & simple: Phylum Americanus, species Marine.

---

*Ferdinand J. Castillo (1917–1993) raced and taught swimming. In 1942 he joined the Marines and saw battle in the Pacific. He fought again when he re-enlisted in the Korean War.

You can hear the men say in mock warning: "don't walk there, those are camouflaged tents!" "Why, goodness, I didn't even see them! What a splendid job of military deception!" Already there are signs in front of tents: "Rose Bud," "Forest Lane," "Garden Row," etc. But one stands out in complete disconformity, forcing me to smile & remember my little blonde. The sign? "Westward Ho House."

There was a part in Bob Hope's picture last nite that to me summed up perfectly the political I-don't-like-you-so-I'll-call-you-something-bad routine in America. Hope was thrown out of a niteclub for trying to borrow money from the manager. He paused at the doorway, looked disgustedly back and sneered in the inimitable Hope manner, "communist!"

The picture was good. Funny, satirical & quick. It was another Damon Runyon tale and even better than the last one we saw together—I forget the name. Hope was a race track tout—the Lemon Drop Kid. If you haven't already seen the picture & can, see it. Your sense of humor will react to it as did mine. The reel only broke about 4 times last nite & the sound went out twice. They served us coffee after the movie.

There was only one thing bad (not really bad) about the picture. It made me terribly homesick & lonely for you. They had some Xmas scenes & I begin [i.e., began] to think about our 2 Xmases together, you, our baby and this Xmas. I thought myself into an even deeper loneliness & fell more & more in love with you. By the time I hit the sack I was almost in tears & missing you so much! I'm always this way—I can feel it in the pit of my stomach. But when something brings it out, there's no breaking my mood. I can only dream.

      I love you & Cinthy
      with all my heart
      your lonely husband—Al
       (& Boondocker)
      XXXXXX
      xxxxxx

MZ 583

    July 1
    Sunday

Dearest Joanne—

Last nite the 2nd Bn. put on a variety show—and it was undoubtedly one of the finest I have ever seen—professional or amateur. It ran for about 2 hours, and, once started, gathered a crowd of about 7 or 800 Marines.

The show started off with a little guy in combat dress shuffling down the field to the makeshift stage. He was loaded with a huge pack, rocket launchers, a machine gun, a BAR, all kinds of ammo, grenades, etc. He walked to the mike & with despair in his voice asked, "do you suffer from combat fatigue?" From there he took off!

There were hill-billy singers, quartets, spanish [sic] singers, soloists, instrumentalists, comedians & a skit. One guy was supposedly a russian [sic] spy. He told about how he was a comrade private in the Soviet army. "You think you have no class hatred here?" he asked. "Then who's sitting in the front on seats!?" A roar came from the audience and lasted for about 3 minutes. And the officers, who sat in the front on "seats" (boxes) laughed the loudest.

One soloist sang Desert Song in a rich, deep voice—the best performer I thought. When the show was over he led the audience in God Bless America along with the other participants in the show. You know, hon, that song has never stirred me particularly when I sang it at a 4th of July program or a phoney [sic] patriotic gathering. In fact I never even really liked it; it reminded me of fat Kate Smith.* Last nite it may have been the sun hanging low in the east; or 800 officers & men mingled together, separated by a silver bar that occasionally flickered in the light, but never by ideals; or the vibrant spirit of the crowd ... whatever it was, the song & the singing did something to me I'll never be able to explain. After awhile [sic] I had to stop singing—so I just listened. Silly, huh? But somehow hearing something like that in a combat zone is different than stateside. It means more & is a great deal more sincere.

Last nite when colors went I noticed that a couple little Korean kids were standing at stiff attention with their hands raised in an American salute. It was a cute sight watching them stand there, seriously, by much taller Marines. After colors I walked up to one of the kids who saluted. "Number one," I said meaning he was a good boy. "Okay, Joe," he smiled. Marines are good to the kids & they love the Marines—consequently they've learned to love the flag. I don't think the kids over here will forget us when this is over; and that makes for better international relations than all the diplomatic cocktail parties in the world.

There's a guy around here (a corpsman) the guys have come to call 'Ridgeway' [sic] in mock respect. Everyone rides him without mercy, because he's always trying to explain the strategy & theories of war. When he's showing deep concern while discussing combat relations, someone will ask, "Hey, Ridgeway [sic], what do you think it'll do to the price of eggs?" That usually ends the discussion. I tell you about this guy to focus another one of the characters over here.

Today marks the beginning of my 4th month in Korea & approximately 3½ months away from you & California. To me it seems like I've been over here years. I've become so accustomed to routine & environment that my mental pictures of San Francisco have to be recalled with effort & imagination; memories of material objects are often hazy. I guess it's nature's way of helping me not to be too lonely. If I could picture things clearly all the time as I do some of the time, I'd be a homesick wreck. I miss you & home enough as it is.

Before I finished that last paragraph I went to Protestant services. He (the chaplain) talked about patriotism and said more or less what I was trying to say in the first part of my letter—that patriotism seems more pronounced over here but none-the-less it exists a great deal at home. A lot of us left our home addresses, which the chaplain said he'd write to & tell our loved ones (you & Cinthy) that

---

*Kate Smith (1907–1986) was an American singer, best known for her rendition of Irving Berlin's "God Bless America." Both her voice and figure were impressively robust.

we're fine & in good health (which I am). So you may expect a note from the chaplain—a fine person.

Talks of peace & cease fire hold the limelight for the men in reserve and, I imagine, on the lines. From what we can gather from news bulletins & grapevine information, a military cease fire is imminently possible. Russia seems to be taking the lead—perhaps another cruel propoganda [sic] trick or maybe a sincere desire for settlement. The men are praying for peace, but only a few seem to be building themselves up for a possible let-down. Personally, I, with the others, am hoping desperately that a settlement is made. Then some of the men over here will have reason to revive their faith in man and peace which has been so bitterly destroyed.

Well, sweetheart, again this is '30'* (when was the last time I used that?) for today. I hope that Cinthy isn't giving you too bad a time—if so, I'll be home soon to correct her. I always say, it takes a man to control a woman! Right now I'll just send both of you all the love in the world from husband & daddy & if you don't behave I'll spank you both. I'll spank Cinthy first (lightly) then deal with you, my shapely wife, at greater & more emotional lengths. If you know what I mean!

All my love & kisses
Al
(& Boondocker, who is,
along with me, praying
for peace)
XXXXXXXXX
xxxxxxxxxx

MZ 585

July 16

Dearest Joanne—

Yesterday at 2 p.m. in a rain that fell off & on, the 2nd Ban. boarded trucks & began a dusty, winding trip on the road to Hongch[e]on,† 80 miles South-west. The jaunt took about 5 hours. We passed through the same territory we had passed thru when we jumped off at Hongch[e]on after our 1-day reserve approximately one month ago. Only this time no one minded the bad roads or the hard, wooden benches. Even so, when we first got on the trucks there was the nervous apprehension that perhaps we would go to the front: no one knew for sure. But when the convoy took the right fork in the road, everything was fine. We were southbound.

We pulled into our area about 7 p.m. & began setting up quickly. We're near the 2nd army division—one of the best incidentally. We've fought with them before. You may be interested to know that the 2nd is from Fort Lewis, Wash. You also may be interested to know that the magazine pub. of America recently voted the 1st Marine division & the 2nd army division as the best outfits in Korea. Anyhow, we're set up right next to them & relations are fine. They got beer rations

---

*In journalism, "30," or "Thirty," was once typed at the end of copy to signify the end of the article. It is not used much today, as "end" or "###" is preferred.

†Hongcheon is a county and city in Gangwon Province, South Korea.

yesterday & shared them with us, and we went to their movies (they have 3). As it is we walk thru each other's areas at will without the chip on the shoulder.

A few days ago we heard the news of the breakup of peace talks with apathy and with the we-knew-it attitude. We heard Ridgeway's [sic] ultimatum of conditions under which the meeting would resume. Talk of home & peace ceased suddenly & a gloomy atmosphere settled. It looked very much like the continuation of hostilities was inevitable. Way before yesterday the Chinese answered Ridgeway's [sic] ultimatum: they accepted the conditions & were quite willing to meet again. I've never seen more general elation than I saw that nite among the men. They stayed up late and talked of home & argued about how long it would take the troops to leave Korea once the war was over…. We haven't heard the news since then, but we do know that the meeting is in progress. I am both skeptical & hopeful. Despite my doubt, I can't help sharing the general feeling that the war is at its twilight and we will never again see the Korean front. They say the enemy has 350,000 troops ready for a counter-offensive. They know, however, as well as we do, that the offensive would never succeed. I can say with belief that the Chinese are morally & physically beaten & are unwilling to loose [sic] lives as they have been for an empty ultra-socialistic dream that can't possibly come true.

The Bn. news is that we stay here 5 days & leave for Wonju* and 8th Army reserve. Wonju is a [sic] quite a ways [sic] South from here & is a good-sized town. The whole division would go in reserve then probably for a couple months. The 1st Bn. of the 7th reg will be relieved off the lines tomorrow; the 3rd Bn. is already in reserve. The 5th reg. is in reserve & the 1st is being taken off the lines. That's pretty straight scoop, but it can change easily. It looks right now like we're due for a long rest—a long<u>er</u> rest, that is. Which all suits me fine.

When I do get home, it sure is going to seem funny getting back to the ways of the civilized. I haven't turned into a savage or anything like that, but I have become use[d] to doing things in a different way. You may have to use a little patience with me, hon, but I think I'll be okay in a short while. It will be a new continuation of an old life for you & I, what with Cinthy & all. I hope you don't have to[o] hard a time getting use[d] to having a man around the house—a maladjusted field Marine at that! Think you can stand me, kid?

I'll write you another letter tonite, sweetheart, but for now I'll close. Things are fine all over and it looks finally like the world <u>may be</u> coming of age. Let's hope so.

All my love
to you & Cinthy—
Al (& Boondocker)
XXXXXXXXX
xxxxxxxxx

[drawing of Marine's face (Al's?) on profile, with caption:] We almost look human again!

MZ 600

---

*Wonju is a city in Gangwon Province, South Korea. It is about 140 kilometers from Seoul.

July 19

Dearest Joanne—

It's 8:25 a.m. & I've been off guard post 5 for 25 minutes. I was on since 4 a.m. I'm only going to write part of this letter now because I'm sleepy; but a couple of interesting things happened on watch & I want to tell you about them while I can remember.

About 5 a.m. I walked by one of the large pyramidal CP tents & glanced in the open side. I was surprised & touched by what I saw: a little Korean girl about 6 years old curled up in an oversized Marine sleeping bag on a stretcher officers sometimes use as cots. I wondered where she had got the sleeping bag until I looked a little closer. On the deck by her side lay a Marine, probably her adopted father, wrapped in an old army blanket. I walked away feeling better about having to be on guard.

Before rev[e]ille this morning another incident took place that made me feel like both a heel & a sucker. Part of my post orders was to keep all Korean kids out of the area. A little boy I had chased out yesterday started to walk between the rows of pup tents. I went over to him and started to tell him to leave. He looked at me in amazement, then with that bewitching smile of innocence that only children have, he grabbed my hand & said breathlessly, "You walk many, many!" thinking I had been there all nite. I started to put on a gruff "kuta!" (leave) but it caught in my throat. I walked away without saying anything, and the kid with Marine dungerees [sic] that were too big & boondockers that were too loose, smiled again. He knew he had me.

Jenkins told me about this one: He was walking his post by the river when he came upon a Korean kid lying asleep in the sand by his shoe shine box. Jenk shook him and kiddingly said "rev[e]ille." Almost as soon as the kid had opened his eyes & before he realized the situation he rubbed the sand from him & said sleepily, "shoe shine, Joe?"

I guess this all goes to prove that as a guard against the enemy I stand on my own feet—but when it comes to chasing little kids away who hold your hand & talk to you, I'm no damn good. For the old men & women who line the roads & carry their loads as they did in an old Oriental world, I have only a conventional pity. But for the children who bear courageously the ignorance & pain thrust upon them by stagnant generations, I have all the sympathy & pity in the world. If the U.N. <u>really</u> wants to do something to insure [sic] future peace, they have a perfect set-up here in Korea with the children & in the countries all over the world— for it is in the young age of impression that wars surely start. Poor, unloved kids are the same all over the world—smile at them, put an arm around them & give them a cracker from your 'C' rations & you're "number one" to them. Give them an American flag & a cracker & you prove to them in their youth that the 2 go together; later on, give them freedom & a chance to earn their own bread & you have the basis for a democracy—and it starts with a cracker. Maybe I haven't said what I've been trying to say, Joanne—but it's something for all of us to think about. After this is over, the U.S. will no doubt "rehabilitate" & rebuild Korea. If you could see the painful work done on rice paddies, intricate rock fences, walls & crude home made [sic] implements & houses, you'd know as I do that for us to rebuild Korea would be robbing them of their work they have learned to do thru generation[s] of toil. But give them some help, give them the promise that they are not building in vain & the enviable patience of the people will rebuild Korea—and they'll know they've done it themselves. It's a rather odd philosophy & one that would undoubtedly fall through in the realism of our nickel-and-dime congressional floor. But I believe it—and I think (conceitedly) that I'm a little ahead of everyone else.

Now that I've solved the world's troubles, I'll go on to something else.

It's raining outside my tent now—and once in awhile [sic] inside. The air outside is fresh & cool, a welcome moisture from the July heat. The dust has settled and the sky is only slightly overcast. I don't think it will rain long—just long enough to refresh an overheated earth.

The peace talks go on & on, and everyday [sic] the rumors start—some good, some bad. From what I gather the talks are going well. And also, I know from reports, the Chinese have 350,000 men (72 divisions) in Korea in case they don't. Our replacements & wounded returnees keep coming in. The company now is overstrengthened [sic]—quite a difference from a month ago. Before, they could hold Fox Co. role [sic] call in the military hospitals—now they can hold it here.

So much for now, darling, I've run out. Got your letter today & I LOVE YOU AND MISS YOU TERRIBLY too. Take care of you & Cinthy, sweetheart. You're all my dreams come true. I adore you both.

    All my life & love always –
    Al
    (& Boondocker)

XXXXXXXXXX
Xxxxxxxxxx

MZ 603

        July 26

Dearest Joanne—

It's a brisk clear 9 a.m.—the sun has broken through the early-morning fog that settled over the hills and dampened the leaves & the shrubbery and made them glisten. I know it's going to be a hot dry day but right now there's still a moisture in the air, and the whole hillside is like a cool glade in the forest. I can smell the earth, rich & black—and the pines and the mixed odor of the vegetation. The insects that sing & add life to the underbrush are awake. And there's a touch of beauty & mystery to life this august morning.

I have a working party and am having them clear away the shrubbery for firing lanes. Writing & watching them at the same time is quite a job. Thus the reason for these little sections. [Each page is marked off in four sections, and each section is numbered.] I hope you can figure them out.

A morning like this (Sunday) is perhaps a vindication for the news we just received. Before us on the lines are the ROK's [sic] & the army—the 2 weakest combat elements in Korea. They are weakening. They are breaking.

Someone has to hold the line, prevent a breakthrough. Thus the news wasn't much of a surprise to us: "turn in everything you can't carry over the hills. Lighten your load, we're moving out in a couple days." That's it, hon. No Inchon, no Japan, no landing. Back to the lines to relieve the army and the ROKs—they've been on a couple weeks and they're "tired." So that's the story. No one has yet said "front lines." But we know. No one has said when we're moving—but it's in a couple days.

But it's Sunday morning, brisk & wonderful even in Korea. Reminds me of home, of Golden Gate Park and of summer camp when I was a kid. It's the kind of day upon which you're glad to be alive & you want to sing and love and be happy.

Because the birds are singing, men talking happily—both Korean & American—and there is peace on the hillside. Even the artillery, which has boomed all nite & day, is still.

Everything is green, and I love you so very much.

I suppose I should rant & rave as I usually do because we are going back on the lines. But I'm usually the calmest when thigs are blackest—even though that has no set rule either. Right now war is incidental. All that matters is we're here—and tomorrow—never comes ...

—later

The afternoon sun has hit this side of the hill, but under the trees where I'm at it's still cool. I just finished looking at a Colliers and one picture showed a young couple standing on a hill overlooking Portland. It made me feel funny & homesick. It could've just as easily been you & I looking over white & beautiful San Francisco. But I can't get homesick, because if I do I'll really feel bad. And I miss you & home enough as it is. Sometime next month or the month after, it starts getting cold in Korea. Then we draw our winter gear. When October arrives, so does the snow. So I guess I'll get a taste of winter warfare after all. Not a pleasant thought, but it couldn't be much worse than rain or intense heat as far as I'm concerned. Around the latter part of November or December I'll start thinking about rotation. I hope to be home in January—that will be 10 months in Korea. Some guys have gotten out in 8—but not from Fox Co. We always seem to have more casualties & fewer replacements. Rotation is non-existent if we're understrengthed [sic]. That's the reason so many guys went home while we were in reserve—replacement drafts.

There's not too much talk about Kaesong* around here anymore [sic]. Seems the hope of success there means little or nothing to the men. Once they had faith, but it vanished when they saw that Kaesong is much like the U.N.: right idea, wrong method. Me? I've always been an idealist. I still have faith.

Oh, about this PIO deal—I haven't heard anything, and when we go back to

---

*Kaesong is a city in the southern area of North Korea. It was the site of peace talks beginning on July 10, 1951, but these moved to Panmunjom on October 25, 1951.

the lines I guess I won't. Oh, well—I had my chance & turned it down.* What I sow, I shall reap ... so on. No one will ever be able to say I'm not a gambler anyhow—however foolish.

Funny how you can sit right in the midst of a war & be so relaxed and peaceful. Only a few miles away from a combat zone too. Planes droning overhead like flies, artillery sounding off lazily every once in awhile [sic]. Funny how these times become commonplace & natural.

Darling, I'm fairly certain I'll be able to write you tomorrow & Tuesday. Wednesday we'll probably move north, so that will handicap writing to you. Once we hit the lines I don't know whether we'll set up in the defense or go into the attack. If we set up, I'll be able to write. If not, you'll know we're moving—so don't worry if you don't hear from me [for] a week or so. Hokay?

Will finish this tonight.

Love ya—Al

—evening

Well, hon, I'm back at our old area. I came back with about 10 other guys to go to church. When I got back I decided to drop in to regimental PIO just for laughs. I walked in the door & they grabbed me. Gave me a handful of copy paper sat me at the typewriter and said "write!" Meanwhile the NCO in charge dashed into regimental sgt. Major's to get my transfer going. Honestly, I was literally swept off my feet. I was looked on by the people in the office as a treasure. It made me feel good to know that my stuff went over good—as it must have by the response. Anyhow, now I'm suppose[d] to clear my transfer thru Fox Co, then battalion. And even if they turn it down, regiment can get me out. PIO wants me to start in an unofficial capacity immediately. So they gave me copy paper. Probably tomorrow I'll talk to the Co. C.O. about the transfer. If it comes thru it will most likely take a month or so. Then again it may not come thru at all. But it's something to think about; and it makes me feel good knowing that my writing has set the 7th regiment on its ear. Gives me an indicator of the improvement I've made & what I can do to John Q.

These pictures I'm sending [no enclosures present] were taken by the top in one of those developed-in-60-seconds camera [sic]. I wrote and said I had gotten good looking over here—I take it all back. It must have been the fury of combat which gave me such illusions. Anyhow these pictures give you an idea of what I look like. I just came out of the field and am grimy, tired & dirty. Don't show it to Cinthy—no use scaring our daughter young.

Well, darling, this is 30 for tonite. Sure hope you're able to read this letter the way it's written.

And hon—front lines or no front lines, I'm alright & I'm going to stay alright. Everyone is afraid of combat & it's only natural to be so. When I'm blue it's just

---

*Al had been offered a post in PIO as a typist, but he turned it down because he wanted to be a writer, not a clerk. He would also be offered a job as editor of the regimental newsletter, but he turned it down as well because he wanted to write bigger stories about the war. Later, he would accept a role that afforded him both roles: writing the regimental newsletter and serving as a combat correspondent.

the way it should be. So, my little sweetie, chin up, keep smiling & love me with all your heart.

I'll be home when I get there & when I do I'm making up for lost time—in many ways.

I love you with all my heart & soul
Al (& Boondocker)
X's all you want

MZ 612

July 29

Dearest darling—

No one can touch me now; none can approach me. It's 9:30 p.m. & still I write. How? I have a candle! The squad got 3 of them today and by process of "you think of a number" I got one. So finally I am able to write at nite. It's only a little candle & won't last long, but while it does I'll take advantage of it. I have a mirror behind it trying to reflect light and it works well.

There's only a very few wandering around the area now. Most have gone to the movies and some are out after sheeba-sheeba (Pussy to us). I didn't feel like going to the movies and I certainly have no interest in the Oriental version of the "call girl," so I remained behind to write to you.

It's a starless, cloudy nite, oppressive with the feeling of rain in the air. The soft wind that blows is moist and everything is damp. It's the kind of nite I like to walk in, feeling the closeness of the atmosphere like a heavy fog. It's a nite of "enchantment," you might say, when you're almost certain that beautiful memories are being carved on young people's minds in our United States. It's really a nice nite—something about it that captures & holds you.

The candle keeps getting shorter & shorter so I'll have to write faster.

Two years ago tonite you & I were sleeping (separately) on dreams of a new life. We were waiting for the dawn of light that would be our wedding day. Two years ago tonite you & I were dreaming such beautiful dreams of days & nites together for the rest of our lives. I remember when I last saw you that nite in San Francisco it was on Powell & Market. I was waiting to put you on a streetcar so I could leave for Richmond. We said, "Just think—tomorrow nite at this time we'll be married…" Remember the nervous awe in our voices & the awkward mannerisms? Tomorrow. Our tomorrow came. And now it's yesterday—a wonderful yesterday, and actually only a little more than a day. I love you, Joanne. I love you very dearly.

Goodnight, my darling…

July 30

Goodmorning [sic], sweetheart!

It's a beautiful anniversary day for me in Korea with the sun a brilliant daz[z]le in the sky and the air fresh and clean. Last nite's rain makes the air smell good & the morning moist. And everything is bright to greet the day that marks our two years of marriage.

—later

All the gear we own is out in front of our tents now & we are standing by for an inspection on Sunday at 7 p.m. Members of other companies come by and can't believe their eyes, but it is the unusual which characterizes Fox Co. In fact, the lieut. is about 3 tents from me now, but (as usual) I can't get worried.

We finally had mail call and I got 3 letters from you (with pictures), one from Dolores, Helen & Bonnie Ralph, oh yes, and Frank Galo. All in all, I took about ⅓ of the plt.'s mail. The guys that didn't get any just looked at me as though I had something that was theirs. They gave me the you-robbed-my-castle look. That one picture of Cinthy where she's lying on her stomach looking at the camera is darling. She's the sweetest little girl in the world. Little Helen is as pretty as ever & who's that little colored guy next to her—could that be my sun-tanned nephew Darrell? All in all, the pictures were good. I love getting pictures! How about sending me more of you?

We went swimming this afternoon—more fun & more tan! Whoops! Here comes the lieut. Will finish this later as I drink my beer. I have a letter to write to you I promised on this date—July 30th.

—later still

Darling—

It's about 8:30. We're sitting by a stream letting our beer cool and I've already reached the first stages of being high: I'm getting sentimental. But that's only natural, because I'm a sentimental guy & my second anniversary is a good nite to get that way. I'm pretty sentimental about us & you and our marriage.

Not many would know it unless they knew me. I can kid about almost anything. But you know and I know that I wouldn't trade our life together for anything in the world. I'd rather be with you even if it meant giving up everything else in life—and I wouldn't say that about anyone or anything else. But the part that makes our marriage wonderful is that I know you don't want me to give up my ambition or anything else.

Joanne, I feel inadequate to say all the nice things I had planned to say. I want to say so much, again, that I get all jumbled up and confused. I'll have to leave much to your knowing me & what I feel about you. You know what I'm trying to say, darling. It's all that I love you & treasure you & our life together. I can't really explain what our 2 years has meant. It's brought a lot of subtle changes in me & taken a lot of the self-pity & selfishness out of my system. You haven't tried to do it—it's the natural change that comes when one wants to [be] perfect for the girl he loves. I am far from perfect. I'm stubborn, proud, concieted [sic] & often foolish—but I'm not insincere. There's a lot of things that can be improved upon—and some perhaps that never will be improved. But however I am, darling, I'll love you all my life. That will never change.

Tommorrow [sic] we move out. But whatever dusty Korean road we travel I'll be daydreaming—about you & July 31, 1949—the day after our wedding. And when I get tired & hot, I'm going to send you a kiss—& one for Cinthy.

From & [sic] husband & father who loves his wife & daughter with all his heart.

> All my love
> always & always—
> Al (& Boondocker)
> XXXXXXXXX
> xxxxxxxxx

MZ 615

August 1

Dearest Joanne—

After a 4-hr. truck ride that took us over mountain passes & along the dusty valley floor roads, we have reached our new area—near Inje & Yanggu.* We reached here about 11 this morning; it's now 7:25 p.m. We set up right at this base of a ridge which is supposed to be our secondary defense line. The general area isn't as good as our last, but this close to a combat zone you can't expect a playground paradise.

I don't feel too happy about backing up an army division. Just a few days ago they lost the high ground to an enemy patrol. They regained the ground, but only because the patrol returned to it's [sic] lines. If they were ever hit in an attack, I imagine we'd be using our secondary line before long.

In your last letter you registered surprise that I give credit to the air force at our manuevers [sic]. Perhaps I failed to mention it, but those planes were Corsairs—our brothers in the sky—the 1st Marine division Air Wing. Our air support, even in combat, is almost always Marine. And it's close support—often only 100 yards ahead of us. Very seldom does the Air Force, per se, give us support & when they do, it isn't close. They aren't trained to support assault troops. Even so, don't misunderstand:—I have a great respect for our Air Force. Without it, believe me, our job on the land would be a million times more difficult.

I may be a little prejudiced in favor of the Corps, hon, but I can & do give credit where it is due. I've mentioned the 2nd & 7th Army infantry divisions. I've also mentioned the KMC's [sic]. As for the ROK's [sic], most Army outfits & even some Marine outfits, I have absolutely no respect. The Army has lately abandoned vital positions when a few mortars have dropped in & our Bn. alone has not only held ground but jumped off in the face of artillery & mortar barrages. The Army loses ground to a patrol; we would no more think of giving ground to an attacking force much less a damn patrol. I wish you could have seen a valley here they call "Mas[s]acre Valley."† We passed through it the morning after an Army bn.

---

*Inje and Yanggu are counties in Gangwon Province, South Korea.
†The Battle of Hoengsong took place February 12–13, 1951. It was one of the worst defeats suffered by the U.S. military during the war. Angry Marines placed a sign along the road where their comrades had fallen, reading "Massacre Valley, Scene of Harry S. Truman's Police Action. Nice going, Harry!" It is unclear whether the sight Al describes was the aftermath of another battle in the same location. He had not yet arrived in Korea by February, the time of the Battle of Hoengsong.

was mas[s]acred in a convoy by ambush. It wasn't a pretty sight. The No. Koreans are jealous victors—you perhaps read about it: the dis[m]embered & bayoneted bodies. I saw it—and drew the line sharper between Army & Marines. If we were ambushed, the enemy would first have to wipe out our flank, frontal & rear security—which is unlikely. And which has never happened in Korea.

Sunday we leave on a Bn. Reconna[is]sance patrol. I don't know where or how long it will last. The last time we went on a Bn. patrol we ran into 60,000 Chinese. I think this patrol is looking for infiltraters [sic] & guerillas. Oh, but we're <u>still</u> in Corps reserve. This is their idea of a rest. How about that!

Just as we arrived here & set up our tents it started raining. It rained fairly hard for awhile [sic] & we had visions of our tent washing away, but it stopped. It still threatens rain, but probably won't until tomorrow nite—we have a nite problem then. Optimistic, ain't I?

As for the truce news—I don't like it. They're dickering again, accusing each other of stalling, and trying to protect national honor. I can't say I'm depending on them too much. Meanwhile the commies are pouring in supplies & troops & artillery in preparation for a counter attack [sic] just in case there's no treaty. I suppose we're doing the same thing—so what can you hope for? A stateside leg wound, my darling. That's what. Not a very pretty picture I painted, but I only echoed the whole situation which, in truth, is not very pretty itself! I hope I'm home by Xmas.

Well, hon, this is the voice of happiness signing off for today. I still pray for peace, Joanne, sincerely & fervently. I definitely do not think it is all hopeless. The situation may look bad at present, but it's been worse & this time there is effort at betterment. I do think the cease fire will come through shortly & the armistice after that. The enemy is not stupid enough to think we are lying idle while they are building—they know that we can build up faster & better. I think this desire for peace is sincere. Given the chance, man can reconstruct a world of faith, hope & peace he has destroyed. I believe a greater power feels the prayers of the thousands warrants that chance—despite the mistakes of the millions.

All My love
always & always
Al (& Boondocker)
XXXXXXXXX
xxxxxxxxx

(P.S.—a big kiss to my little Cinthy)—daddy

MZ 617

Aug. 9, '51

The purple liquid twilight pours
Across the waste of bloodless sand
And drowns the tears in evening lull
That weep across this no man's land;
The peace of darkness is at hand.

Dearest Joanne—

> Oh, yes—I often get the urge to write poetry ... still.
> The streaks of scarlet in the sky
> That fade into the evening brown
> The thunder from the Northern front ...
> The streaks of scarlet on the ground.

War is an incentive for poetry—a grim one. The beauty it perceives is only in its prose, not in thought. But to one who thrills at the drum beat, poetry has a way—

> The hills tear open with the flame!
> That pounds the earth to molten dew –
> The roar of thunder's in the air:
> Stand by—Marines are coming through.

And in every movement of life & nature in Korea, a poem is born—a poem the potential of which is limitless. But what bothers the poet, is that all it encompasses spells death. And loneliness.... But if death is beautiful, as Poe would have it, here is the height of poetic beauty! Here is death by the bloody handfuls.

Aug. 10

Dearest darling—

Tonite I am not so poetic. I am not even alive. I am exhausted. Only the pain in my feet, legs & muscles is alive. Why? Today the 2nd plt. went on a patrol: we have a new 2nd lieut. plt. leader; it was raining. Put them all together, they spell murder—and murder's what it's done to me.

Let me reconstruct the scene of the crime.

Rev[e]ille went at 0530 for us. At 0630 we boarded trucks & went about 16 miles south. The object of the patrol, they said, was to look for enemy guerillas & strag[g]lers in the hills. When we got off the truck I saw how ridiculous it was—army units were set up all over hell. All this time it poured and I, without a poncho, felt the anger well in me for such a stupid & senseless patrol.

After breaking our necks climbing up & down treacherously slippery ridges for about 2 hrs[.] came the rub. We went up one hill that was 400 meters (1350 ft.) looked at the grinning skulls of dead Chinese & the debris of death & destruction & came down completely to the valley floor. This in itself was a feat—rocks (10 & 20 lb ones) roaring down on you at a freight train speed when dislodged by someone behind you, slippery trails, mines, booby traps & rain. When we reached the bottom we almost immediately started up a sheer rocky bluff of at [sic] 600 meter hill (2050 ft.), the lieut. carrying a pistol & forgetting that we carried 20 lb. BAR's, M-1's & cartridge belts loaded with ammo. He therefore set an impossible pace.

Anyhow, we climbed the damn thing after about 2 hrs. At the top he gave us a break for chow—one of the first breaks incidenteley [sic]. Chow consisted of assault rations—or practically nothing.

Darling—I'll finish this letter tomorrow. I'm beat.

—Aug. 11

Hi sweetheart—

To get on with the above, we came down off that hill to the valley floor again, only to start up, nose after nose, a gradual slope which reached 800 meters (2700 feet) into the air. It was a torturous climb over loose rocks & precipitous ledges. Each nose was higher & steeper. Two men dropped out, 2 passed out. After 8 hrs. of sweating & soaking in the rain, we dragged ourselves over the last ledge & to the top. As P.O.'d as I was, I figured we were finished. But no. At 6 p.m. the lieut. said, "We have about 4 or 5 hours to go from here. All those men who think they can't make it, can go down to the road from here & catch a truck."

Now I've gone up 1200[-]meter hills before with 40 lbs. on my back and people shooting bullets & mortars at me. But always with a purpose. There was no purpose to this patrol. So I (& 18 other men) said, "Okay, we'll go back." And back we came. The rest of the plt. stayed out in the rain & darkness, got lost, and finally arrived at the company area about 11 p.m. So the most worthless patrol in Fox Co. history was over, and I'll bet more than one officer got chewed out for it! I could have made it—but I've been around long enough to know that nothing would be accomplished by it. This morning the lieut. apologized to the plt., & envied us that came back. I think he'll be okay. Just learning about patrols the hard way.

Today it is still raining. The weather is miserable, and I'm still tired. So forgive me, hon, if I stop now & do better tomorrow. When I get home, we buy a car. I'll never walk anywhere if I can ride.

> All My love
> always & always –
> Al (& Boodocker)
> X's by the millions
> to wife & daughter.
> I love you both.

MZ 626

[ca. Aug. 12–18, 1951]

Dearest Joanne—

A lot of these men are ones you knew—friends of mine, whom you met at the Dog Co. party in San Clemente. You may not remember them, but that makes little difference to everyone concerned—in a few years it won't make any difference to the world that they died on a napalmed-charred, ugly hill in Korea. To me it makes a great deal of difference. I want a lesson in life to be burned white-hot on my brain. I want to remember them when they laughed, the way they laughed—I want to torture my memory until I can see them clearly … then I want to cut them off, let them die as they did in Korea. Then I want to write about it and tell America—here are your sons! Torn apart, mutilated. Dead, perhaps, for a noble cause. Dead nonetheless. Wave a flag & try to revive them. Here then is the consequence of a righteous war.

> Al

MZ 629

IN MEMORIAM

SEVENTH MARINES

Col. Herman Nickerson, Jr. USMC
Commanding

August 12, 1951
Korea

Cover of booklet for memorial service honoring Marines lost in battle, August 12, 1951 (The Huntington Library, MZ 629, p. 1).

Aug. 15
(I think)

Dearest Joanne—

Well, as the chaplain would say, the depredation has hit the ventalation [sic] around here for Fox Co. Two men have gone over the hill and were covered up

ABSHIRE, Ruric T.	FRIZZELL, Gerald K.	LANE, Monty J.	RODRIGUEZ, Rubin C.
AINSWORTH, Homer R.	FUGITT, William D.	LASSLEY, Loyal G.	ROEHM, Emanuel G.
ALLEN, Walter H.	GAGNE, Gerald J.	LATHEM, Paul W. Jr.	ROGERS, Warren, W.
ALVARADO, Eulalio	GARDNER, Ralph H.	LEAVER, Thomas J.	RUSSELL, Clifford U.
ARTHUR, Bobbie R.	GAYLE, Howard	LEE, Kenneth R.	SACSON, George B.
BAGALE, John D.	GEDDES, Nelson R.	LENOIR, Edward	SAGDAHL, Rolf J.
BANKSTON, Bobbie R.	GINGLEWOOD, Leon R.	LEWIS, Richard S.	SALAICES, Carlos L.
BARNELLO, John	GOODING, William E.	LITTLEFIELD, Gordan A.	SANCHEZ, Leo C.
BARNS, Jim B.	GOUDELOCK, Felix W. Jr.	LIVAS, Santos	SANDERS, Harry W.
BEAN, Jackie R.	GREGORY, James A.	LUNSFORD, Ronald D. L.	SCARBOROUGH, Harry E.
BELTZ, David L.	GROSS, Donald R.	MARINO, William J.	SCHAEFFER, Malcolm J.
BERG, Richard W.	GUNTER, David L.	MARKEY, Leo P. Jr.	SCHERZINGER, Herbert A.
BOWDEN, Willam E.	HAMILTON, David L.	MARSH, Howard Mc C.	SCHWEGMAN, John J.
BOYD, Hugh W.	HANSEN, Lawrence D.	MATERNE, Lafe H.	SEMAR, John E.
BRIGGS, Merton E.	HASKETT, George N.	MATTEI, John R.	SEWARD, Stanley J.
BRIZIUS, Martin C.	HATFIELD, Theodore I.	MATULICH, Joseph S.	SHADDOCK, Ronald F.
BROOKS, Robert F.	HAUSMAN, Theodore F.	MAY, Donald L.	SLY, Donald D.
BUCHANAN, Edgar L.	HAYDEN, James A.	MC BETH, Donald	SMITH, Alfred Jr.
BUCHMANN, Robert E.	HEATER, Howard W.	MC GOWAN, Robert F.	SMITH, Donnelly F.
BUHS, Richard D.	HEINZ, Erwin G.	MC WAIDE, Patrick J.	SMITH, Jimmie R.
BUTTON, Charles D.	HERMOSILLO, Carlos	MEDLIN, Billie J.	SMITH, John L.
CAMPO, Joseph S.	HILGENBERG, Robert H.	MELTON, William R.	SOMJAI, Stephen R.
CASTILLE, Felix A.	HILL, Griswold M.	MILLER, Vernon E.	SPEEDY, George Jr.
CHURCHILL, Robert A.	HOILES, William H. III	MILLS, Robert J.	STIDHAM, Henry C.
CLARK, Edward L.	HOLT, Melbourne, G.	MISLER, Russell G.	STOCKHOLM, Lee Carl Jr.
COLLINS, Calvin R.	HOPKINS, James R.	MISOVIC, Michael Jr.	STRAWHORN, Delmar E.
CONLON, John J.	HOUCK, Jack A.	MONCRIEF, George E.	STRICKLAND, Asa W. Jr.
CORRELL, Bobby D.	HOVATTER, Donald J.	MOORE, Claude A.	SUMMS, Arthur C.
CROWLEY, Charles S.	HUNTER, Millard H.	MORRISSEY, Richard E.	SURRETTE, Joseph B.
CURRY, Charles M.	JACKSON, James E. Jr.	MOSELEY, Marvin E.	SYKES, Forrest D.
CURRY, Wiliam F.	JENNINGS, Robert E.	MUER, Frederick M.	TARDIO, Harold M.
DAMON, Robert V.	JOHNSON, Randolph A.	MUNGER, Luman E.	TILLEY, Louis H.
DANIELS, Donald R.	JONAS, Bernard C.	NEWTON, James E.	TOVAR, Julian T.
DAVIS, Nubern D.	JUDSON, Stephen H.	NICKLOS, Ronald C.	TOWN, Edwin J.
DAVIS, Robert E.	KAISER, Raymond R.	NOTSUND, Harold N.	TROVILLO, Alfred J.
DAWBER, John L.	KANE, James J.	OFSONKA, Robert S.	URABALEJO, Antonio Y.
DE MEO, Anthony F.	KEATING, Charles E.	ORTEGA, Jesus M.	VALESQUES, Angelo M.
DE WERT, Richard	KENNEDY, George Q.	PASSERO, Guerino Jr.	VAN LOO, Paul E.
DRUZIANICH, John C. Jr.	KIEFER, Yale S.	PEAKE, Thomas	VERBANAC, Carl J.
DUNCAN, Raymond E.	KING, James D.	PETERSON, Udell L.	VILES, Robert L.
DUNLAP, Albert H. Jr.	KLINKERMAN, John W.	PETERSON, Robert S.	WATSON, Byron E.
DURHAM, Richard W.	KNIGHTLINGER, Jack C.	PITTMAN, Clark L.	WELCHES, John E. P.
ELLIOTT, "R" "J"	KNOX, Joseph J.	POWELL, Harry A.	WHATLEY, Charles L.
ELLISON, Harold E.	KNUTSON, Jerome F.	PUTMAN, James E.	WHELAN, Leonard J.
FALATACH, Anthony J.	KOPCZAK, Joseph A.	RASPANTI, Robert J.	WHITE, John E.
FIEDLER, James T.	KOTT, Daniel B.	REGAN, John L.	WILLHITE, Frank B.
FISCHER, Ralph R.	KROLAK, Chester A. Jr.	REYNOLDS, William R.	WITHERSPOON, Joseph R.
FITCH, Robert S.	KUBISTY, Robert L.	RICHARDS, Ralph L.	WOODRING, Elmer J.
FLACK, Jack E.	KWADER, Louis P.	RITZ, Jack D.	YATES, Richard L.
FLORY, Rene J. Jr.	LAND, John H.	RIVIELLO, Frank V.	ZELLER, Robert W.
FORD, Francis E.	LANDERS, Homer J.	ROBLEDO, Ramon C.	

Inside page of booklet for memorial honoring Marines lost in battle. Al has marked the names of those he knew (The Huntington Library, MZ 629, p. 2).

for by a fake muster—consequently, three plt. sgts. have been run up & the Co. command group is on the carpet by the Bn. C.O.—which means the peons catch the hell. Secondly, our area didn't pass an inspection; thirdly, we made fun of the Col. The last one was really funny. We were having close-order drill in our usual apathetic way when the Col. appeared. To instill the pride of Marines in us he shouted in a gruff voice, "march! be proud!" No one dared laugh outright, but the assembled hushed laughter was heard & the company mimics who mumbled in impersonation "be proud!" were undone. The Col. walked away, but we've had no peace since: inspections, forced marches & practical restriction to the area ("check out with the Cpl. of the guard, the duty NCO, the squad leader, plt. guide, plt. sgt, gunny, top, plt. leader & C.O."). We don't go anywhere.

> Thy Will be done, if Thou decree
> That I shall die afield.
> But let me go face to the foe...
> Sustain me, lest I yield.
> Let no man cry he saw me fly
> The battle's agony.
> And let me die as a man should die
> In a fight for Liberty.
>
> G. E. Lord, Pfc
> USMC

Back cover of booklet for memorial honoring Marines lost in battle, containing Al's letter of ca. August 12, 1951 (The Huntington Library, MZ 629, p. 4).

Something else happened the other day which I have beaten: you have to carry some kind of weapon everywhere you go –the head, showers, chow— everywhere! Lots of the guys have 45 automatic pistols in shoulder holsters they carry—which is acceptable. They wrap their pistols in old socks to keep them clean ("aha" you say, "the plot unfolds!"). Yes, I got an extra shoulder holster someone had, cut the exact duplicate of a .45 pistol out of wood, wrapped a sock around it everyone thinks it's a .45, so my wooden pistol & I go to chow everyday [sic]! Of course, if an officer ever wanted to see the pistol, I'd be in a hell of a spot and you'd be addressing letters to PFC again. But as it is, I don't have to carry a rifle everywhere. Time for chow right now, hon. So will you excuse my wooden pistol & I?

later

Hi hon—

I have just witnessed as part of a howling[,] bloodthirsting (they got it) audience, a thing known as a "Marine" smoker.* The word "Marine" is necessary, as it distinguishes between the Stateside smokers of women, etc., these were boxing matches, I believe they called them—where 2 husky youngsters don trunks & pound one another to the tune of a gong which always rings just in time. There was one particularly brutal fight where a squat dark muscular fellow beat hell out of a sorrier and wiser adversary. The name "Tony" fit this guy, because it recalled something ancient with a tail and a stone axe—driopithecus [sic] Cro-magnon, you know the type. I expected him to growl. He just punched! Tony will get you if you <u>don't watch out</u>!

Darling, it's getting dark, candle hava-no (Korean)† and I want to mail this today. I hope you won't mind this one millionth time if I make this short.

Joanne I want to tell you something before I close—and I hope you understand. I had a chance to get in PIO and turned it down. Here's why: PIO offers me only the chance to punch a typewriter as a clerk for some officers. Yes, it's a rear echelon job, but when I thought about it I knew it wasn't what I wanted. Before, I was impatient—and that impatience lost me a lot in writing. Now I have a chance to write only for a mimeographed Bn. sheet—and believe me the urge to write is killing me. But I've learned patience, Joanne. The war I want to write about is the war <u>I've seen</u>. I can't write about it from the rear. Darling, please understand & trust me. I'm sacrificing my desire now—writing (<u>plain</u> writing)—for something much bigger later on. I'm no heroe [sic] but when my readers see the war, they'll see a PFC with an M-1 & a heavy pack scared as hell over the Korean hills and muttering, "I wonder what the poor people are doing." They'll see the heroes & the cowards, the living who so rapidly become the dead. Believe me, sweetheart—I want to write something I've seen & felt down to my toes. I'm sincere—this is going to be <u>my</u> story—of a guy named Joe Citera. It may mean a hole in the head (just kidding), but it will be a hole in the head of a man who knows what he's doing.

Trust me.

> I love you—
> All My heart & soul
> to wife & daughter—both [of] whom I want to be proud of me!
> Al (& Boondocker)

P.S.—I still may get a transfer somewhere anyhow. I don't know.

MZ 630

---

*A smoker is an unauthorized fight or boxing match.
†"Hava-no" is the English-language rendering of the Korean mispronunciation of "have no," meaning "don't have any."

Aug. 20

Dearest Joanne—

This letter from necessity must be short. I have guard again in a short while and I've been busy all afternoon. I've been writing stories for PIO. No, I'm not in there yet. But the officer in charge has read my qualifications & wants my stuff. He wanted to see what I could do. That was yesterday afternoon. This afternoon I handed him some 15 feature stories of different natures. He said to just do a half-assed job. But I couldn't. I put my heart & my ability into every one of them, and the old spirit beat back in my brain—the fire returned. The stories were far from my best. But I'm wonderfully happy with them. They prove what I only thought—I'm coming of age as a writer, Joanne. My humor is real, my diction colorful or serious without being elaborate or frilly. I've experienced life, and now for the first time I'm telling a story which every violent sense in my body has reacted to. It was as though I just closed my eyes & <u>remembered</u>—not "imagined"—and my pen acted accordingly.

I don't give a did[d]ly damn if I never get into PIO. For I've discovered a poignant fact: I can write. Darling, I <u>can</u> be a writer despite the competition in the world. There'll be heart-aches & set-backs—many of them. But I feel confident that once I hurdle the conventions of that tight clique, I can bring an honest sincerity into writing. I can make them read me—<u>and not forget me</u>!

Honey, share this moment with me—you & Cinthy. Share my feeling—a new, wonderful feeling which humbles me & makes me fiercely proud of the challenge in the profession I've chosen. War, in its horror[,] provides death—but for one who survives & observes, it creates experience. Into that latter category I must inevitably fall.

Darling, this is it! I've accepted that challenge. I can be patient. I have the incentive, the experience, the ability. I promise you & Cinthia security and happiness you've never know[n]. I swear it! I promise.

      I love you with <u>all</u> my
      heart & soul—
       Al X's by the millions.
         love me always—as I
         love you.

MZ 635

Aug 23

Dearest Joanne—

I guess the inevitable has happened. From what we've heard, the Kaesong conferences have been called off completely. The No. Koreans are counter-attacking along our Eastern front. What we feared worse [sic] has happened. There is still hope that a miracle—a[n] inconceivably fine miracle—will happen, and the holocaust will end. But the word "inconceivable" is just the word. Peace has failed as we knew it would. There are 70,000, maybe 700,000 or 7,000,000 Chinese waiting to destroy us. It doesn't make any difference how many. One can squeeze a trigger—one can pull the lanyard on an artillery piece—one can man a mortar.

It's been raining hard all day. We were soaked, our rifles rusted. We walked over the hills & worked hard all day. No mail came in. We heard the news up on the hill of the Kaesong failure. Yet we sang as we slid down the slippery trail & knee deep through mud & water of the soggy rice paddies. We laughed when we saw our flooded tents. Why? Because a cold, solid fact is at least staring us in the face: no rumor, no scuttlebutt. We have no further dissilusions [sic]—no more false hopes. I suppose this is something the newspapers would call high Marine morale—and the will to fight. They're so horribly wrong. This is fear, bitterness & heartache, summed up in the violence of a song, harsh & loud, giving way to the disgust of the men, which dreams [sic?] of no tomorrows—only the yesterdays that, with the whine of artillery, may come no more ...

But the men sing & laugh. Because at last we know.

A person not use[d] to seeing death every day, of listening to the beat of his heart tick away the minutes of his life, could never understand the feeling which now prevails. It is a feeling of finality, of eat, drink & be merry for tomorrow we die. It is the feeling characterized in glamor & fiction as the picture of a brave man. It is the feeling of nothingness with which neophyte writers end their novels. No one would believe it. It's phoney [sic]. It's celluloid & tinsel, fake fog & paper stars. Yet it exists, here in the ragged land of Korea, 6,000 miles from the dreamers whose idiotic minds plot ways to demonize wars. And the cinema heroes fall.

The wet ground before me is real. My rifle is steel reality. And I know you & our Cinthia is [sic] real. Nothing in fancy can blend them together. They are seperate [sic] entities, things apart. You & Cinthia are beautiful in memory & imagination—preserved in love & held above all this. War in Korea, the hills, my rifle are real—the present, substance hard & certain. But they mean nothing to me in values determined. You & my baby are the things that count—<u>really</u> count. You two are all I hold dear—<u>nothing</u> can change that.

I can't really say I'm bitter. No one has been cheated. Man has violated all rules of life, and by so doing is reaping just punishment. I'm no fatalist, and I do believe that some of us are entitled to the chance to build from the ruins of the past. But perhaps it is the will of God that we learn a lesson never to be forgotten. I've trusted in God when fear blinded me: the trust calmed me. I had faith in him when things looked good. And now because a more treacherous turn has taken place, many will lose faith. I won't. I refuse to denounce Him. And I never shall—despite peace, tranquility or physical wealth. I've learned my lesson. A lesson which deception will never change.

No one has ever considered me a brave man, darling. But no one will ever call me a coward. I'll do what I must. I'll be afraid, and I'll think of running. But I won't. I'll watch, & I'll remember. Without diary, without record—oh, yes—I'll remember.

This sounds too much like a "goodbye-I'll-see-you-in-Heaven" note. It certainly isn't. It's a letter explaining to you how I feel, what I've seen in the face of new events. I want you to see the picture, because I want you to know the truth. I sincerely want you to go out of the way to show <u>anyone</u> this letter. Show it to the Jaegers, to Mrs. Rozelle, to Margueret [sic], to my family, your friends. I want everyone to get the picture—but especially you.

Let them look & read! Here is a new generation, damning war, living through all the horrors the past has given us to nurse our present. Yet we will not lose faith in God or man. It's a terrible new courage, foolhardy—like hot-rods & French bathing suits. Warm—like hot coffee on a cold night. As realistic as a bayonet, as sentimental as love.

Here is a new generation. One which will only be remembered, perhaps, because it is unusual.

Let your friends read this letter then go home and say I'm crazy, smart, saddistic [sic] or anything they will. Let them feel sorry for you, Cinthy or me—let them shake sad heads in hollow mockery. Or let them read it & teach their children the ways of life which are true, fair & sincere. Those are the only ways.

Oh, I've got a story to write. And believe it or not, they'll read it because I'll cram it down John Q.'s throat. I'll paint a picture that will make them vomit with disgust & distaste for writer & plot. But they'll read it and it'll sink in like a 30 cal bullet.

Darling, this is it. Maybe I'm over dramatizing, maybe I'm going off the deep end again. But to me the following months will mean more than ducking a mortar round or making the next hill. It will test the endurance of an ideal: of that ideal which says that our sons will never go to war. And I'm betting my life on that ideal. Because I love you, Because I love Cinthia. And because I'm Al Martinez.

> All My heart & love
> to wife & daughter
> Always & always—
> Al   X's

P.S.—I'm in a good mood, believe it or not. Just trying to show you that we can take it and have faith—no matter what. Like a poem I wrote:

> Give me the strength to live, oh Lord
> A strength to face failure & dread –
> A power to pity & banish the sword
> And fight when my chances are dead.
> And give me this above all, oh Lord –
> When life does others condemn –
> The power to issue a deed or word …
> To bring faith to the heart of men.

Yeah—I'm an idealist.
    I love you—
        Al

MZ 638

Aug. 25

Dearest Joanne—

Finally I feel good tonight despite everything—I got 4 letters from my honey today, 2 from Galo and one from Mary. It's been my first mail in three or four days and has made quite a difference in my moods and general outlook.

The letters I got from you were awfully sweet and made me smile just to read them. Especially the one with the little airplane in it. I'm going to return it with a kiss on your kiss and an extra baby kiss for you to give to Cinthy.

I don't remember telling you when I didn't feel good, but I feel fine now, hon, so don't worry. Thank your mom for the compliment, and give Tony my best on his venture in TV—he'll need it.

I'm glad you're feeling good, darling. It makes me so much more at ease knowing everything is fine with you. That's what counts. And you won't be so nervous when I come home. I'll see to that. I promise.

I love you too, cutie …

Darling, it's dark, we're in a blackout zone (no candles) so I have to close. I'm alright, dearest, so don't worry about me. When I get blue, I can't help it—it's just me.

I love you with all my heart & soul. On this little plane I return to my home is my love, my heart & my very life. Take it—it's yours.

All My heart & love—
Al (& Boondocker)
X's

MZ 640

Joanne planted a kiss on this cardboard airplane and sent it to Al. He kissed it and returned it to her in his letter of August 25, 1951 (The Huntington Library, MZ 640).

Aug. (either 27 or 28)

Dearest darling—

Honey, I'm sorry I teased you so much about your typeing [sic]. I was only kidding, honest, sweetheart. Gosh, if I were serious, you'd certainly know I've got no room to talk in either typing or spelling! I'm the world's worst at both! Don't be hurt if I tease you about it, because that's all I am doing. I love you, angel, and the thing that counts is receiving <u>all</u> your wonderful letters. You can write them in Korean, if you want to as long as you said "I love you." I'm still an "old tease."

You asked me to mention if anything you wrote bothers me. Well—I guess I'm still jealous even though I haven't mentioned it for quite awhile [sic]. What's with calling this guy "Al" (a hell of a name) and letting him hold my Cinthy? Of course, I don't expect you to call him Mr. Jaeger!—But couldn't you kind of say "hey"? As for him, holding our Princess—there again, I don't expect you to leap at his throat when he suggests it, or crouch in a corner. But couldn't you tie her on your back when you're helping Barbara (Mrs. Jaeger?)? Seriously, hon, it did bother me a little—just the combination of his name being Al & him holding Cindy Lou. Jealous? You aren't kidding! It makes me jealous just to think that when I come home & you're waiting at the docks other guys will whistle at you from the ships. But, that's just me, and it all goes to show how much I love you ... but still—couldn't you just say "hey" to him?

I don't know how to begin this next paragraph, because it's so damn confusing. However, I've got to tell you, so here goes.

When I wrote you the last letter (with the pictures) you remember I said I went from where we were on the Wichita line (building bunkers) back to where we were in the first place where regiment was. Well, after I finished that letter (at regiment) I went back to our company area on the Wichita line. (All this is yesterday.) When I got there, everyone was packed & ready to move out. I rolled my gear frantically, threw everything into a pack & got aboard a truck. After an hour of riding, we ended up back at regiment (our old area) where I had been two hours before. We slept there for the nite. At 4 a.m. this morning, we moved east. They said to the lines so I threw everything away including the shelter half with which we make tents. After some 8 hours of riding we got nowhere. It's been raining all the time—pouring! They put us in a valley at nowhere (130 miles east) & said pitch tents. With borrowed ponchos I put together the awfullest looking "tent" you've ever seen! So now I am soaked to the skin with no dry change (I threw away the extra dungarees I had), no tent to speak of (threw away the shelter half), a leaking house & a thoroughly confused mind. I do know this: we are about 15 miles from the east coast, behind our lines and under the protection of Naval gun fire. I hear that 2 regiments are going into the attack & one is staying in reserve. They say we (the 7th) are staying in reserve. None of this is verified. It does look as though <u>someone</u> is going into the attack—I don't know if it's an all-out offensive or a limited one for better positions. However, if they're having the Marines move you know it's fairly important or they expect stiff resistance. So here we are in a muddy rice paddy, rain dripping in and the floor like a muddy pig pen.

If you can figure it all out, you're a better Marine than I am. I'm still confused.

Because we have moved out, it looks like PIO is passé. They're miles behind us and always will be while we're near the front. Unless they pull my transfer thru in a line company I shall remain.

A pat on the back for the army: they gained a thousand yards where we went 85 miles. Hooo-rah!

I don't know why I'm in such a ridiculously good mood—I feel wet & miserable. But I'm so confused I feel good—you know, like dope. One, two, three, four—I love the Marine Corps! Yeah, I do like …

Honey, keep telling me you love me like you have been in your last three letters. It's wonderful. You always do tell me it, but recently you've said it so sweetly & nice—like you were kissing me on the side of the lips the way you use[d] to. Telling me how much you love & miss me gives me that funny feeling & makes me feel like crying—it makes me feel warm & good. It does wonders to my spirits and makes combat seem just like another job that has to be done until I can be home with you. And knowing that Cinthy smiled & tried to talk when she saw my picture gives me the exhilaration only a new daddy knows. By the way—sure she wasn't laughing?

As for Cinthy having my ears & your saying "poor thing"—well! After all, young lady, that sort of thing isn't conducive to the proper morale of our fighting troops (me) and I just may drop the hint of your communistic activities around! After all, a "friend" of mine in the reserves said my mother mentioned you had the "communist manifest[o]" in the house! Now—aren't my ears pretty?

Come to think of it, if a censor ever got ahold of this letter there'd be hell to pay, huh? We'd both be screwed! No!—I'd be screwed! Not you (get me?—well love me then!)

In lieu of the possibility of censorship, I shall insure personal an[d] familial tranquility by the pledge: "I pledge allegiance to the flag …" Oh, hell, that's too long. This will have to do:

[Drawing of an American flag on an eagle-topped flag pole with the following captions written on three sides]:

God Bless America"

Long Live Capitalism! (Gung Ho!)

E Pluribus Unum

Think that'll convince him?

Well, darling, I've rambled all over, drawn pictures, teased you, cried on your shoulder, been jealous, explained to you, teased you (again) and complimented you. There's nothing left I can do in this letter, so I'll trip off the stage in a grand finale whispering softly and sincerely to my one-person audience (you): "I love you." And, Joanne, I mean it with all the power man has to love his wife. No one (including the Chinese) will ever take it away.

Take care of yourself, honey, and watch our little darling Cinthy real close.

Two. Through Mud, Mortars and Hell

You're doing a wonderful job raising her. You're a <u>wonderful</u> mother. I love both of you to pieces!

> All My heart & love
> forever & always—
>   Al (& Boondocker still plugging
>   along—the gamest toy turtle
>   in the world! A real buddy!)
>   X's—literally by the billions!

MZ 641

Sept. 19

Dearest Joanne—

It's dark at 7:30 p.m. and the stars are alive in a frosty sky. It's Christmas weather—where you can see your breath and the glare of lights through a cold haze. Men have lit small fires throughout the area and they glimmer from a distance. Candle light [sic] shines from the crevices of evenly-spaced tents. Some men sing—and the different songs they sing mix in a single thought: that they are at peace and tomorrow is only vaguely remembered.

Night in reserve retains a quality which is far different from any I have ever known. Because there is usually so much fear for us at nite, here there is so much peace. And because there are no disturbing thoughts, there are lonely (but pleasant) ones. And warped to the extreme of the moment, we can laugh. Because now there is reason to laugh.

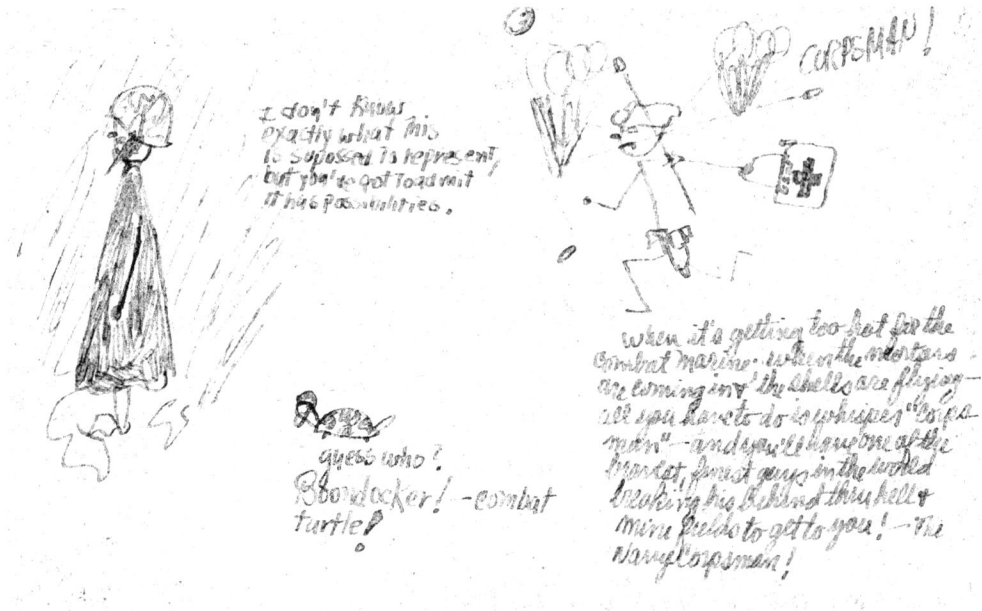

Al Martinez's drawings at the close of his letter of August 31, 1951. The letter is not included in this book (The Huntington Library, MZ 644, p. 3).

Our Bn. area is situated at the top of gradually-slopping [*sic*] rice paddies which suddenly rise into a rugged ridgeline directly above and behind us. About 500 yards from us is a road which stretches from Pusan to the Yalu—the main supply route. It is lined on both sides with trees, tall and narrow, magnificently green. The road is always busy, since convoys with troops and supplies move back & forth from the fiery eastern front. Right now there are convoys moving both ways, the stream of lights flicking in and out of the trees which partially block my view. It looks like 101* between San Jose & Santa Cruz at nite ... only the houses that line that road are healthy & happy. The ones that line this one are usually sad little grass and brick huts, usually deserted, often burned to the ground. But the impersonal stream of trucks moving by doesn't even look at the unhappy little houses which dream of a peaceful yesterday.

Far on the other side of the road are the high mean peaks which once represented valuable high ground—but which now are sullen in their unimportance. They rise & rise into steep climbs then drop suddenly in no particular pattern onto rocky crags. From here the mnts. look green. But I'll venture that beneath the tops of the trees which meet the eye is ugly charred earth, cratered by explosives and nurtured by violence. This is the "green" earth, a tourist's view.

Sometimes I feel sorry for Korea. The insignificant penninsula [*sic*] houses a war which in proportion is out of its "class." The land isn't prepared for war. There is no frame of mind, no national patriotism which fired the liberals. The people live in small communities of two or three houses miles from any semblance of cities, in valleys bordered by nature at its most protective. They are undisciplined folk, quiet with the external peace which has come with an apathy handed down from generations rich with a humble acceptance of life & servitude. The Koreans are unparticular people, and in their lack of fickleness we could well learn a lesson. They live by a crude method of hand, yet the children are happy and the adults expect no more out of life. Poverty? Not as they know it. The loneliness of their houses is crowded with an unnassuming [*sic*] kind of love. And a tenderness which may yet outlast the pugnacious, young United States ...

But Korea has been hit by war, and the crude homes which shuddered in the rain have died by the shell. The valleys bear only the wheat of battle—tasteless & bitter. The mountains protect the hunter & the hunted, and the small rivulets wash out the blood of the quick & the dead. The old men & women who wander endlessly along the roads are questioned, forever suspected & hungry. The children, alone in a world of adults, have prostituted themselves to the circumstances of war, and thus accepted the decline which will inevitably follow. This now is a country whose people are quietly bitter, not caring who wins the conflict, unfooled by our propaganda. They smile when they are told to, and die because we force them to. Their lives & homes are shattered—only a peace of mind remains intact. Korea is a land which does not care. And who can blame her?

Poor little Korea.

---

*Highway 101 is one of two major arteries that span much of the full length of California. The stretch between San Jose, in the southern part of the Bay area, and Santa Cruz, further to the south, would have heavy commuting traffic in the evening.

Just received a letter from you (mail call at 9 p.m.!) and I feel better. When they first came with mail they said I had none. I went into a fit of dissapointment [*sic*]. About 15 minutes later they brought me a letter and a package from you. Now I feel much better.

So Cinthy had her first shot, huh? I had my first shot about the same age. Four feathers* I believe. Seriously, you're right about the Marines knowing all about shots. I've had every shot from anti-pregnancy to double diptheria [*sic*] and compound ghongorea [i.e., gonorrhea]. I doubt like hell whether I'll ever cont[r]act any of the above, but it all follows the staid old Corps policy that if a Marine dies he is going to die at fixed bayonets & not of some chicken-s__t disease.

I'm glad you saw something at the doctor's wonderful enough to counteract the sight of two underfed, apparently uncared for kids. Your description of the blind colored woman & her child made me feel real good. Love knows no race. Nor physical handicap. It's sights like that which keeps [*sic*] this old world on its feet.

Darling (as you always say) it's late & I'm tired. The gentle hand of the sgt. will roll me out at 0615 & I want to be at my best. So for now, sweetheart, I love you & goodnight—my dearest wife & daughter.

Sept. 20

Hi sweetheart!—

After a hard morning of lectures & 2 hrs. of the afternoon spent in digging a rain ditch, I can relax at 3 p.m. in the afternoon. Yeah, our training schedule has started again. This morning it was map-reading & compass. We also received the situation as of the last operation. On the 12th of Sept. when Fox jumped off we were scheduled to tie in with Easy Co. But as I said before, we were hit & forced to retain the hill we were on. Thus, Fox Co. is officially accredited with making the first U.N. nite assault of the Korean campaign. The next day we were relieved on the lines after securing the commanding terrain and were presently defending it. The 1st Reg. relieved us in the attack. The 5th Regiment joined it. The 1st & 5th continued the assault for 2 days & consolidated the line of ridges. They are presently set up in the defense. And that's the news of the 1st Marine division.

The sun this morning was reluctant in coming out, but not so the frost & the cold fog.... However, at 10 a.m. the warm sun appeared[,] and all was bright. Right now, it's hot & lazy. So off with the winter gear until this evening.

Darling, I'll close now, mail this & write more this evening by candle-light

---

*The Four Feathers is a 1902 novel by A.E.W. Mason about a British officer who is disgraced by resigning his commission during action in Egypt. His three fellow officers and his fiancée each hand him a white feather, symbolizing his presumed cowardice. He disappears into Egypt and Sudan, where he undertakes acts of great courage, to redeem himself. Among several film adaptations, the 1939 movie directed by Zoltan Korda is perhaps the most highly regarded. By referring to this story, Al is commenting humorously on the courage babies need to withstand shots at an early age, and perhaps he includes Marines, who are subjected to a significant number of shots.

[*sic*]. Take good care of yourself & our princess & think of me—I <u>always</u> think of you. I love you.

>All My heart &
>love always &
>forever –
>from the guy who
>loves you more than
>anything in the world –
> Al (& Boondocker)
>X's for my family
> (you & Cinthy)

[enclosures: three clippings:]

"Marines Hit Waves Of Screaming Reds In Punch Bowl Tilt"

"Fighting Explodes On Half Of Front" [At first paragraph, about Marines, Al has written] "Us!"

"Korea: 'We're Coming Out as Marines!'"

MZ 654

          Sept. 22

> Starlight, starbright [*sic*]
> Mem'ry on an icy night;
> Kinda lonely, kinda blue
> Dreaming of my prescious [*sic*] you
> Far away across the sea
> Darling, do you dream of me?
> Starlight, starbright [*sic*]
> <u>How</u> I love my wife tonite!

Dearest Joanne—

 Another clear, crisp night in Korea—a lonely night—and nature responds and tries to ease our pain with all the natural beauty at her command. She has done her job well. It's a beautiful star-filled nite. Even in Korea one expects to see a young couple holding hands on a beach or a lonely road. This is a night created for love & perfume, lipstick and whispered promises. You can't blame nature for war. She has given us this nite. And we violate its solace with destruction.

 I wish there were something I could say to describe all the enviable calm of this nite. There's something about a nippy evening which recalls everything beautiful and fresh in my mind. Perhaps that's what makes me lonely. I remember too clearly. But that which I remember are things I don't want to forget. So I'll bear the consequences until we can be together again.

 Received another letter from you this evening with an enlarged picture of Cinthy. She's an awful <u>pretty</u> little girl—with all the beauty of her mother and the devil of her father. She looks so precious and cuddly that I believe I could just hold her in my arms until she disappeared in my heart. I know I can be a good father to such a nice little girl. But I'll leave the correcting to you while she's little. I just won't have the heart to bawl her out. She'll look at me with those big eyes, say "I'm sorry, daddy," and I'll be like putty in her hands.

I'm so impressed with her photographic beauty, that I thought I'd write her a note. Read it to her and though she doesn't understand all of it, she's a Martinez—and will find it in her heart to give her daddy credit for trying.

My dear Cinthia—

This is a letter from the daddy you've never seen, but will before too many months have gone by. I'm writing it now because I'm sort of a writer and not much of a speaker.

The world you've been in for some 4 months now is kinda confused. It's really a good world, but sometimes the people in it don't understand each other as well as they should. The only life you know right now is the one shaped by your mother—a beautiful, warm kind of life—surrounded by a love you'll never understand until many years from now, because it's so great and enduring.

A lot of people will say that it isn't fair to bring you into a world such as this. But your mother and I are great gamblers. We believe that it's little girls like you who will one day make life better. And because so many generations have failed, we're betting our futures on you.

As you grow older and are more able to understand things, you'll encounter perversions from the norm which will confuse, hurt, anger and often embitter you. You're [sic] mother and I have met these [illegible word]. The only intelligent thing to do is to understand them and conquer all the anger & bitterness with love & understanding. You'll find in later years it will pay off. You'll have something which so many of us lack today: peace of mind.

You're [sic] first experience with religion will leave you wonderfully awed and humble. As a child you'll try to do things He'll approve of. We won't try to frighten you with nonsense about the devil. And don't worry if you make a mistake now & then. God understands little girls and knows that sometimes they're awfully mischievious [sic] (your daddy can't spell either.). As you enter high school, you'll begin to feel pretty big & important, and you'll brush God aside as part of childhood—then maybe you won't, I hope not. But if you do, that's all part of growing up. When you grow older, human experience will teach you a religion of life—and perhaps you'll learn to worship God as I have—in the vastness of nature's own beautiful cathedral & by putting your faith in man and all his dreams of peace & happiness—and by trying to bring comfort in a world where there is always someone who needs it. When you learn life & try to better it, you'll learn all the wonders of God.

Then Cinthy, sometime during your high school career you'll enter a whole new experience. Something wonderful & daring known as love. Once, maybe twice or several times (you are pretty) you'll feel that only <u>he</u> is the person that matters. His words and looks create a new kind of Heaven, a life of roses & bright shiny stars. You'll know all the wonderful thrill of a first kiss—and of heartache and tears. It will be easy for your mother & I to comfort you –because we've been through the same thing. And despite all your doubts, you'll survive many an episode to become a beautiful young lady. Love, princess, is a wonderful thing. It's soft music and beautiful memories. But it has pitfalls. It has experiences which are left for married couples. But I'm no preacher, and because of intelligent bringing up, those are bridges you'll pass gracefully when [you] reach them.

Then one day, when you least suspect it, you'll meet a man—a special man. Maybe in college (I hope you'll go to college), maybe at a dance or party, maybe on a bus. He'll be a nice person, the kind you can talk to, understand and respect. The type of person you can trust under any circumstances. You'll love him and share his joy & sorrow, his ambitions and dreams—as he shares yours. You'll dream of a life together. And you'll make plans for it. Then, Cinthia, God & man will unite you in marriage.

Marriage sometimes is an ordeal for young people. But if you can laugh at life and believe in it, love and [word omitted] each other, there is nothing to fear. Because marriage is a wonderful, lasting experience with something new for each bride & groom. But that's where I stop advising, young lady. You'll be a wife then.

When you have your first child, you'll perhaps understand then some of the mistakes we've made—you're [sic] mother & I—in raising you. And I hope you'll profit by them.

I hope, Cinthy, that you'll be the type of girl who is laughable, loveable, sometimes naughty & mischieveous [sic], stubborn (sometimes), haughty, proud, humble, happy & healthy. I hope you'll know how to accept life as it is and love it nevertheless. I hope that once in a while you'll say "the devil with convention" and be a little different. I hope that you'll be a dreamer, a realist and an incurrable [sic] optimist. I want you to be the finest little girl in the world. But it's your life.

I don't think you'll have to worry about wars when you're old enough to worry. There's still a few people left such as I who are bound & determined to inject a little milk of human kindness in the world. I suspect we can do it. We've had a lot of experience at trying.

Anyhow, welcome to life, Cinthia Louise –my pretty daughter. It's a grand feeling watching the sun rise & set, watching the season's [sic] change, feeling the movement of nature under your feet. This is a heck of a thing to receive when you're only 4 months old, but your daddy's a writer and unstop[p]able . All this is just to tell you I love you, princess—as no father could ever love his daughter. All I do from now on I'll be doing for you—so you can avoid some of the ruts in the road I fell face flat into.

In later years from now, if you can read this, understand it and <u>still</u> say "the rest of the world be damned"—then I'll be happy. Because I'll know I have a daughter just like my wife and a man couldn't ask for anything more!

All My love—
your father.

Sept. 23

Dearest darling—

It is evening & I am drunk—or maybe high, I'm not sure which. Why? Simply because I want to be high and because I'm in Korea nobody gives a damn. I saw the divisional PIO chief today & I don't think I got the job. He didn't say no, but I just think that I wasn't gung ho enough for him. But that's the way the ball bounces, and why be bitter? So I'll get higher! Perhaps I should have screamed "God Bless the Corps & Country!" But nuts. I've got more sense than that, and the devil with the Corps! I can live longer than anybody on the lines or in the rear! So, pass me another beer, Jenks, & let's get drunk. Eat, drink & be merry for tomorrow—for tomorrow, darling, we'll be together and I can forget about all this terrible mess. Forgive me for being high, sweetheart. But tonite I just want to forget war!

I love you & Cinthy with all my heart and soul. Love me always—even if I am a damned derelict.

All My love forever—
Al (& Boondocker)
X's by the millions

MZ 657

Oct. 5

Dearest Joanne—

Just received 3 letters from you and now I feel much better as I haven't heard from you for a couple days (that sentence is all fouled up, but you understand). I'm <u>awfully</u> glad you're dating your letters now. That's something I've always wanted to ask you to do. Now I'm happy!

Doggone, I don't blame Cindy for crying when you give her to this Nunno character to hold. She doesn't want any male but her daddy to hold her and she's mad cuz her daddy's in Korea & Nunno & Al Jaeger are home trying to impress somebody by holding <u>my</u> baby! (Got me so upset I spilled ink on my inspection dungarees). No kidding, these men have no right to hold my princess. When I come home <u>no</u> man will hold her but me. Jaeger & Nunno ought to be over here replacing me. Heck, I wouldn't wish this on anyone. I'm just a jealous daddy.

I'm sorry you had to receive that letter I wrote to Frank, Joanne.* I had a sneaking suspicion that I had done that, but wasn't sure. I don't even remember what I wrote him, but I know I usually let myself go a little more. It's unnecessary for me to write a lot of the violent details of each operation to you, Joanne. Sometimes I do for an unexplainable reason of my own, but I never feel quite right about it. I realize that you have a pretty good idea of what's going on, but nonetheless I don't like to worry you by elaborating. Sorry the whole thing happened, hon. Just one of those confusing things from a confused mind.

Today the 13th Marine replacement draft joined us, fresh & vibrant, nervous and ill at ease—a strange bunch of semi-civilized men who, even though bearded and dirty, looked strangely apart from us. The Bn. received 200 men, Fox 81—and we're <u>still</u> understrengthed [*sic*]. Our plt. lacks about 5 men, our squad one. Only

---

*The letter written to Frank Galo and mailed to Joanne in error has not survived.

1500 men came over in this draft—the smallest yet! The Gooks keep knocking off our companies like they have been, the Corps might as well send over a whole new division & send the remainder of the 1st home. But I guess they won't be satisfied until they write <u>another</u> post mortem on the glorious finish of the 1st Mar Divy [*sic*].

After reading that letter I wrote to Frank, you might as well know something else: about 25 men in our company cracked up on the last week of our last operation; complete psycho-neurotics, blubbering, crying, screaming or just staring into space. I don't think the people at home fully realize the tremendous strain placed upon the men fighting in this type of terrain against such a fanatic & versatile enemy. Even those who came through the rugged Pacific Campaign in the last conflagration proclaim it mild by comparison. The mountains here are not made for foot travel, much less for a man with a pack on his back who's been moving all day, who's emotionally upset & who's being shot at all at the same time. At nite there is equally no rest. There's a 50% watch in each 2[-]man foxhole & it invariably turns into a 100% watch at the first sign of trouble or low visibility. And when we're hit, it's usually in silence (unless banzaied [*sic*]), by an enemy who is invisible, noiseless and who gives one the impression that he's been watching just <u>you</u> and he's waiting…. After a sleepless nite you awaken & move again. Under such conditions it's no wonder there are so many pitiful cases of "combat fatigue"!

When I come home I will still be in a combat frame of mind for one more operation. I am personally going to kick the shit out of one postal clerk who has been giving you a bad time at 16th & Mission. I'm not kidding. Somebody's going to get knocked square on their ass and I'm not kidding. It may be me, but he's going to know he's been in a tussle when I'm through. That really P.O.'s me. I'd like to have his nasty behind in my fire team. He'd be on his knees to you before I was finished. Just shooting off my mouth again? Wait & see! (P.S.—I'm sorry about the harsh language, hon. Just makes me so damn mad!)

Did you realize that on your letter dated Sept. 30 you wrote the return address as "Mrs. Joanne Martinez["] instead of ["]Mrs. Al Martinez"? Just observation. First time you've done that.

Give all my love to your dad. If he does write I'll certainly answer him, but I won't count on a letter right away. I too hope I'm home by the time he visits the coast. And it's entirely possible.

I can't understand what's happening to my mail. I've written to you every day since I've been in reserve (almost every day). What a fouled-up system. Hope you eventually get them all. I love you too, my little sweetheart.

Tell Donna I said "hello" too.

Who's Donna?

I sure enjoy reading your descriptions of Cinthy. By your writing & my imagination I can picture her clearly, sleeping so snuggly by you—a little girl in such a big bed. My darling little baby. Cinthy's like me & she wakes up in a good mood? Honey, do I detect a note of teasing in your statement?

Goodnite for now, my darling. Will write more tomorrow. I love you—Al.

—Oct. 6

Hi sweetie—

This morning we had a company commander's inspection and all went well. Except for one thing: Our haircuts. Yesterday when we were all in a frantic rush to get a last-minute trim, the one barber we have had a line-up a mile long. So we borrowed clippers and a pair of siccors [sic], picked one man at random & said cut!

And cut he did.

This morning the C.O. asked one man what the hell had happened to his hair. "My buddy asked me if I wanted a haircut so I got it, sir," he replied. "Man, you <u>really</u> got it!" As he walked down the ranks his amazement grew at the odd assortment of haircuts. By the time he got to Jenkins, that was it. For his cut hair is the most horrifying blasphemy to the American male I have ever seen, front-line troops notwithstanding. Honestly, it's … it's … <u>inhuman</u>! I'm a misfit with mine, but <u>his</u>! Poor Jenk. He'll never live it down.

Anyhow, the 2nd plt. stands out.

I have become a compass & map reading expert. Since one time last week where I explained to a class something I had learned in map reading, the lieut. has elected me to explain it all to the new men. So I lectured them this morning. Seriously, it's amazing what I've learned about grid co-ordinates, triangularization and azimuth readings. Difficult to some, I seem to have developed an interest in it and hence picked it up. I can read maps with ease, pin point [sic] emplacements, locate my unknown position by cross azimuths and generally work the map & compass to the best advantage. I'm surprised I've managed to comprehend something so precise. Wonders will, in answer to the hackneyed question, never cease.

The replacements we received seem to be the best yet. Older, quieter, more willing to learn & co-operate and take orders. They're a deviant from the salty brood we usually get. Already they've caught on to the close friendship which is always with us. None I've seen are tight, one-way or sarcastic. That's because of good indoctrination on the part of our officers & men. They've learned the inter-dependency of combat troops & I think they'll profit by it. As far as I'm concerned as a fire-team leader & NCO, I'll do everything I can to see they know all I know about front-line existence.

When most men get "no duty" slips from sickbay for various ailments, they still carry out the little formalities of military routine. But when a member of Fox Co. gets one, he completely dissassociates [sic] himself from anything Marine and considers himself <u>out</u> of the Corps for the number of days he's on no-duty. This morning one such man failed to salute a major. When asked why by the major, he, for some incomprehensible reason, replied, "I'm on no duty." A look of rage crossed the officer's face and Fox Co. is in the dog house again. As the chaplain once said, "the depradation [sic] has hit the ventilation." No wonder we're always in the attack!

We were looking at advertisements in a magazine the other day when we came across one of those "naughty-naughty-peekaboo-come-sleep-with-me-nightie" things. The lace & laceless parts of the garment weren't bad, nor were the anatomical conditions of the gal modeling them (she had a mole on her left breast). But the <u>pose</u> she was in was one of the oddest things I've ever seen. She had one hand above her head extended palm down. The other was extended over her rear like a hootchy-kootchy dancer. Her legs were apart & bent like she was attempting a half-assed pirouette [*sic*]. The look on her face was naturally seductive—that "I-wouldn't-try-it-if-I-were-you-but-I'm-not-you." look. I don't know why the pose fascinated me except that it is a fine job of contortionism! Hat's off to the "naughty-naughty-second-look-bosoms-nightie" hucksters! They've done a fine job!

I understand the newspapers have been carrying a lot about the 2nd Army division's "Heartbreak Ridge."* They should. The Army pumped 27,000 rounds of artillery into it in two days, and spent the next week making sure there was no one on it before they climbed it. Then when they did get on top, they lost it 3 times to Gook patrols. You might be interested to know that the 7th Marine regiment was allotted 75 rounds of artillery support in the attack of a hill commanding a 50-mile view. Yeah, we took it in about half a day. At the cost of about half of the regiment's lives. Why couldn't we get the support. "Each round costs $90.00!" was our answer. Human lives are cheap. So much for "heartbreak [*sic*] Ridge."

I suppose you know that Ridgway refused to continue the talks at Kaeson [*sic*]—and here's why. Kaeson [*sic*] lies in the path of the army's movement & would block advancement in that sector. The commies know that & could use the Kaeson [*sic*] ruse to stall off our offensive. As a parallel, now that the talks are off, we're moving toward Kaeson [*sic*]. The truce fiasco would make that impossible. As the nonchalant rear-echelon major said when he was first shot at, "<u>this</u> is war!" Uh-hu[h]!

The latest is that we move out Wednesday. Supposedly the 1st & 5th regiments were relieved on line by the 1st army cavalry division. The scuttlebut [*sic*] that counteracts this "moving out Wed." is that we're in "floating reserve" to be used to plug up a gap anywhere along the front. But that's what it all is—scuttlebut [*sic*]. No official word.

Well, hon, that's about all for yesterday & today. Am not sick unless you consider sick of Korea as an ailment. Hope you begin getting my mail. Take care of yourself, chin up, pip pip & all that rot (English schizophrania [*sic*] too).

All my Heart & love from husband & "daddy" who loves you both dearly.

My love Forever—
Al (& Boondocker)

MZ 667

Oct. 13

Dearest Joanne—

Build 'em up, tear 'em down! That's the corps. We had perfectly fine bunkers on the reverse slope with fighting holes on the forward. It was fine for the 5th

---

*The Battle of Heartbreak Ridge was part of the Battle of the Punchbowl, q.v.

Marines. But did it suit the 7th? Why, I should say not! We tore them down today & rebuilt our bunkers on the forward slope! Oh, they really make a beautiful target—for the Gooks. A flat trajectory piece could lift the logs like toothpicks! Oh, well—the Col.'s after a silver star again.

You asked me a question in a letter I received from you (a <u>very</u> sweet letter) which I feel I can answer partly: "Why can't we push these people back? ... Are we so underequipped, poorly staffed or are the odds so great?" It's all of those, darling. And a lot more. Here's the main premises [*sic*]: the U.S. is losing the war in Korea. Our casualties are <u>proportionately</u> higher; theirs are greatly exag[g]erated. We do not have the equipment for this terrain; we are not trained well enough. Our tactics are World War II variety, flat land, good observation, tank support, accurate artillery fire.... Our tank support is nill [*sic*]. Observation is practically non-existent. Artillery? It's great if you catch 'em in the open; it's fine if you know where they're at. But here's an example of the ineffectiveness of artillery: we were on a low knoll in a valley dug in under the full observation of the enemy. In our stupid, American way we became careless (which the enemy very seldom does) & gave away our exact position (which he <u>never</u> does). The Gooks pounded us with artillery for hours—about 200 rounds. Sure, it pinned us down as long as they threw it. It came right on top of us. But as soon as it stopped we got out of our holes. Casualties? One. One man nicked with shrapnel in the arm. We pound their positions with <u>thousands</u> of rounds. And lots of times when we go on the hill we just pounded we're apt to find that no one has ever been there. You know why newspapers scream "Chinese loose [*sic*] 7000 men"? Because an artillery observer says, "'there's a ridge that can hold 10,000 men. Hit it." They pound it for days. Then he observes without basis, "Must have killed at least 7000 of them!" <u>That's</u> how they get their casualty reports. Air strikes? A direct hit will tear up any bunker. Napalm covers quite an area. But miss the bunker, throw the napalm into the wrong hill, and you might as well save the ammo. Because it doesn't do a <u>damn</u> bit of good.

Both are demoralizing as hell. And they keep 'em pinned down for awhile [*sic*] while we move up and if they catch 'em in the open, it's a slaughter. Even if they're in bunkers a lucky strike by air or artillery will tear them up. I wouldn't be without air or artillery support. It saves our lives. But as for wiping them out, the powers of those 2 are greatly exag[g]erated. The Gooks move at nite. And you can't observe at nite.

And we are underequipped. Hand grenades—the combat man's left arm—are short. Ammo is often at a premium. Machine guns are scarce. Mortars (our <u>close</u> support weapon) & ammo is [*sic*] scarce. Chow is sadly lacking. Front-line medical equipment is poor. We are actually under-equipped. It's almost impossible to get nite illumination from artillery sometimes. We are better equipped than the enemy man to man. But this is <u>his</u> country—he is use[d] to fighting without equipment in this terrain; we are not.

Yes, we are poorly staffed. From Ridgeway [*sic*] on down. The combat individualist seems to be passé. All the brass work by rote command & imagination is lacking when it comes to unprecedented situations. The officers I have worked with in Korea are exceptions to the rule. Their brilliancy [sic] has saved us many a time. I think the 7th regiment is lucky in this way. But the caliber of army brass (and Marine too in many cases) is rock bottom. The strategy now, I understand, is to sustain a limited offensive during the peace talks. Supposedly, this is to retain the initiative. If the talks fail, we will then go all the way to the Yalu. Then what? Then we wait. We wait while Red China builds up to counter-attack as it inevitably will. We wait while the jet MIG's [sic] race from their air sanctuary in Manchuria to pound us then return, unharmed, combat justice looking the other way. We wait, while our casualties mount & the men grow lax. We wait until we are hit by force, wiped out, sucked back or both. Then when we finish licking our wounds at another Pusan perimeter, we start all over. Pretty huh? And another 13000 Marines die.

"Are the odds so great?" The odds, <u>generally</u> speaking, are 10 to 1—against us. But I've been in instances where they were 30 to 1! The odds are tremendous. We are fighting not only a numerically superior enemy, but one which is smart, rugged & versatile. He is easily adaptable. He is able to move at nite,—our weakest time. He is a master at compounding fear & harrassing [sic].

And here is one thing Americans overlook. He is fighting for <u>his</u> country.

The North Korean is a viscious [sic] fighter. But now we are in North Korea—65 miles. He is fighting with the determination of a man who sees us trespassing into his land. He's fighting for his <u>home</u>! It's the same as the Russians fighting for Stalingrad; the English & their courage during the bombing raids; the Indians in America. The North Koreans are living humans, who love, have families & want to live. What reasonless propaganda pushed them into So. Korea, I will never know. But that's gone. Their past perspective is dim. All they can see now is the present, fortified again by propoganda [sic] & the fire of patriotism: <u>we</u> are the aggressors, moral purpose & ideals notwithstanding! Who's right, who's wrong? So. Korea is liberated so why don't we quit? Let the historians argue that thought-provoking question out!

So, in the long run the U.S. is loosing [sic] a battle. Why? Because it is a battle which can never be won the way it goes. We have com[m]itted our troops in Korea & can't find an honourable [sic] [way] out. We are expending our magnificent strength on a peninsula!

I hope I've answered some of your questions, hon. If you have any more, ask 'em. If I can't answer them, I'll find someone who can. You're my wife (as you probably know) and have more than a perfect right to know the truth above [sic] this situation from a battlefield viewpoint.

I'm glad my letter of jealousy explained itself, darling. Loneliness & homesickness have a lot to do with jealousy—too much time to think, imagine & feel sorry for oneself. You understand, hon. I have too much faith in you to be really jealous with reason. I love you, darling & I know you love me. That's what counts.

I cut this little paragraph out of a clipping you sent. Who is Shrdluun?

>   All My heart
>   & love forever
>   & ever—
>   Al (& Boondocker)
>
> X's for both
> I love you &
> Cin very
> very much.

[Two clippings enclosed:

[First:] Gen. Bradley, chairman of the U.S. Joint Chiefs of Staff, made the comment at a Korean airport from which he flew back to Tokyo after a two-day tour of the front. man, who is SHRDLUUN

[Second:] Careful Man
A Marine replacement draft had just arrived in Korea, and the men were billeted in adjoining tents for their first night near the front lines.

"Say there, corporal," a voice said, "come here just a minute, will you, corporal?"

Immediately the reply came back, "Dammit man, don't call me corporal over here. You know the Chinese are looking for us NCOs."

MZ 671

Three

Cpl. Al Martinez, Combat Correspondent.... How About That!*

> Honestly, darling, if you could only feel the surge of being useful again after 7 months of murdering inactivity. For me, nothing is worse than feeling useless. The hum & speed of journalism has caught me again & I love the jumping tap of the typewriter as I always have; I love that last story being typed out at nite; I love to watch the type & paper form into a living message; I love the feeling of accomplishment that comes with another story, another issue. It's me again, learning, experimenting, profititng [sic] by slow degrees— It's me again, Joanne—and after months of non-entity I can believe it again. (letter of October 20, 1951)

When Al was suddenly transferred to the Regimental Public Information Office, it was the answer to his dream. He had already passed on a PIO post, because it would have made him merely a clerk typing documents for others when he wanted to be a reporter and writer. He had also declined a position that would have involved writing just for the regimental newsletter, since he wanted to write the larger stories of the war. But he had been able to get samples of his writing under the eyes of the PIO officers. With the transfer, he could undertake the writing he so loved. The frustration, boredom, and stress disappeared as he swapped the muddy foxhole of the forward lines of combat for his favorite and more familiar position at the keyboard of a typewriter. He was in a place of much greater personal safety than he had been while on the front lines, but he was still not completely out of danger. The PIO operation was close to the battle front, bringing mortar shells and artillery barrages on him and his colleagues, and he often visited the front lines to interview the fighting men and to gather material for stories he would write. He entered a two-fold position: writing, editing, and printing the regimental newsletter, the *Ridgerunner*, and serving as a combat correspondent sending news items to newspapers and press syndicates in the United States.

In these roles he drove his newly-acquired jeep to the battle front to gather information and to interview Marines on the front line. Al's superiors liked the

---

*"Cpl. Al Martinez...": Letter of October 20, 1951.

THREE. *Cpl. Al Martinez, Combat Correspondent.... How About That!* 145

Al Martinez, 1951 (The Huntington Library, UDID 324238).

fact that he had served in battle, as this gave him special insight. Most other PIO men had been assigned this duty right after finishing boot camp, while the correspondents who arrived from the States had not been to the front lines for more than brief visits and knew nothing about fighting. In contrast, Al could write from his own experiences and was able to understand exactly what Marines in combat were going through.

Al's love of writing and of journalism are evident in the obvious lift of his spirits after he arrives at PIO. As he plied his writing talents, and as he grew increasingly accomplished in planning each issue of the newsletters and in simply operating the old and temperamental mimeograph machine, his pride and confidence grew.

He proved himself from the beginning and the issues of the *Ridgerunner* that he produced met with increasing approval from his superiors. In addition, his pieces of journalism appeared stateside with increasing frequency. (These newspaper articles almost never carried his byline but appeared anonymously.) Al's writing also appeared frequently in publications such as *Leatherneck*. The *Ridgerunner* was the only newsletter produced at the regimental level (all others issued from Marine divisions), and other regiments sought to emulate his success. As his work began to be known more widely, Al shared this news with Joanne, writing in a letter of February 25, 1952, "And they are still working on the story about the only front-line paper in the first Marine Division, ours natch. They're going to send the story and pictures into a new Pacific Edition of Leatherneck, the Marine Corps magazine and also to Stars and Stripes. Once we get that kind of publicity, and the old man sees it, the Ridgerunner will be a part of the 7th Marines for life. Incidentally, the 5th Marines are thinking of starting a similiar [sic] paper." During his months writing for the PIO, Al's accomplishments netted him a promotion to sergeant.

Al's letters naturally focused largely on his writing for the PIO, but he returned to subjects of combat in several ways. As mentioned, he was not entirely out of danger and incoming shells shattered the peace and sometimes brought injury and death. In addition, Al finally learned the names of the battles that occurred when he was at the front, and he was able to take pride in specific accomplishments of his unit. He also used some of the extra time at hand to recall and record his experiences in his letters and his diary excerpts. The diary excerpts he copied into several of his letters are vivid and constitute an important record of his and his comrades' actions in battle. Many of these written recollections are long and read like the drafts of essays, presumably with future publication in mind.

After he joined PIO, Al's letters tended to become longer, because he was happier, had more time to write, and had a typewriter at hand, increasing the speed of his epistolary output. In addition, especially at first, he had more to write about, telling of his happiness and new responsibilities, and relating stories of his new buddies, colleagues and officers. However, even as Al was happier and feeling much safer, the strain of their long separation began to tell on both Al and Joanne. It was more difficult to keep their spirits up and Al not only missed Joanne dearly but was less able to tolerate both Korea and the military. As the weeks wore on, Al observed the schedule of men being shipped home ever more closely and with increasing impatience, watching for his rotation and anticipating the happy day of his departure.

In a high-stakes poker game, unusual for Al and his buddies, he won sufficient money to buy a camera. From then on, he often added "and camera" to his signing off, so it would read "Al and Boondocker and Camera."

◆ ◆ ◆

Oct. 15

Dearest Joanne—

I wrote you one letter today, but the events of 3 hours earlier deserve telling immediately. I'm writing this from a pyramidal tent, under an electric light. A radio is playing music. I've just eaten evening chow of steak, mashed potatoes, coffee, vegetable, etc. How? Why?

Because as of 3 p.m. today my transfer to Regimental P.I. O. was affected [sic]. I am no longer in Fox Co. I'm in the rear at last.

Here's how it happened.

I was sitting by my foxhole when the plt. sgt. set down the phone & hollered over at me: "Martinez, get the hell out of here!" I looked up, amazed at his sudden confusing outburst. "Roll your gear, man, damnit, you're transferred!" I felt anger well up in me with indignation at a mean trick. "Another trick like that & they'll take you off the hill feet first," I threatened. "I don't like your sense of humor!" About 15 minutes later I was convinced. 2 minutes later my gear was rolled & I was on my way to the company C.P. to check out. I shook hands all around and, for the last time as a foot slogger, I came off the hill. My tenure at the front [is] over. From there I rode to Bn. C.P.[,] then rode a jeep to regiment, 6 miles behind the lines. I checked in with the regimental Sgt. Major & came to my tent to thank the guys who've been breaking their necks to get me the job because they thought I "had it" and because they liked me. So here I am at the 7th Marine Command Post on the staff of the Public Information Office. I'm out of the hills.

When I told the men of Fox Co. goodbye & good luck—Jenkins, Nunn, the lieut.—and came off the line I felt happy & sad in one emotional tension. I'm not fool enough to be sad to leave the assault front, even though at one time I felt differently. But it wasn't the way I wanted combat to end for me. When I came off the lines I wanted all my buddies, all the fighting men in Korea to come with me. Jenkins, Nunn & all the old men left in the squad & myself were tied together by life & death. Jenk & I especially. We felt as long as one of us was alive & unwounded, we'd both be. And when one got it, we both would. We kept each other alive & safe, sharing the same happinesses [sic] and fears, living for the day when we'd have to fight no longer. Now, the bond is broken, and my wish has come true, my prayers are answered. But I don't feel right about it. There's a lot of good men left up there on the hill, and I don't want to see any of them hurt. We formed comradeships that was [sic] more than the shallow stateside variety; these were deep, sincere, where one hinged his life on their value & was willing to give it to maintain that value.

I don't suppose one who hasn't seen war could realize the sentimentality attached to two men who share their last drop of water, their last can of chow. I don't suppose one could get nostalgic over a kid from Kentucky who plays cards & laughs when the mortars are coming in & all hell is breaking loose. But I can, and whatever I do in PIO, I'll do for them. Because they're the ones that count. They're the ones who climb the hills, watch the nite & hold the line. They're the ones who assault the enemy, cry with fear & exhaustion at a final effort then stand on their objective, proud in the wind and the face of combat that they had taken their objective—and it was theirs, all theirs!

I'm in the rear now, darling, and probably will be until I return home. But part of me is still up on 749, praying for the lives & the safety of the finest men in the world. It's not important what I do. It's Fox Co. now that counts, up there alone.

I prayed hard and God heard me. I'll continue praying all the time that this war will end & all my buddies will come down off the hill. Until that time comes when I can say to Jenk, "Well, you made it, kid," and when we'll leave for the USA together, I won't feel right about my transfer. I'll feel that I don't deserve this as much as a lot of guys.

Tonite Joanne say a prayer for them, not me. Thank God for being as good to you & I [sic] as he has been. Then pray hard that a nice little guy from Kentucky & a lot of others will be talking about the "old days" in a little 'Frisco bar when the first division pulls into California.

  All My love
  forever & ever
  Al (& Boondocker)

P.S. Tell Cinthy that Daddy knows he'll keep his promise now—he'll be back.

X's

P.S. #2—forget about that I don't love you letter. I didn't like the idea in the first place & now it's unnecessary. [One of Al's buddies had suggested that Joanne should write Al to say she didn't love him and wanted a divorce, as a way for Al to be sent back home. Al had relayed the idea to Joanne, but it was clear that he didn't like it and would not pursue it.]

I love you
Al

MZ 673

Oct. 16

Dearest Joanne—

At 6:35 p.m. I have completed my first day with regimental PIO. It's been an unusual day, quite different from the ones I knew only a short while ago. I met the major in charge of PIO & several others. I worked on my first publication of the Ridgerunner, the regimental mimeographed paper, I took news off the dictate radio & re-wrote it, traced cartoons on stencil paper, wrote heads & pounded out 4 feature stories. One of my stories had to do with the "incoming mail" incident I wrote you about—you know, someone throwing letters at me & scaring me out of 10 yrs. growth. They liked that one particularly. The other three will be published on successive days I imagine. The Col. & Sgt. Major go for the idea of feature stories on the men in the companies. And they like the fact that I'm fresh from the lines. So far, so good. Once I hit a stride I'm sure I'll impress them with my writing.

The chow here is out of this world. It's the best I've eaten since I've been in the Corps. Even better than Pendleton or boot camp. Last nite when I got here I had steak, tonite roast beef, and everything is seasoned for once. And good? I can't praise the food enough. It's living!

Today 4 casualties (wounded) came into regiment from Fox. I haven't found out what's been happening up there yet, but I'll wager it's incoming artillery. Now that it's started it will come fast. Looks like I got off the lines just in time.

Even here at regiment there's been a few incoming rounds. We're set up near our artillery & I suspect the Gooks are after that. Most of the guys here have never heard many enemy shells & a resultant panic is usually the outcome when one swishes over. Since I've heard quite a few of them, I can tell by the sound whether they're near enough to take cover. So far they've gone <u>way</u> overhead so I've ignored them. This kind of makes me appear like a cool character, but also makes anyone I'm near look like an A---hole when he hits the deck with me standing there—if you know what I mean. So hereafter I'll take to doing what the romans do & scream in mortal fear when artillery hits a half mile away.

I forgot to put my new address <u>in</u> the last letter, so I'll write it now: S-1 section, H & S Company, 7th Reg., 1st Marine division, etc. Got it? Want it? Like it? Keep it.

Got a letter from you today but only because I know the regimental mail clerk. He use[d] to be my plt., sgt. & recognized me yesterday. This morning when I got mail everyone was highly amazed because it usually takes a couple weeks for mail to catch you when you're transferred. But, fortunately, I know the mail clerk so he just yanks my letters out & puts them in the H & S Co. section. Good, eh?

Glad you got to go to Mary Lee's wedding. Also glad you missed having me around. Here's a big kiss for not taking a ride with just anyone: X.

About your allotment. I put in for Cinthy's increase the <u>same day</u> I heard that she was born, which was June 3 when we were in 4-day reserve at Hongcheon. Check me. I've checked my diary & I <u>know</u> I'm right. Write all the nasty letters you want to the general. He's a damned fool anyhow. Darling, buy all the shoes & clothes you want to. I don't like the idea of your having to buy from Goodwill, but that too will be remedied. I love you, honey. Anything you do is fine by me. I trust you & you're [sic] judgement sincerely.

I guess Galo's letter did burn me a little more than it should have, but dog-gone it, it's none of his business what I do. In regards to journalism I feel it's right for me to give him advice & criticize—if he wants it. Just as I'm willing to accept some from someone whom [sic] I think knows more than I about the profession. But when it comes to a more personal matter, such as religion, I repeat, it's none of his damn business. I think that if Frank ever outgrows his prolonged adolescence he'll come around. Tell me—does he still blush & giggle when you mention sex? He's as bad as a 14 year old in her first period. Tsk, tsk.

Darling, I'm going to try to get a few more letters off before hitting the rack, so I'll stop. It still looks as though it won't be until March or April before I get home. Wait for me (a silly statement). Love me, miss me & take care of yourself & the princess. Give our prescious [sic] a kiss for me & tell her daddy is a combat correspondent. Sounds good.

> All My heart &
> love forever &
> always—
>   Al (& Boondocker)
>   X's by the millions

MZ 674

Oct. 20

Dearest Joanne—

Five days ago I was a miserable, unimportant, expendable infantry man. Today I am one of 2 PIO men of this regiment. Beginning Monday I will bear the spec number of a combat correspondent, will be editor of the Ridgerunner & the only official PIO man & military correspondent of the 7th Marine Regiment! Let me catch my breath.

It all started today when Ernie Martz (my cohort) was ordered transferred to division. He was asked all sorts of questions about me, my work was looked at &

considered, I talked to the S-3 (operations) major & the S-2 (intelligence) major & tomorrow I see the <u>Regimental Commander</u>! It all happened so fast I still can't believe it. Me—a combat correspondent! One of about 6 (military) in the whole <u>division</u>! I'll have assistants stationed at all the battalions, assistants (typist, locater, file clerk) here at regiment & connections in division & the 1st, 5th & 11th regiments. The joy of it is, I won't have to go on the lines. I go to the Bn. C.P.'s & get all the dope & sometimes I don't even go there—telephone work. I do all the writing, channel it through division & from there it goes on the wires—AP, UP, etc.* Now a military correspondent <u>seldom</u> gets by-lines. But the good part of it is the experience, the connections and (most important to me) the right to say that I was a Marine combat correspondent for the 1st division in the Korean War. Think of the weight that will pack in civilian life when I apply for a job! And on top of all that, I'll be able to keep in touch with journalism <u>per se</u> by editing the Ridgerunner. Incidentally, the Col. told Ernie that he wants one of my features in it everyday [*sic*]. I left it out today & he noticed it immediately.

Gee, hon, I don't know what to think. The change has left my head spinning & a little afraid. I'm certain that I'm up to any task confronting me, but the whole sudden[n]ess of it all.... Gee! Oh, it's all probably not as important as I consider it, but to me it's a chance to get back in the saddle—and a self-gratifying fact at progress that I haven't lost the old touch. Remember last New Year's eve in Richmond when we were crossing the street from the show to drink a Tom Collins in that Harborgate Bar—I said "I've got a feeling this is going to be a good year." Maybe the prophecy in that optimistic statement bore more truth than I suspected. Could be that here I'll have my start in the professional world. I'd rather not have it during a war, but since the circumstance exists and I can do nothing about it, I may as well make the best of it & I will.

I'm still in a fog. Cpl. Al Martinez, combat correspondent, 7th Marine Regiment, 1st Marine Division. <u>How about that</u>!

Again in today's Ridgerunner you can see the effects of Martinez makeup—the 2-column masthead & the right column going all the way up; the 2 colum[n] lead on the left. Incidentally, all the page 1 stories are my re-writes; I got the facts then pumped up the leads, etc. But I suppose you can tell that by looking at them. Also the overline (—optimism runs high—) and the step lead on the Right column are my ideas. Al Hearst,† they call me.

As I look back over this letter, I can see it's (as usual) all Martinez & all about writing. But at least you can see I'm happy—for the first time in 7 months. Honestly, darling, if you could only feel the surge of being useful again after 7 months of murdering inactivity. For me, nothing is worse than feeling useless. The hum & speed of journalism has caught me again & I love the jumping tap of the typewriter as I always have; I love that last story being typed out at nite; I love to watch the type & paper form into a living message; I love the feeling of accomplishment that comes with another story, another issue. It's me again, learning,

---

*The AP is the Associated Press, and the UP or UPI is the United Press International, the two leading news syndicates in the United States.
†This is a reference to Willian Randolph Hearst, q.v.

experimenting, profititng [sic] by slow degrees—It's me again, Joanne—and after months of non-entity I can believe it again.

Somewhere in the hearts of men & in the spirit and substance of love, understanding and coureage [sic] our God was created. He was born to create the simple & most beautiful ideals of life. He came to bring us the coureage [sic] to hang on, to move ahead, to laugh at our darkest hour & to have faith. I did that. Many a time I seriously contemplated shooting myself in the leg, dropping a heavy boulder on my foot, faking a crack up. But moral discipline and the will to hang on kept me going—I never wanted to have my wife or daughter think of me as a coward. And other times I wanted to fall back, but I moved ahead. I got pretty bitter, but I could still laugh. I wanted to crack up—but I couldn't—and look you or Cinthy in the eye. I believe my efforts were rewarded. And now I believe that when this war is over & I can evaluate my gains & losses, experience will come out the winner. And when I can hear someone in his darkest hr. say, "there is still hope ..." Then I'll feel certain that with my experience & his faith in life we two can combine & plan a future. Because only with a faith in man & his ultimate intelligence can we hope for lasting peace. And there is always hope.

    I love you
      Al   X's for you & Cinthy

MZ 678

          Oct. 21

Dearest Joanne—

It's been a hard day. It's now 8:30 p.m. & I've just completed my daily routine. The reason things were so hard today is that I put the paper out myself. Writing doesn't phase me; headline writing doesn't bother me; even makeup is fun. But cutting a stencil* & have [sic] to count each letter you type, gets me down! Also the headline drawing—we have a stylex (like a plastic stencil) off which I trace various letters for the headlines with a pin-like object. As yet, I haven't learned the touch, so I keep pressing too hard & tearing the stencil paper. Really fun. 'Bout drives me bats. Consequentely [sic], today's Ridgerunner isn't worth the paper it's printed on. I don't have today's with me, but I'll send you two tomorrow—and you can judge for yourself.

Tomorrow Ernie leaves & I'm on my own.

I meant to mention that there's a fellow here (a chief clerk) that I went to high school with—one Sgt. Ted Childress. He told me that if he'd known I was in the 7th he could have got me in the rear right away. Now he tells me. Oh, well.

---

*"Cutting a stencil" refers to the creation of the form used to print using a mimeograph machine. The operator types onto a stencil, which, as a result, has holes cut in it by the typed letters. The typing must be completely free of errors, as they could not be readily corrected. As the stencil is run through the machine on an ink-filled drum, ink goes through the cuts, thus printing the text on paper. A mimeograph machine is far smaller than a conventional printing press, so it would have been easier to transport into battle zones in an era before photocopying was developed.

"Our Miss Brooks"* is on the radio now. Almost like old times. But it could never be just like old times—not without you next to me.

We've had a 5th of Canadian Club in our tent for 4 of us for a week now, and every nite we each take a nip. Wonderful on cold days!

Speaking of cold—it snowed today for the first time this winter. Just a very slight flurry, but snow nonetheless. The days have been gray, still & icy—the nites pitch black & freezing! But I don't mind it—now. It's the guys on line I feel sorry for.

Got your package today, darling, and here's a big kiss for being so sweet: mmmmX. I love you, Muggins. Our Princess too.

I lost my lighter about 2 days [ago] & practically tore things apart looking for it—but without success. I was heartbroken. So I put an add [sic] in the Ridgerunner & today the Sgt. Major found it & handed it to me. Elation! I live again.

Hon, there's not much more to say, so I'll close. Life is semi-happy, I'm feeling wonderful & I love you with all my heart. Think of me, darling, miss me & love me. I do you all the time.

> I love You With
> All My heart &
> Soul Always &
> Always—
>   Al (& Boondocker)
>   X's for you
>   x's for Cin.

MZ 679

Oct. 22

Dearest Joanne—

I got quite an unusual story today, which will go all the way to the US via division. I should say we because Ernie & I collaborated on it. The story is this: 2 swabbees [sic] jumped ship at Inchon from the USS Es[s]ex & decided to see the war. They hitch[h]iked to the lines, dodging the MP's, and joined the 2nd Army division. They didn't get the desired action, so they traveled on the lines to the 5th Marine sector. They went on patrols & participated in all action. Everyone thought they were replacements so no questions were asked. The 7th relieved the 5th so as they were walking down the road then they passed the 7th—so they fell in with the 7th going back to the lines. They went with Easy Co. until they were discovered & sent back here. We interviewed them today, and the guys are really sincere. They wanted to see what the war was like, so they left. In their words, they "… liked the comradeships [sic] of the Marine Corps. No dog-eat-dog stuff. Everyone gave us clothes, gear, sleeping bags & chow. A wonderful bunch of guys. If I had it to do over again, I'd join the Marines. Sure, it'll mean a court martial—but

---

*Our Miss Brooks was a popular radio show on CBS from 1948 to 1957, about a humorously cynical high-school English teacher, starring Eve Arden and Gale Gordon. It was adapted for television in 1952 and ran until 1956.

we don't give a damn. If some of the guys in the rear could see what the situation was, their attitude would be a lot different." That was their attitude. Quite a story. We'll have it in the Ridgerunner tomorrow probably. I'll send it to you.

—Oct. 23

Hi darling—

Sorry I didn't mail this yesterday, but I was beat last nite. Just had to hit the sack. It's 8:30 p.m. and I'm confronted by the same situation plus an added gripe: I'm sleepy & I got 2 shots today which made me feel "icky." So, pardon my brevity if this letter isn't what it's cracked up to be.

Today's paper showed some improvement & tomorrow's (which I've been working on) should be better yet. You can see the feature story on those sailors on Page 2 of today's Ridgerunner. Wasn't the way I'd have run it (make-up, wording, etc.) but military restrictions & orders will have their way. It's good experience, however, to pin down my wild, free journalistic soul.

Got 5 letters from you today (including one "miss you["] card, a Hallow'een [sic] card, a letter from my folks, Dolores & aunt Helen. A wonderful letter day. I love you, darling, and miss you with all my heart. But the months are passing. Won't be long now.

I'm afraid my pen has seen its last days, & this one I borrowed isn't much better. But it's SNAFU as the men say—<u>S</u>ituation <u>N</u>ormal <u>A</u>ll <u>F</u>ucked <u>U</u>p. Pardon the vulgarity, but there just isn't another way to say it.

Honey, I'm not questioning your way of bringing up our Princess. You're absolutely right in having her get use[d] to men being around & holding her. Just my paternal jealousy. But I love you both.

Darling, this pen is getting me down as are these shots in my stiff right arm. Love me? Love ya both. Love ya, Love ya, <u>Love ya</u>!

        All My Heart
          —Al (& Boondocker—no shots, the
              lucky turtle!)

MZ 680

Oct. 25

Dearest Joanne—

Our generator is being overhaul[e]d tonite, so I'm writing by candle-light. But that I am use[d] to.

I got a letter today from Jenks that made me feel kinda sad & good at the same time. Instead of being bitter that I got a rear job (he's been on the lines since January) he wrote about all the guys & said he wished I was there to address his letters for him (he likes my handwriting). All in all it was the kind of letter you get from a good buddy who's glad you got a break even if he didn't. At the end of the letter he wrote, "…Kid bayonet—we all miss you." Jenkins isn't usually a sentimental guy, so that really touched me. The whole letter sounded like he sincerely missed my companionship. The letter was 3 pages long—he seldom writes even one page to his mother or girl if he writes at all.

Jenkins and I have always been buddies—ever since I made the long climb up the hill on the Kansas line; up through the Quantico line on "Killer"; back to Hongchon [sic], Honchor, Honjin, the punchbowl, "mous[e]trap," Punchbowl, Yanggu, Hwachon—through every operation for 6½ mo.'s we've looked out for each other, laughed at our misery and thanked God that we came through alright. After every patrol we'd shake & say "that's another one we lived through." And each time we came out of reserve after stoutly proclaiming all the time we'd never go back again, Jenk would say with a scared smile, "here we go again."

There grew a bond between us that was welded together with understanding, common misery, appreciation of the small pleasures and a mutual sense of humor that kept us both going when the cards were stacked against us. We talked continually about our homes and Jenk had the greatest interest in our Cinthy. Remember the money he use[d] to send for "the baby's beer"? It was just one of his gestures to show he was interested.

I suppose you've heard a lot about "front line" comradeship. I know I've mentioned it. But the friendship between Jenkins & I [sic] is the actual proof. He's a nice little guy—with a pug nose & light brown hair with streaks of blonde. He talks with a Kentucky drawl and likes to drink beer. I never want to see the lines again—but if I have to, I'll know there's at least one advantage about being there: the friendships one forms; where a guy will not only give you his last cigarette—but his life.

That's my buddy Jenkins …

———

I'm eating (we're eating) the popcorn you sent in your last package. Dee-lisc-ious [sic]!

Makes me feel kind of funny what the major says to me. We've been working on getting another PIO man to assist me and yesterday we got some guy down for an interview. I naturally took the guy to the Major & he sent him back to me saying it was up to me. I turned the guy down—no line experience, no journalism experience, no typing & a complete anti-social dud. So I told Major Sedgewick & he said "It's up to you, you're the boss. You're the PIO man." So I have that power in my hands. I can transfer whom I please. I've been thinking about getting Don Roper off the lines. He's had 2 yrs. of college, can type, & can get along with people. Of course, he's had no journalism experience but I may be able to use him as a typing clerk to cut stencils, etc. I don't know yet, so don't mention it to Pat. I've still got to think about it & besides, I don't know if the 2nd Bat. will release him. I'd sure like him working with me, but I have to consider carefully if he'd help manifest the major's trust of my judgement.

Every day I take 2 papers to the Regimental C.O. I usually just rap on his door & walk in without waiting for an answer. I did that today and walked right into a staff meeting with General Thomas, commandant of the 1st Marine Division!*

---

*General Gerald C. Thomas (1894–1984) was appointed commander of the 1st Marine Division in Korea in April 1951.

Plus staffs of intelligence & operations. Colonels up the gigi! I was dumbfounded for a moment. I meekly laid the papers on his desk, half whispered, "good afternoon sir," and began to back my way out, bowing slowly. But instead of being bitter, the Col. said to the group, "this is Cpl. Martinez, our PIO man." I smiled sheepishly, handed them each a paper with shaky apologies & left. It was quite an experience. But after this I think I'll knock & <u>wait</u> for a "come in" before I take military courtesy in hand & slap the Col. on the back!

Some of the guys I knew who were wounded in the last operation came back today through regiment to rejoin Fox Co. They thought I was quite a wheel, rubbing elbows with to [sic] major, etc. Wish I could have them all with me—but ... that's the way the ball bounces.

That's all for now, darling. Love you, my little Muggins! Love you, Princess.

   All My heart
    —Al (& Boondocker)
  X's all [sic] I've got.

MZ 682

Oct. 29

Dearest Joanne—

Sorry I didn't write you last nite darling, but I had one of the most violent headaches I've ever had in my life. Left me sick & weak & feeling generally lousy. Went to bed at 5 p.m. & woke 5 hours later feeling great. I've felt fine all day today with no aftermath, so I guess yesterday's venture was just one of those things.

Got your letter yesterday where you found out I had been transferred to the rear. Gee, you sounded happy. I bet Cinthy was surprised when you danced her around the room. It must be a relief to you, darling, as well as it is to me. I know when I finally got back to regiment a heavy blanket of worry dropped away—and I could see things clearer in a sharper perspective. Whenever I was up on the lines I was in a constant dither, so many things to think about & watch for. There was never any mental rest & very little physical rest. So when I was transferred to the rear, I could look back & wonder in all e[a]rnestness how I ever survived it. So I can share your relief, baby, and we can both be happy.

Yesterday I went out to the third Bn. again & the 1st Bat. also. Got some good stories. Today I went out to the 2nd Bat[.]—<u>my</u> outfit. They came in reserve about a mile behind the lines—all, that is, but one company. Guess who? Fox Co! It never seems to fail. Whenever one company gets the rod, it's Fox. I feel sorry as hell for the guys up there. Everyone says they have a good deal, but the most poignant of facts remains: they're on the lines. And there, anything can happen. But, as I always said through clenched teeth, "that's just the way the ball bounces." And it is.

But anyhow I got to see a lot of my buddies from the other companies in the Bn.—Don Roper being one of them. He got transferred to the Bn. C.P. I could have gotten him into regiment as a clerk, but he likes the job he has. I hope he doesn't regret his choice. Bn. gets hit—and hit badly—too often. But my best wishes are always with him.

I've been half-listening to a program on the radio called "Town Meeting On [i.e., of] the Air."* Two jokers have been arguing about war & communism. The program is usually good and educational, but tonight they ruined their record. It stunk to high Heaven. "We have the will to fight!" this one old geezer proclaimed over the networks. Always reminds me of Bill Mauldin's† cartoon captioned, "I say it's war, Throckmorton, and I say let's fight!" It boils my blood to hear them. Two old farts fighting an arm-chair war when the guys over here are fixing bayonets for the real thing—without a will in the world to fight. Someone's got to pound a few brains into the fixture on the slopping [sic] shoulders of fiery Mr. John Q. They say there's a guy named Al Martinez who's willing to give it a damn good try.

The Ridgerunner is coming along just fine. I haven't got a copy of yesterday's paper, so I'll send you today's. [No enclosure present.] It's improving. The story on page one about the tipsy Gook is mine. Got it in my travels to the third Bat. I'm sending it to Division for Stars & Stripes and Leatherneck tomorrow. Should make it easily. I'll send you a copy.

Not much more to say, sweetheart, so I'll close. I'm anxious to hear you're [sic] other reactions in my good fortune with PIO. Been looking forward to seeing how happy you'd be. Kind of gives my "battle weary" shoulders a lift. If you're happy, I'm happy. And if we're happy, Cinthy will be. Doesn't it sound like a wonderful formula for a wonderful life. Let's always be happy.

> I love you, darling—
> you know it now, &
> I'll see that you
> always do.
>   Al (& Boondocker)

X's [sic] for you
& Princess.

MZ 684

Nov. 2

Dearest Joanne—

Well.

Yesterday was one I shall not forget. Nor today. Yesterday we were shelled by Gook artillery—badly. Today it snowed—hard. The shelling on the 1st of November, [sic] came by surprise with the routine efficiency which the Chinese usually apply to their heavy artillery: 2 hours of it, stopping work and creating the gloom of thoughts with the gloom of the day. We had casualties—non-serious. But most of all it showed that we should be aware of war's dangers, a vital lesson was learned here in the rear. And I relearned it. Tomorrow we move the CP to a safer place.

---

*America's Town Meeting of the Air was a radio program that ran from 1935 to 1956 and dealt with public affairs.

†Bill Mauldin (1921–2003) was an American editorial cartoonist who received two Pulitzer Prizes. He was best known for cartoons of soldiers in World War II.

Today, nature sent a chill up the spine of Korea and it snowed. The hillsides were blanketed in white like a worn quilt, with the black earth showing through. The limbs of the trees were heavy with snow. The valleys became soft & slushy. The tents shone under the morning sun, a crystal white. And as the day wore on the snow vanishes [sic] from the low hills & the valleys, but remained capping the high peaks of the north. So now it's winter, cold and real. The air told us it was coming, but the snow said it's here. And it's pretty, Joanne. Something clean on the ground, something fresh in the sky. It's refreshing & rich and good to feel crunching under your shoes. There's peace in the silent snow. Something to think about.

The paper WED [i.e., Wednesday] was one of the best yet, and I forgot to bring one up (come to think of it, I guess I sent you one.). The paper yesterday was fairly good also. The one today is lousy (I'll send it tomorrow). But I'm so fouled up I'll just end this paragraph & send you the paper I have here. [No enclosure present.]

(more—let's
start anew)

The cartoons in the Ridgerunner I usually trace on a stencil. Recently, however, I've been doing a little free-hand—sexing them up for the boys: the breasts a little tilted, the dress higher, the legs more inviting. Kind of fun. Gives me a chance to work out my frustration. Today's paper (I mean yesterday's paper which I'm sending today) is a good example.

Honey, you'll have to excuse this whole letter. I must be shook or something. I love you, darling & miss you with all my heart—that, I can say with sense & meaning. I love you & our Cinthy <u>very much</u>. Forgive my confusion.

All My heart & love
forever & forever –
Al (& Boondocker)
X's [sic] for the family I
love so much—you
& Cinthy.

MZ 687

3 November 51

Dearest Joanne—

Covered a bridge dedication today across one of the swollen Korean streams. And who should be there but 2nd Lieutenant Eddie LeBaron,* ex COP [i.e., College of the Pacific] all-America quarterback. I talked to him for quite awhile [sic], both because he was platoon leader of the man in whose honor the bridge was being dedicated and because he was in the same outfit I was in back in the

---

*Eddie LeBaron (1930–2015) was an All-American football player at the College of the Pacific (COP). He served in the Korean War as a Marine lieutenant in the 1st Battalion, 7th Regiment, 1st Division. Later he was a quarterback for the Washington Redskins and Dallas Cowboys.

States—the 12th AmTracBn. Since we're from the bay area we had something in common, so we talked. He's really a nice guy, unconcieted [sic] and very friendly. He's built peculiarly—short, muscular with unusually long arms. He doesn't talk like he's very intelligent, but that's no criterion for judgement, because no one talks natural [sic] when they talk to the press. And I represent the regimental press. After we talked for a while, he loosened up and became more natural.

This ceremony I covered today was quite impressive. It was in honor of one Sgt. Frederick Mausert,* killed in action after personally assaulting a hill and practically capturing the objective himself. He's up for the Congretional [sic] Medal of honor, and he well deserves it. The bridge, incidentally, is in the shadow of the hill upon which he was killed doing his extraordinary job. And the river it crosses is the one he was first to cross in the assault. So naturally I had 2 good angles on which to base my story and made the most of it. Turned out a pretty good news feature. You'll probably read it in one of the SF papers.

Got two letters from you today, darling. Thanks for loving me like you do. Same same [sic for repeated word] for me too. Nice wifeo, as the gooks would say. Tocsan nice wifeo. Also got a letter from Dolores with pictures of Emily and Ed's new car. Geez! What a boat. I now am justified in refer[r]ing to her as my rich sister. That is the biggest damn car I've ever seen. And to think they started with the green hornet. See. It's possible to do.

Two days have passed now since the shelling of the CP, but the memory of it all is not yet erased from the minds of the men. For two days they've been working on bunkers. Me? I play it cool. I've had a bunker all the time. I spent to[o] much time on the line to tempt fate now. Cool, that's me.

Your reference to Cinthy's eyes being normally crossed made me feel a lot better, but I still certainly hope they don't stay that way. Not that I'd love our angel any less if they did, but for her personal sake I hope they don't. If they do, we can take her to a specialist immediately. Even if she has to wear glasses, a little sweetie with her looks will never have to worry about a social life, I am sure. She's my darling, and she takes after her darling mother. I just know it. Think she'll make the movies. Bet she wins something.

I meant to send you Wednesday's paper tonight but now that I'm looking forit [sic], I find that (I mean for-space-it) all I have left are the file copies. So Wednesday will just have to sink into oblivion as far as your getting the Ridgerunner is concerned. I'll send you today's and hope that will make every one happy. Incidentally, how do you like my "Take 'em or leave 'em" football prediction column? Causes quite a sensation. Not because everybody likes it so tremendously well, but because they usually just disagree with me so fervently. Last week I only missed about three games, that is predicted three of them wrong. My method is usually hit and miss, because I know so little about most of the teams. But that's what makes it interesting. For instance, I like Cal as a football team so I pick then to win; I like Stanford and Notre Dame, so etc. I pick because I like 'em, and

---

*Frederick Mausert (1930–1951) earned the Medal of Honor for many acts of heroism and for ultimately sacrificing his life at the Battle of the Punchbowl on September 12, 1951.

sometimes I pick 'em because I know something about them. It's really fun and amazing how close I come. I think the guys know that I use a rather ragged system, and it enfuriates [sic] them all the more because it's so ac[c]urate. However, the bulk of my readers probably think I'm some kind of an expert at it all. Oh well—God bless the anonymity of free journalism.

I sent in three features to division wanting to know how they liked them. Lieut. O'Leary called back and said they were 4.0, perfect in Naval slang. Wants me to send some more. Naturally, I'm very smug about the whole thing because I don't think division has any feature writer[s] which are worth a damn. That's not just conciet [sic], that's a well-shared professional opinion. I've learned since I applied for a job with division PIO that they were afraid to accept me because I had no professional experience. All the men they have there are ex-newsmen, etc. One of my purposes here at regimental PIO besides turning out good work, is to make O'Leary wish very much that he had me on his staff. It's not purely for revenge, because I like O'Leary. I just think he needs to be taught a very valuable lesson—that experience is experience whether you're getting paid for it or not. And sometimes you can profit more from amatuer [sic] experience, because you have no restrictions. I think even now he's wishing he had me there. A division man should have covered the bridge dedication—it was big and impressive. They did have a division photographer there, but he asked me to write the story. How about that!

All this space skipping and non-spacing is due to mechanical difficulties and not my own mistakes. Honest. This typewriter (which incidentally had a purple heart ribbon tapped [sic] on it) is about due for rotation. It's been with the regiment since Inchon. It is deffinetly [sic] shook.

Rotation is humming right along. A reserve draft went out about two weeks ago, and a regular rotation draft is going out in two days. The way it looks, the fourth draft is supposed [sic] to get out of here by December, the fifth draft in January, the sixth in February, the 7th in March. In this reserve release thing, since I was called to active duty in Sept. I should be discharged in March or April. So no matter how you look at it, I should be leaving Korea in February or March, no sooner <u>I don't think</u>. But that too remains to be seen.

Well, sugar, as usual it's late and I'm a wee bit weary. Had a rough day in the field. Wrote a big old story and went up to the front (two miles behind the lines) and had to ride a bumpy old jeep all the way. Incidentally, we have our own PIO jeep, to be used at my discretion. Actually, it's the major's jeep, but he put it in my hands—plus a driver. Walk, me? I ride. Even if it's 50 feet. How about <u>that</u>?

Love you and Cinthy with all my heart. Hope you get the radio fixed. Love, love, love you—and Cinthy. Take care of yourselves, darlings, and give each other a big kiss for me.

All my love forever and
forever and forever.
Al (and Boondocker)—combat
correspondents.

November 17

Dearest Joanne—

Hi, hon. Sorry I didn't write you yesterday, but I got involved in a million and one things that left me very little time to do anything. Thought about you all the time though. I haven't recieved [sic] a letter from you for three days, so I wouldn't have much to write about anyhow. Got a letter from Galo, my mom and Emily however. But none from my favorite girl. Whassamaatter?

Yesterday morning two civilian correspondents from the Cleveland press came out and wanted me to brief them on a "ski-lift" method of evacuating the wounded the Marine Corps is using.* I didn't know a damn thing about it, so I had to find out. Then they wanted six men from Cleveland to take pictures of and write a Joe-blow story on. I checked the roster and found there were none at regiment, so I had to get them from the second Bat. All this time it was raining which made things very uncomfortable. These guys were the dullest, most confused individuals I've ever seen. Completely in a fog, knowing nothing from nothing. But I guess that's why they send them overseas.

After all that, I had to get the paper out and that took until late at night. That's why no write. No time.

The cartoons, as you can see by the two issues I'm sending you [no enclosures present], are improving. There's only one fault. Our cartoonist has ideas, but they're all bad. So I think up the ideas and he draws the cartoons. He doesn't go for the idea, but of cours[e] there's nothing he can do about it. He did a couple on his own and I got the word that they went over like a le[a]d balloon. That's when I started getting on him to turn out better ones. I've got a million ideas.

This letter from Galo asked me to write some stuff for the Golden Gater. Norma Swain (the editor) seems to be in a dither for the material. I hardly think I'll be able to do too much, but I have written two stories. Emily wants to put my experiences in some neighborhood paper in Oakland. Celebrity, eh? By the way, did you ever find time to do anything about my letters in the way of publication? Just wondered not impatient.

Yesterday Jenkins and some other kid from Fox came out here which added to the confusion. Couldn't spend much time shooting the bull with them, but it was nice seeing them. The 2nd Bat[.] is scheduled to go back up to the lines in two days. December 1st or 5th we all go into Division reserve back at Inje for Xmas. But it's going to be a lonely Xmas without you ...

Well, darling, not much more to say except I Love You and I say that all the time. I don't have to say it anyhow, cuz you know it. But it's nicer to say it. Think of you all the time, dream of you and miss you. Here's a big kiss for you and Cinthy—X. Love you both with all my heart.

All My Love Forever
And Forever—honest ...
Al (and Boondocker)

---

*The better-known innovative method of evacuating the wounded in Korea involved the use of helicopters and mobile hospitals close to the front.

P.S. I Love you.
[Drawing of a man's face (Al's?) in profile, captioned:]
Rich [i.e., Bob Richardson, the cartoonist]
INJE, KOREA
11/17/51

MZ 698

November 20, 1951

Dearest Joanne—

Across the burning, thundering hills of Korea he went, a combat Marine, an inimitable individual, suffering out the dark and dreadful days of the attack when all around him fell, but one he depended on. His buddy, the one he watched with the vigilance of devotion, carried this combat machine into the fight, and where he went THEY went, one and inseparable, bearing out the fine tradition of combat comradeship. When the night settled over the land, dangerous and decieptful [sic], this little Marine stayed awake, staring out into the shifting ebony of shadows, keeping wathc [sic] over his Marine for a girl that loved him.

And now his buddy, Al Martinez, is safe so this little Marine can rest. But something is discovered: he's wounded, a casualty, a leg is gone. The sturdy little man trudged silently in all that is horrible with a pain of which he bore no mention. We can only now decorate him with the Marine Corps' Medal of Honor, The Purple Heart, the sign of a combat Marine who has given his flesh and his blood for the ideals under which dictatorships fall. To BOONDOCKER MARTINEZ, my buddy, my luck, I proudly present the Purple Heart Medal, for wounds received in action against the enemy from 1 April 1951 to 16 Oct. 1951. Cpl. BOONDOCKER'S actions have been in keeping with the highest traditions of the UNITED STATES MARINE CORPS.

Boondocker actually is a casualty. I discovered that aside from being rather flat, his left hind leg is missing. I have gotten him a purple heart medal, enclosed [no enclosure present] is the campaign ribbon which he wants to send to Itchy Pup; he wears a purple and white ribbon on him now. You know, Joanne, I've gotten pretty well attached to little Boondocker. He's been with me through a lot, accepting his fate in the animated silence of one without life or heart. And yet I often wonder if the inorganic things which exist only by our vision are not the prototype of a better man, who live[s] by loyalty and silence, two virtues which so many of us in the field today don't have. Herein, with the green and yellow little turtle is a story: a story of stamina and intestinal fortitude which so few of the homo sapien[s] have. In the story of Boondocker, who now sits on my desk for the world of men to look at, there is a lesson in life.

I'm afraid our Cinthia isn't going to like the idea of lying on her back too much pelvic bone or no pelvic bone. Babies always like to lie on their stomachs and kick. I know, I always did. Hope they line up okay; hope her right eye is okay; hope our little darling is alright in every way. But with such a wonderful mother watching over her, how could she be anything else? She wieghs [sic] 14 lbs. 5 oz., huh? Gee, that's little. Twenty-four and one-half inches sounds pretty tall though. I really wouldn't know, but anyhow she's just right whatever she is. My prescious [sic].

Who the devil's Eric? You keep mentioning men I don't know, have never heard of and am going to beat the heck out of when I get home. Why? Oh, I don't know. Just on general principles. Only kidding. I know who Eric is—the Jaeger's baby, isn't he? What a memory. Sure am anxious to get these pictures of you and Cinthy you've been talking about. But since you're being so teasy about Christmas, may I add that I have a little surprise planned for you for Christmas too. First let me say, however, that the surprise is not that I'll be home then—don't want you to get your hopes up. But if all goes according to plan, it will be a nice surprise. Curious? Nyahhhh.

My battle's won? Why, because the Jaegers like me? Never knew I had to battle to get someone to like me. Come, come, dear wife, am I that much of an anti-social. Had to battle to get you, I admit, but that was a sweet battle. I liked it. I like the Jaeger's [sic] too from what I've heard of them. Just one big intelligent family.

Had a sexy dream about me, huh? I have tocsan (many) about you. Proves that you're the object of my affections and intentions—purely honorable, of course. In a lovey sort of way.

<u>A Poem, not composed, but copied:</u>

>A woman is an awful thing.*
>   I like her.
>She'll never pet without a ring.
>   I like her.
>To some he-man she loves to cling,
>Until his sense and roll take wing:
>Then you just watch her crown her king!
>   I like her.

<u>Comments</u>—*my own:*
'Tain't true—<u>not</u> mine, anyhow.
Yep.
Cigarette?
Yep.
Me? He-man? Well, whaddayaknow?
You never married me for my money, anyhow.
Me, honey?
No. I love her. You.

—Curtain, Music, Finis—

---

*This poem remains unidentified.

> A wonderful bird is the Pelican!*
> His mouth can hold more than his belican.
> > He can take in his beak
> > Enough food for a week –
> I'm damned if I know how the helican!

That's enough of poetry or whatever you want to call these cute little whosamacllits [*sic*]. Fiddedlehops [*sic*].

Honey, I think you'd better stop putting dates on your letters. Just confuses me when you remember, because I'm so used to your forgetting. Just kidding, sweet. I get a kick out of your little comments, "Nov. 13 or somewhere thereabouts." Who's confused? Not me. Not you. Must be Cinthy. No, not Cinthy. She's too sweet. Truman, yeah, he's always good for a kick in the teeth.

Warren† is going to run for president, huh? Good. Wonderful. I couldn't think of a man I would rather have for president of the US than Earl Warren, I mean it. And that includes Taft,‡ Eisenhower,§ MacArthur,¶ Truman or anyone else. I don't know how good his chances are from Stateside opinion. But over here it's close between Warren and Ike, with The Earl of California getting the nod. I'm all for him. Now I don't want to start a political argument between us, but what do you think?

They've got the rotation blues around here again. One of the fellows in the tent is going home the 27th of this month with a reserve draft, and a regular rotation draft is leaving for the US the 5th Dec. Might even be one going out the last part of December. Rolling along pretty good.

In a different vien [*sic*], here's a story with kind of a tragic alliance. May the 29th in the Punchbowl a fellow by the name of Strickland was shot in the neck by a .45 automatic when he went to wake up his buddy for watch one night. He's in the Oak Knoll Hospital now, paralyzed. About three days after that, another fellow named Strickland in the Fox Co. mortar section was killed by a direct hit from a mortar. Last night, the last of them went—one Bob Strickland, killed in action by a probing attack. Three Stricklands were in Fox Co. when I was in it,

---

*This famous limerick has long been attributed to humorist Ogden Nash (1902–1971), but it was actually written by Dixon Lanier Merritt (1879–1972). Al slightly misquotes it. One version of the correct verse is:

> A wonderful bird is the pelican.
> His bill can hold more than his belican.
> He can hold in his beak
> Enough food for a week,
> But I'm damned if I see how the helican.

†Earl Warren (1891–1974) served as governor of California (1943–1953) and was appointed Chief Justice of the U.S. Supreme Court (1953–1969). In 1948 he was the nominee of the Republican Party for vice president, running with Thomas E. Dewey. He unsuccessfully pursued the Republican nomination for president in 1952.

‡Robert Taft, Jr. (1917–1993), sought the presidential nomination in 1952, his third unsuccessful try. He was a Republican Congressman from Ohio from 1963 to 1965 and a U.S. Senator from 1971 to 1976.

§Dwight D. Eisenhower (1890–1969) became the Republican candidate for president in 1952, defeating both Warren and Taft, and he was elected president, serving 1953 to 1961. He had served as a five-star general in the U.S. Army in World War II and as the Supreme Commander of the Allied Forces in Europe, in charge of the invasion of France and Germany. He was popularly known as "Ike," especially during his presidential campaign.

¶Douglas MacArthur (1850–1964).

none of them were related. In each case when they became casualties, only one person was hit—one of them. What's in a name?

That's all for now, darling. Think I'll write to my folks tonight and possibly my sisters. Love you, love you, love you—loads and loads, Cinthy too. Give my hello to your friends the Jaegers, and tell them I'm really not as intelligent as they think, but intelligentlererer [sic]. Concieted [sic] too. Any friend of yours is a friend of mine, honey—all except The Thing, Lowene—and I like even her over here. Just goes to show you what a war can do to a man, either make him or break him. Then there's me. No one has made me, no one has broke[n] me. Guess I'm the exception of the rule. Love you anyhow. Love me? Better.

(P.S. Have you heard the latest song, "My Wife Is Out with My Best Friend, And I Miss Him.")

All MY heart and Love—
    Al (& Boondocker)I love you

Thought you might enjoy the humorous side of the Corps.
    Love ya—
    Al

MZ 702

                    December 1

Dearest Joanne, My darling—

Received quite a long letter from you today much to my pleasant surprise. Most of it was concerned with the raising of Cinthia, and for some reason it almost sounded like a challenge to me to contest the book method of raising a child. I certainly do not feel that the way my sisters have raised their children is entirely correct; nor do I feel that it is entirely incorrect. But rather than argue or expound on a subject which I admit I know very little about, let me say this in a very unlearned attitude:

I suppose reading books, majoring in child psychology or being a child counsellor gives one a better basis for raising a child, something to go on. Yet, I daresay, it certainly makes one far from being an expert as you have already said. Darling, I want our child to be healthy (physically and emotionally), happy, secure and content more than anything in the world. But above all I want her to be natural.

You're in a better position to know how to raise our daughter than I am, darling. But I hope that when I come home you'll make allowance for my ignorance and my lack of book reading on how to raise our daughter and go along with me when I want to spoil her and love her just once in awhile [sic]. Okay? I promise I won't spoil her—too much.

Now it can be told: you may address your letters: SERGEANT Alfred Martinez, up-and-coming young man in the United States Marine Corps Reserve. Yep, I made it. I made it on both proficiency score (which is the highest for sgt. than it has ever been, a-hem) and on conduct rating and on TO—training Operation; in other words, they rate one Sgt. for PIO as nco in charge. I am it. So up and up and up your little honey goes ... even if he did cut a couple classes in college. Oh,

I admit that being a Sgt. is far from being a top man in the newspaper field. But it shows a change of personality which I hope you can understand: I can lead men.

I'll send you my warrant as soon as I get it.

Sounds like you had the typically nice Thanksgiving at my folks['] place in Richmond. Your description was so vivid and cute: kids hollering, throwing things around and just being wonderful kids. I suppose you, being in there [sic] rowdy mi[d]st at the time, can't exactly share my exultation at kids. But somehow over here, they seem like wonderful little people—or pipples, little pipples.

I suppose lately you've been hearing Truman, etc[.], rave that no cease-fire was authorized in Korea the other day, that all reports by the Associated Press stating there was a cease-fire are incor-

Drawing of Al at his typewriter by Bob Richardson, the cartoonist for the *Ridgerunner*, included in Al's letter of November 22, 1951. The letter is not included in this book (The Huntington Library, MZ 703).

rect. If you haven't seen it, ask the Jaegers about it. And tell them that I am one of three newspapermen who know the documented truth on the whole subject, and I could make a liar out of the president of the United States. Here's what actually happened:

Three days ago, the company commander of Howe Company, 3rd Battalion, 7th Marines, for a joke sent their Korean interpreter out to holler at the North Koreans (whose positions are only 80 yards away[)], and asked them how they would like being not shot at. One Gook private said he couldn't talk, but if the interpreter brought an officer back in one-half hour they would discuss it. Later, the interpreter brought the officer back and the Gook private re-appeared with two high North Korean officers. The officers proceeded to tell the Howe company commander that the Marines were bad and that they should go home. He said they didn't mind fighting the army (this is in [i.e., on] record, not just personal prejudice) but they wanted little or nothing to do with the Marine Corps. They wanted a cease fire on the Eastern front. They told the CO of Howe to bring many officers and meet by the river and they would talk. It sounded like a trap, so the officer let the word of the goings on get back to division. Division, horrified, tabued [sic] the idea and tried to kill the word. Too late. Corps got hold of it[,] then the 8th Army, then Ridgeway [sic] and finally President Truman. All hell was raised with the officer and all such proceedings were tabbed snafu. But the North Koreans have quit firing at the Marines and vice versa. It is quiet on the day-time Eastern front—only at night is there any activity of mention. And that is nil. They holler back and forth at each other, they throw each other chow, and they sing back and forth. The reason I say I am but one of the three newspaper men who know the truth is this: Lieut. O'Leary of Division PIO is one, an AP war correspondent got it partially, and I saw the S-2 Intelligence files on it by permission of the Adujant [i.e., Adjutant] of the Regiment, Major Sedgewick [sic]. There are more facts to the story even now than I have told, but at the present they must remain with me. I could really tell a story if I were given permission—but I wouldn't dare do it without it. The brass of the regiment trusted me enough to show me officials [sic] files on it, and I certainly won't violate that trust. I hope you don't spread it around too much. It's okay to tell Barbara and Allen if you want, because I think the whole thing is rather amusing and unusual. But see that it gets no further or I may be a private again—on the lines.

Bob Richardson's drawing of Al Martinez going after a rat, included in Al's letter of November 27, 1951. The letter is not included in this book (The Huntington Library, MZ 708).

I feel that the most significant thing about it, and one reason they killed it, is because it would make the truce delegates in Panmunjom look like what they are: muddled old fools who can't punctuate or pin down a point if they had to. It shows up in black-and-white negatives just what the peon, the citizen, the average man thinks of war when he has to fight it: he hates it. Propoganda [sic], even the strong Russian type, can't convi[n]ce him that he's dying for a cause when bullets are flying. Think of it, Joanne: small incident that it might be, it serves to show the deeper thoughts of men when, in the midst of a very terrible war, they can talk about a common subject with each other and still desire peace, even though the night before they had been killing one another. There is hope for men, here in Korea and all over the world. The will to live in peace is there. And in years to come, perhaps, as a dominate [sic], desire it will overthrow the words of the war mongers. And I can see it happen. I have a feeling, a wonderful feeling, that all is not as black as it appears. And when the revolution for good will and understanding hits the world, you can bet your last pair of nylons that Al Martinez will be waving the saber. Pray with me, with all of us in Korea, Joanne, that what happened on the Marine sector of the eastern front will happen all over Korea. And when it finally does happen, I'll know, and write, just how it happened.

We have our little houseboy living in the tent with us now. He's the most intelligent kid. We're learning him to speak English, to have manners and to be a little Americanized. He's really willing to learn. He's always picking up books and asking us words, asking us to show him how to type, etc. He's writing a Korean-English dictionary and doing it well. When we call him a houseboy, he says, "Me no houseboy. Me study boy." I asked him why he wasn't going to school, and he gave me a reason which explains who [i.e., why] so many korean [sic] youngsters who are so eager to learn aren't: it costs the equivalent of $16 a month. Of all the people in the world who are so willing and anxious to get an education why is it the half-assed characters like Al Martinez get the breaks then sluff off? If I decide to go back to school, I'll remember Lee, and put a little more effort into what I do for him. Now I know why so many returning veterans after the last war were such good students. Again, I've learned a lesson.

Love you with all my heart, darling. I think you'll be pleasantly surprised when your don't-worry husband comes home. "It takes a war to wake you up," they use[d] to say to me. Okay. I've had the war. Good morning.

>Love and lots of
>kisses to my wife
>and baby ...
>
>>Al (and SGT. Boondocker—when I get a
>>rate he does too.)
>>Love you,
>>>darlings ...

(P.S.—has Dr. Bock* or whatever his name is got a book on how to raise husbands? Or don't you think you'll need it, sweetie?)

MZ 711

Dec. 7

Dearest Joanne—

I felt pretty good all day today. I felt like writing you a real long letter. That was up until about 5 o'clock. Then I found out something from the S-1 office.

---

*Al means Dr. Benjamin Spock, whose *The Commonsense Book of Baby and Child Care* was the most popular book on the subject beginning with its first publication in 1946.

One artillery shell had rocketed into Fox Co.'s position today. Two men were killed. One was a fellow by the name of Seabloom—I didn't even know his first name: he was a nice kid about 18, blonde, young-looking. He was the 'baby' of the machine gun section attached to the second platoon.

I came to like him alot [*sic*]. A hell of a nice kid.

He use[d] to kid me about my wife & daughter. Use[d] to say he would go home before me & look up my pretty blonde wife. When I got transferred to PIO I almost forgot to shake hands with him & wish him good luck. He was hurt. But I remembered. Then everything was okay.

Seabloom & I never hung around each other too much. But when we were together, or when we stopped to talk on the road, we were the best of buddies.

Self-portrait by Al Martinez, in his letter dated December 2, 1951. Joanne had recommended to Al that he smile when things were bad. The letter is not included in this book (The Huntington Library, MZ 713).

Picture this, Joanne—a young kid with a baby face—from Cincinnati I think, I don't really remember—laughing, always kidding; a kid that's never really been in love & hasn't experienced life. One minute he was writing to his mother. Now he's dead, horribly dead.

In three days we go into reserve for Christmas. A nice little guy by the name of Seabloom won't be around & I'll miss him.

Casualties were light today. Two KIA's [*sic*], just two. One of them I happened to know …

All My Love
Al

P.S.—Sorry for the letter, darling. I'm just feeling badly. Love you. Cinthy too.   Al (& Boondocker)

MZ 718

Three. *Cpl. Al Martinez, Combat Correspondent.... How About That!*

December 12, '51
In Reserve

Dearest Joanne, My darling—

It's sleeting (such a word?) outside, and the wind is howling something terrific. And it's cold. Inside, it's sleeting (holes in the tent), the wind is howling something terrific (through those holes). And it's cold (out of fuel oil). But none-the-less, a[n] I'll-fight-on smile plays about my lips, and I'm happy. That's cuz my boys of the line companies are in reserve, and because I got two real wonderful letters from you this morning. I don't have them with me, so I won't be able to answer them word for word. But I'll try to remember some of the things you wrote about.

You said I love you, I remember. Love you too. Cinthy too. Itchy Pup too. And everything you laid your eyes on that said I Love You to me.

The reason I haven't written for a couple days is this: Monday I had one of my terrific headaches and wasn't worth a damn. Tuesday we spent moving to this present reserve area, and today is Wednesday, an' I'm writing. This new area is about 35 miles behind where we were. It is a permanent reserve area, fully equipped with squad tents (with wooden floors), electric lights and cots for the troops as well as for the headquarters personnel. All of the 7th Regiment is in reserve. In answer to your question, yes—we go back when the line companies move back. It certainly wouldn't be a rest for us with guerillas snipping [sic] away, or with artillery shells whining in. Of course, we don't have it nearly as rough as the boys up front, but we do have casualties sometimes—though very seldom.

When we moved (on trucks, natch) I had about as much gear of my own as the whole S-1 Section. I've somehow managed to accumulate 8 sets of dungarees, three flannel shirts, all kinds of underwear, socks, winter gear, and accessories—plus my packages, books, two sleeping bags, typewriter, desk, stencils, paper, boxes of junk, file copies, etc.—and all since Oct. 15. Honestly, I've got more gear than I know what to do with. Nobody understands why I carry toy turtles and tops around with me. Deadbeats.

In this area, we have two tents. One's a working tent, the other a sleeping tent. Right now I'm in the former. This is where we do our work on the paper and write our letters. Today, the Major presented the PIO section with a fifth of Bourbon (all officers get an issue) and tomorrow Lieut. Guice is giving us another fifth. We intend to have a merry Christmas or float away in the attempt. S-1 is planning a party too, so that's two we have scheduled, including our own. Now, honey, I'm no drunk—but if a man can't get a little high on Christmas then what's this war coming to?

We didn't have to put out a Ridgerunner yesterday because of moving, so we didn't. Today we didn't have to either. But I got the bug that we were last night, so we did. It didn't dawn on me until that time, that we had nothing to put in it. So today's product isn't the best. But it's a paper, and I have the satisfaction of knowing I expended a little bit of effort (until 2 a.m.) for the boys who've done such a fine job of holding the military line in the hills. I think it was worth it. And oddly enough, the Colonel liked the paper. He was in a tremendous mood this morning when I took it to him. Just goes to show you, that you can never tell. When you get this Ridgerunner you can undoubtedly see the Martinez creative touch in almost every story. I padded and rewrote like mad. My cartoonist kept falling asleep, putting the headlines on crooked, and my other typist (Hopkins) couldn't do worth a damn with a typewriter and stencil. But that's all water under the river, and I'm not complaining.

In a discussion with Guice and the Major the other day, I learned that they are very well satisfied with the progress of the RR. Bless them.

Remember one time when we were waiting for a Greyhound bus in Oceanside, and I introduced you to a kid named Rogers? A guy with a long face who lived in Sacramento. He was a good friend of Pete Mamaril's; went rhough [sic] boot camp with us and training at Pendleton. He was killed in action December 10. Another guy who "had a feeling" he'd never get it. A lesson in life is worth repeating.

Jenkins came through the last time out okay, as did Nunn, Lutke (he got transferred today as a regimental mail clerk), and all the rest of the boys. Jenkins won't see the front lines again—he'll be on his way home soon. I saw most of the guys today.

Darling, I can't think of anything more to say, so I'll quit. I'll bring your letter down tomorrow night and really answer it. I love you honey,—more than you could ever quite realize. And I love our little Cinthy more than she'll ever know. It's wonderful being in love, and knowing you've got some one real wonderful to return to. Maybe (though I can't quite see it) a little absence is good for two people. It certainly showed me how much I took for granted. And I'll never take it for granted again. I love being in love with you …

Honey ……. I'm cold.

All My Love Forever and
Forever to my adorable
wife and daughter …
Al (and Boondocker)
XXXXXXXXXXXXXXXXXXXXXXXXXXX's [sic] by the millions.
Love you, love you, love you.

MZ 721

December 18

Dearest Joanne, My darling—

Enclosed [no enclosure present] you will find an exact copy of the citation which was finally passed and awarded to the 2nd Battalion, 7th Marines for meritorious duty from 1 April to 1 June 1951, the time that I was a part of it with Fox Company. I told you about this citation before, but then I lost track of it. It is a naval citation, the highest unit citation of its kind, and the 2nd Battalion is the (one of the) smalles[t] units to recieve [sic] it. We were offered an 8th Army citation but turned it down to try for this Distinguished Service Citation.

I know the citation will probably sound phoney [sic] to you in the wording. But what it says without all the pretty words is true. Those were extremely dark and treacherous days when we came northeast and attacked the Hwachon Rese[r]voir, Yanggu Valley, the Punchbowl. We suffered every kind of torment an armed unit should be subjected to.

I for one most definetly [sic] feel that the 2nd Bat. earned the award in the hardest way imaginable—by sheer force of guts against a numerically superior and a stragically [i.e., strategically] superior enemy. We went after him, and though we had the intitiative [sic] and the moment of the attack, he had the protection and the well-fortified positions.

So when I com[e] home, sweetheart, I'll have a blue ribbon, lined in gold with a gold battle-star that only members who fought with the 2nd Bat. during that period will be entitled to wear. Oh, it will be a pretty ribbon and will look nice on a uniform. But it will mean much more to me. I'll be extremely proud to wear it, just as proud as I was to be a member of the 2nd Bat. when they threw the Chinese and the North Koreans back with a terrible venge[a]nce; just as proud that I am in the Marine Corps. Just as happy to be in the rear and on the lines no longer.

Nothing new[,] different or unusual has happened today. Didn't even get a letter from you. So, don't have nuffin [sic] to write. 'Cept that I love you and I love Cinthy, and I always do that—always love you, I mean. Will try to write a more interesting letter tomorrow …

All My Heart and love
Forever And Always …
Al (and Boondocker and
Our Camera)

I love you!
XXXXXXXXXXXXXXXXXXXXXXXXXXXXXXXXXXX's [sic]

MZ 725

December 20, 1951

Dearest Joanne, My darling—

Looking up into the smiling faces of you and Cinthy sitting on my PIO desk, I seem to see a question in your eyes: "Daddy (and husband) what have you been doing all the time in Korea?" I heard your question, and decided tonight I would answer it. It's an awfully long story that might have started in boot camp, at Camp Pendleton, aboard the USS Thomas Jefferson in the Middle of the ocean, in Japan, Pusan, Hoonsong or on the Kansas line with an infantry regiment. I prefer to have it start with me, a boot, staring up to a hill 1000 meters high and knowing I had to climb it. I looked at my 7th draft buddy and muttered, "If that isn't the highest damn hill in Korea, I'll put in with you …"

I'd've had to put in with him. It wasn't.

By the time I had reached Fox Company on the Kansas line, I looked like I had just been through the battle of Chosin, I was beat. But I was a veteran. Salty?

Why, you have never seen a saltier Marine than I was. I reeked of Calcium sulphate. I litterally [sic] dripped with the spirit of the Corps' saltiest Marine, Lou Diamond.* That was before we jumped off. Then I stepped into it.

Operation Killer,† Operation Mousetrap and Operation Yo-Yo‡ flew by and left me a humble critter. Boondocker and I had had our fill of walking, waiting, fighting and getting P.O.d. We were sick of night wathces [sic] of two months on C rations, of rain, sun and Korea. We didn't think that war was such hot or dangerous stuff. Sure, guys got wounded, some went psycho, but few, very few. Where's the hot-to-go fire of the Corps, I thought to myself. Then we moved east.

The Punchbowl, Yanggu Valley, Mortar hill, Buchmann Ridge,§ Hamlin Hill, Mortar Gulch,¶ Banzai hill**—Mortars that whipped through the air and shells that whinned [sic] into our lines. Flat-trajectory explosives that punched at the hillsides and exploded in the tree tops. Land mines, throwing lives and limbs and bodies into the air with an inconsistnet [sic] consistency. An enemy who, rejecting our attack, came in the night and left with the lives of a lot of nice young guys. Objective 10††, a high, jutting land mark at the end of the Punchbowl, calling death on top of us. X-Ray,‡‡ and the fight to stop the whole North Korean Army. Pvt. Joe, a nice guy who held our luck on Banzai hill, and died when we didn't need it anymore. Hamlin, who saw a platoon on the verge of anhililation [sic] and gave a leg to the fortunes of war to save us.

What have I done in Korea? I've listened to the cough of the heavy machine gun, hacking like a man with TB; I've heard the chatter of the light .30 Calibur [sic], warning angrily, the powerful punch of an M-1, the feminine bruuup of a burp gun…. I've been watching the Corsairs scream at the hillsides and blossom into flame with a napalm; watching the artillery shells errupt [sic] on the ridges in their white phosphorous, high explosives, incinderary [sic]. I've been writing a book about things and people …

I've been thinking.

I've been doing a lot of thinking. I've had bitter thoughts, pleasant ones, cowardice ones, brave ones. I've thought about you, Cinthy, death, hate, killing people, freedom, war, my buddies, peace, home and life. I've thought of how funny a lot of things were and I've laughed to the point where people thought I was a

---

*Lou Diamond (1890–1951) was a career Marine who rose to the rank of gunnery sergeant, serving in both World Wars. He was known for his exploits in battle.

†Operation Killer began the second major battle against the Chinese Communists and the North Korean Army, from February 20 to March 6, 1951. It was planned by General Matthew Ridgway.

‡Operation Yo-Yo. In June, 1950, the North Korean government claimed the entire Korean Peninsula as its own territory. The United States fought back along lines that stretched all the way from Pusan at the south end of the peninsula to the Chinese border, changing constantly between those two areas. Hence, the fighting in the first year of the war was known as "Operation Yo-Yo."

§Buchmann Ridge. There appears to be no ridge by this name. It is probably Al's private name for the ridge where a platoon leader named Buchman distinguished himself. Similarly, Al named Hamlin Hill for Sergeant Hamlin, who had shown considerable bravery.

¶Mortar Gulch. No battle found by this name. It is likely Al's private name for a battle.

**Banzai Hill. No battle found by this name. It is likely Al's private name for a battle.

††Objective 10. It is unclear whether this is a named battle or location, or Al's private name for part of the Punchbowl Battle.

‡‡X-ray. No battle found by this name. It is likely Al's private name for a battle.

psycho. Maybe I was at one time, I wasn't sure myself. But I never screamed or cried hard or cracked up.... I Just [sic] looked ahead and laughed. It was funny.

It was a long war for me up there in the hills. It's far from over, I know, but for now at least I'm comparitively [sic]. I'm not climbing up ridges anymore, I'm pounding a typewriter.

What've I been doing in Korea? Wishing to hell I was in San Francisco, and thinking of you ...

I Love You
Al

MZ 727

December 20, 1951

Dearest Joanne, My darling—

Sexy, huh? The stationary [sic], I mean. [See illustration on page 189 showing Marine stationery described here.] That campaign ribbon to the left is the Presidential Unit Citation, where [i.e., which] the First Division earned on the places, Korea included. I can wear the ribbon as long as I am a member of the Division. The last blue ribbon is the Korean ribbon. So far, I can wear that with one battle star; the Marine Corps only gives a battle star for very MAJOR engagements—the Army has five in the same period; they get one every time they retreat. However, I feel certain that they'll judge this last operation a major engagement and therefore give us another battle star. Also, I have our battalion citation with a battle star which I'm entitled to wear. I also rate the reserve ribbon, a proposed UN service ribbon, possibly the Asiatic Pacific ribbon and whatever else they decide to throw out. All that with three stripes and a hash mark (which I now rate) ought to look pretty good, eh?

Guess who I got a letter from today? Dr. Alfred G. Fisk,* professor of philosophy at SFSC. Boy, was I surprised. He complimented me on the article I wrote and sent the greeting of the faculty to me. It was really a nice letter. I'm surprised he remembered so much about me. He also told me of his travels in Pakistan and what he thinks of the situation there in relation to the Anglo-Egyptian feud. All in all, a nice letter which I answered immediately.

Well, the mimeograph machine finally broke completely down, which I expected it would for quite some time. We have one side of the paper out, and one side blank. What to do? I dunno. Everyone's fussing over it now, but I think it's seen it's [sic] last days myself. Do I care? Naw. It's about time they bought a new one anyhow.

I'm not the only [one] who gets toys in packages. One of the fellows in here (speaking of packages, I've still got most of the little ones you sent me way down in the bottom of my wooden box so I won't be tempted to open them) got a package the other day which included a jumping Frog and a little mouse that does somersaults. Cutest darn things. More fun.

---

*Alfred G. Fisk (d. 1959) taught philosophy at San Francisco State College.

Love you loads and loads, baby. Cinthy too. Kisses for my family: Jo and Cin.... XXXXXX

                          All My Heart,
                              Al (Boondoc[k]er and Camera)

MZ 728

SEVENTH MARINES DAILY RIDGERUNNER REVIEW

Vol. 2, No. 88   Friday, Dec. 21

FILM DEVELOPED IN JAPAN

Personnel in Korea authorized to posses Military payment certificates may have regular black and white roll film developed and printed by mailing it to: Yokohama Main Store, Japan Central Exchange, APO 503.

Enlarged "Jumbo" prints will be made on single-weight glossy paper. The "Jumbo" prints size will depend upon the negative size.

A flat rate will be charged for developing, printing and return postage. The rate charged will depend upon the number of exposures on the roll.

No. Exp. roll	Cost
8	$0.40
12	.60
16	.80
20	1.00
36	1.80
40	2.00
72	3.60

Reprints or additional prints will cost 5-cents per print. Not more than five prints or reprints per negative are permitted.

A postal money order payable to Custodian, Japan Central Exchange Fund, must accompany the order. Current regulations prohibit sending MPC through the mails. No refund will be made for unprintable negatives except in cases of total failure.

Approximately two weeks will be required for developing, printing and return. All orders will be returned by Air Mail.

PREPARATIONS FOR PARADE TOMORROW NOW UNDERWAY

Final preparations are being made for the award presentation to 37 men of the Seventh Marines tomorrow. The ceremony will be held on the Regimental parade grounds and is slated to began at 1330.

An honor guard composed of members of the First Battalion will participate and plans include the Division band.

Actual presentation of the combat awards will be made by Col. J.J. Wermuth, Regimental Commander.

Nineteen men from the First Battalion are slated to receive awards. Of those, 2 of them will be awarded the Silver Star; 11 will receive the Bronze Star; and six others the letter of Commendation.

One Silver Star, six Bronze Stars, and two letters of Commendation, will be awarded to members of the Second Battalion.

The third Battalion awards are: two Silver Stars and five Bronze Stars.

A Bronze Star will be awarded to a member of H&S Co and a Silver Star to a member of 4.2s.

The season spirit is continuing to flourish as members of the Seventh Marines busy themselvs with trimming little trees, their tents and mess halls.

COMMITTEE FALTERS ON POW EXCHANGE

Panmunjom---Peace in Korea within seven days seems to be slipping from the hands of truce delegates at Panmunjom, as the one prospect of progress--the exchange of prisoner of war lists--settles into an old familiar.

This morning the sub-delegates to the POW committee wondered what to do about exchanging the prisoners themselves. Progress was practically nonexistant.

Twenty-three days ago, UN and Communist delegates began the race anew for a settlement of the Korean question. The armistice hopes took a new lease on life by what appeared to be an earnest desire to end the conflict. However, the meetings of the full-dress delegates fell into an old familiar pattern of accusations, stalls and eventually sub-committees.

Twenty-three days ago the delegates began an inspired race for peace by stepping into the Supervision of the truce issue. They are still working on it.

Two sub-committees were formed; the exchange of prisoners of war and the supervision of the truce. Both have showed alternate signs of hope, but stalled hopelessly.

PLEASE PASS THIS PAPER ON.

The first page of the *Ridgerunner* for December 21, 1951, with Al's letter of December 21, 1951. The letter is not included in this book (The Huntington Library, MZ 730).

December 22, 1951

Dearest Joanne, My darling—

It's early afternoon and unus[u]ally warm. There's a breeze that blows right through the S-1 tent because both doors are open. There's a touch of laziness in

The second page of the *Ridgerunner* for December 21, 1951, with Al's letter of December 21, 1951. The letter is not included in this book (The Huntington Library, MZ 730).

the air caused by the summer-like weather. A plane is droning overhead like a big bee, and every low voice seems to be alone in the sleepiness of the afternoon …

We got the paper out this morning, but not without difficulties. We put the wrong title (Skylarkin') on the Chaplain's Corner, and didn't notice it until about 500 page 2 copies were run off. So we had to yank the stencil off the machine, use correction fluid on it and start all over on the headline. Naturally, since the stencil had been inked, it turned out lousy. But I hate to think of the consequences if the error hadn't been caught. It would have been saddle-up, PIO—back to the lines. That's the constant terror we live under. Oh, for the happy days of civilian journalism where all they can sue you for is criminal libel …

As it is, I may be going back to the lines anyhow. Or at least, giving up my sergeants' [sic] stripes for those of a Corporal. It happened this way. Our stove wasn't working so well, so we stole (Thomas stole) a carburerator [sic] out of the stove in the movie. Unfortunately, it was a brand new one and easily recognizable. They came to each tent looking for it and stopped at ours. I told them the thing had been there all the time, as did all the rest of the guys in the tent. But they knew better. They took it, after identifying it positively as the one stolen. Now there's talk about court martials for someone. I don't think there will be, but there's always the possibility. Troubles, troubles, troubles …

Today a surprise rotation came up when division said they had planes to fly to the UNited [sic] States, some men out of the 4th replacement draft, both officers and enlisted. So they left this moment, dumbfounded by the sudden[n]ess of the thing, but nonetheless happy. Wish they'd surprise me like that.

Glad you finally got my birthday card. Thought I had forgotten, huh? Not me. Love ya too much. So you think ice cream in the middle of winter isn't such a good idea? That's funny. The Corps does. We always get it when it snows. All the letters I received from Aunt Helen I answered. It's very possible that it could have gotten lost somewhere. I'll write her one anyhow. Tell Barbara and Allen that I hope very sincerely and with all my heart that I do not receive a card from them next easter [sic] unless it is addressed to MR. Al Martinez [several strikeovers] (how do you spell that last name?), 2023 Folsom St., San Francisco.

Me worry? Humph. I don't worry, you know that. But I'm glad you love me, and sometimes when I don't get a letter, I just get blue. Love, love, love you, darling. Love Cinthy.

All My Heart Forever and Forever,
Al (Boondocker and Camera)

MZ 731

December 23

Dearest Joanne, Darling—

With two left to go before Christmas, I'm working myself into a fizzle. We are putting out a four[-]page Ridgerunner for Christmas, and though it seems like an easy task, it has its complications—particularly when co-operation from various sources is lacking. I've had to direct almost everything that has been done, including the art. I've had to have the damn thing okayed by everyone from the PIO officer, to the adjudant [sic], to the Regimental Executive officer to the Regimental Commander. And, naturally, they all take their time about checking it. Now the problem has come up that we have no regular sized paper to run them off on. So we are using long paper which we have to cut with siccors [sic]—EIGHT THOUSAND PAPERS. Not that that's too bad, but we left a half-page open for the chaplain, and he hasn't even turned it in yet. Not that that's so bad, but we've got a story on a USO show that's supposed to be here Christmas that we can't run until the Colonel okays it. Not that that's so bad (there's power in repitition [sic]), but the Major wants the paper out tomorrow and we've only got two pages out, with those [a]forementioned articles holding up the other two. Not that—nuts. After all that we've got to staple the pages together and get 4000 copies of the four[-]page paper to the troops. What do I think about it all?

I love it.

It's finally the old dazzle of newspaper life and speed which I've missed so much since I left the Gater. It's the long nights and the short stories and the harsh words and the chain-smoking over a motionless typewriter. It's all of that and more, because when the paper comes out it's going to be a good paper, you can bet on that. And it's Martinez, right from the COLONEL's message on down! I loved every minute of it. Hon, there was a pause there. Lieut. Taylor, the Special Services officer, just called and said it was okay to run the USO story. So that means I can start on the other stencil. Have to stop now. If the Chaplain come[s] through now we'll have it knocked. HOW ABOUT THAT?

All My Love and
Kisses always
Al (Boondocker & Camera)
XXXXX's forever …

MZ 732

December 25, 1951
Christmas Day …

Dearest Joanne—

Merry Christmas, darling. Last night and all week we've been singing, "I'm Dreaming Of [sic] A [sic] White Christmas," and this morning we've got one. It's snowing, that soft, fluffy stuff from the sky, powdering the ground with a layer of white that grows thicker and thicker. It's a white, cold, crisp Korean Christmas.

Well, our special issue of the Ridgerunner came out on time and fairly successful. I was a little dissapointed [sic] when I first saw it, cuz I expected something better. But the result [i.e., reaction] from both the men and the brass was gratifying. The Major was very pleased, and when I took the paper to the Colonel last night about 11, he was overjoyed. I had been drinking all day (shots from all the officers and a bottle that Lieut. Guice presented to the PIO section) and was high when I took him the paper. Consequently, I had no hesitancy at all about talking to him. He said, "I'm very well pleased with the paper, Martinez, and it shows that a great deal of effort was put in on it." That's all I needed to start talking, and we had a nice chat. As I left, I hollered back at him "Merry Christmas," and he laughed and hollered back the same. The Major last night came in and started praising "his" PIO section, and saying how much better than division PIO we were. He then stated, "you don't have to bother about putting out a paper on the 26th—you deserve the rest." Lieut. Guice was equally overjoyed. And since 9 a.m. this morning, there isn't a paper left. Circulation, over 4000. I personally took the paper down to the H&S messhall [sic]. And 100 went while I was waiting in line for chow. So, you see, I am realatively [sic] happy.

Last night we did work like dogs. Had to cut with siccors [sic] 8000 papers and staple them them [sic] to make 4000 copies. We finished completely about 11:30 p.m.

I phone[d] Brunn and We[i]land up last night and wished them both a merry Christmas. Brunn came over this morning and we had a nice long talk. I sure like both of those guys. I'll be glad when we can all celebrate our homecoming party.

Paul Douglas,* Jan Sterling† and a cast of stars were at the 7th Marine Regiment this morning. Let me tell you a story about that. We know [sic] (Regimental PIO) knew they were coming by virtue of the Col. We spent weeks trying to get all the dope on it and finally did about three days ago. Then it turned out that we were the only ones who had any information on it. Division PIO called and got the dope, Division Special Services called, regimental special services called, as did everyone else. We scooped 'em. Wizard PIO (division) is eating right out of our hand now. We scooped 'em on the Bell[e]vue‡ story too, so what all the wire services carried was MY story from the Ridgerunner. They use[d] to send photographers out on their own. Now they check in with me first. Wine (Regimental) PIO is coming unto its own. And it's here to stay.

I was sure lonely last night, hon. Kept thinking about you and missing you and talking about you to everyone I was too busy to write then too high to make sense. That's why I put it off until today. I do hope you had a nice Christmas, sweetheart. I can't complain under the circumstances, but I wish I were home. You know, as high as I was last night, I was surprised to notice the looks and the attitudes of some of the guys. Downright bitterness. They'd make fun of any Christmas message, any Christmas program and any group singing carols. And actually they have nothing to be bitter about. If they were on the lines, or if they even were in a line company, then they'd have something to be bitter about. But they're not—they're poges.§ Doggone, I can't understand it. They've spent all their time in the rear, never been shot at, never had their right to live challenged, and yet they're bitter. Personally, I think a lot of it's an art—the glamorously-portrayed embittered Marine on Christmas Eve—you've read the plot. Being in Korea on Christmas is certainly nothing to shout about, but I believe in being thankful

---

*Paul Douglas (1907–1959) was an American actor who performed on Broadway and in films.
†Jan Sterling (1921–2004) was an American actress who performed on stage, film and television.
‡The Bellevue story is not identified.
§A poge or pogue is someone in the military who works in the rear, in a noncombat role. Among front-line Marines and soldiers, it was common to view such personnel in a negative light, or even with scorn.

for small blessings; such as being in reserve, being in the rear—and being alive. When I hear these jokers sound off, I keep thinking about little Pete Mamaril, Rogers, Seabloom ... and a lot of others [sic] guys that would have gladly given their right leg to protect their lives.

I think a lot of people are going to be surprised when I return home. If anybody should be teed off at the whole situation, I think I should be one of them. I've seen about as much if not more than any combat Marine in Korea today. I'm as emotional and as idealistic as any of them. But despite all that, I'm completely unembittered. I realize how much I do have to live for, and how far a little faith, guts and determination can bring a man. I hung on a long time when things were getting me down, because I had a picture of you and Cinthy in my mind that even the physical proximities that faced me couldn't break. And because of that force, I lived out each day, forced myself to listen, to stay awake, to move when every muscle in my body hurt me. And that little perserverance [sic] paid off in the long run.

By the time you get this letter it will be New Years, Joanne. Not like the one last year. We're not together, going to the show, drinking a Tom Collins in Richmond. But at least there is certainty in this year and we have a little more to look forward to. Last year we had Korea to look forward to, and we knew what was coming. Now we have my coming home to look forward to, and it's a little more pleasant prospect. Also, we have Cinthy to raise and I have seeing her ahead of me, I said on January 1st. 1951, that I had a feeling it was going to be a good year. And who can deny it, but the dead of Korea, that personally I have progressed some, froma [sic] childhood to a manhood. Of those who died, nothing very significant can be said. Of those who will die, all we can do is pray.

It's a new year, darling, a fine, clean, new year despite all. We have much to look ahead too [sic] and nothing can swerve our determination in planning. When our job is done here, and the prospect of a better life for our children is ahead, then we can die and not regret it. But until then, we have a definite purpose in life. Had the generations before us done a better job, then we could have spent our life time [sic] really living an enjoyable life. But as it stands, we have to correct their mistakes. And though we have to fret a little, when you stop to think that it may keep our pretty little Cinthy happy in years to come, it's worth the effort.

Happy New Year, to you and Cinthy, darling. Keep your hope up and your dreams alive.

> All My Heart and Love
> And Faithfulness for the
> New Year and for the years
> to come ...
>   Al (Boondocker and Camera)

I love you both!
XXXXXXXX's [sic] Christmas
& New Years kisses.

MZ 733

January 13 1952

Dearest Joanne, My darling—

It's almost midnight and the ingenuity of the Marine Corps has mellowed me to a nice warm state. With powdered milk, powdered eggs, vanilla tablets and water (plus a dash of whisky) we had egg nog [sic]. It was really good. We didn't have enough of anything for any of us to get drunk or even high—so there's no worry on that score. We just had enough to feel, well, mellow. We sang the rest of the evening away until now the fellows are going to sleep one by one, the radio is playing low and here I am and there you are—away, in a sense, but together.

The infernal bend of the spotlights about a mile to our rear have [sic] formed an arc of the regimental CP and is glistening on the always-reflective snow. Artillery rocks the area occasionally with a blast about every five minutes—then really slams away with Time On Target, with every big gun in the area sending its shells miles into enemy area. But even so, despite the noisey [sic] silence of the spots, and the tremors of artillery, there's a funny kind of peace in the air—a quietness which the infantry men would call a dangerous noise.

Today packages came in from Portland, Oregon, with clothes for the Korean kids. Really some nice stuff. More are destined to come in—many more I'm afraid. I got a bathrob[e], asweatshirt [sic] and a little black hat out of the deal. No, I'm not robbing the clothes off the Korean kids' backs—just a little something to add color to an otherwise dull existence.

You know, honey, I'm homesick again. As usual[,] I suppose. Nothing new to either one of us. Sometimes I get moreso [sic] than othertimes [sic] and that's tonight. Could be the egg nog [sic], but I doubt it. Could be the bright moon and the stars. That's probably part of it. I think—I know—that it's because I love you and want to be with you. I'm not especially feeling sorry for myself, nor am I bitter. I just feel the way I do, and I'm not trying to talk myself out of it. I'd rather face it and accept it and feel a little lonely. Because that's when I picture and think of you the best and remember all the details of our days together—right from the Art Blum* era on down—or up. I can remember the first day we rode on the streetcar together to the Polk Gulch† Times; how I waited for you when you were in buying that yellow summer dress; how you bought my coffee; how I told you I didn't want to have anything to do with you; how mad you got when I said that; how we parted.... And how suddenly I knew that I loved you very much and there wasn't a darn thing I could do about it. I like to remember those things here in Korea even though it makes me miss you so awfully—and kind of hurts me to be away.... But if I can't face a beautiful memory, then what can I face? It all adds up ... when you're away you're away and there's nothing you can do[.]

        The Lights Are Out Darling and
        I'm typing in the dark. So goodnight,
          my precious [sic], goodnight....   I Love you.... Al

---

*Art Blum (d. 2003) was known as the "king of public relations" in San Francisco, representing a wide variety of clients.

†Polk Gulch is the area around part of Polk Street in San Francisco. The name stems from an old stream under the street. It was the city's primary gay area for about thirty years beginning in the 1950s.

Three. Cpl. Al Martinez, Combat Correspondent.... How About That!

January 14 (the next day)

Hi darling!

Something is in the wind. And it's good. It all started out yesterday when a Master Sergeant rushed in and said the General was here and wanted some papers so the Colonel could show him. So we sent the paper. This general is the one who took over from General Thomas as Commander of the 1st Mar Div. He's an old PIO man and really hot to go for that aspect. Anyhow, he liked the set-up we have on our Regimental level. That was the last I heard of it until last night. Then a Master Sgt. (the NCO in charge of division PIO) came out here[,] asked for me and wanted to know about our set-up, etc. He was the guy who usually gives us a bad time and was reluctant to accept us as an official PIO set-up. Well, quite suddenly he has taken the time to visit me, talk to me, do favors for us and compliment us on the paper, etc. Then today comes the clincher. The new Lieut. who took O'Leary's place came out PLUS (now get this) a Stars and Stripes Correspondent, two radio correspondents and a Division PIO man. Where do they go? Right to me. Before, Division use[d] to take it upon themselves not to bother to contact us at all when they were in the area or when they wanted a story—consequentely [sic] they would have missed out on a lot of good stuff had it not been for us. But today they introduced themselves, asked for our help and did a lot of talking with us. I got a good deal off my chest in relation to the Regimental-Division PIO set-up. In the first place, I have never thought much of Division PIO. They've got a bunch of individualists who call themselves combat correspondents and who couldn't write a story to save them. They have no more perception of a story or an angle than Toni Robinson. They've refused to co-operate with us in the past and it's ired me no end. But instead of giving them a bad time, I just ignored them. Also, I mentioned the fact that I didn't think a man was qualified to be a combat correspondent unless he actually had an insight on what was going on in the minds of those guys who were doing the combating—namely the infantry. And I personally don't feel that a man can know what's going on unless he's actually been there. I take nothing away from a good correspondent who can be up there and really try to write what this war is like from the infantryman's point of view or at least from a good objective viewpoint. These guys from division don't seem to be able to do either. Anyhow, I told him all that and the amazing part of it was that he agreed with me. So now they've promised all co-operation they can possibly give, contact when their correspondents are in the area, and an eventual build-up of regimental PIO. And in return, we'll send in to them for publicity purposes all stories we think rate down-town publication. It's a good set-up, and the Lieutenant means what he says, I'm sure. I like the sudden change, and I think I can trace it to this: the general gave somebody the word that Regimental PIO is a wonderful thing when it's handled properly, and I think I'm handling it as well as anyone could. Things are clicking: Division offered to take all three of us back there to work; they want a Ridgerunner every day; they're thinking of putting out a paper such as we have (which is the only one in the first Mar Div) on a division level to compete with Stars and Stripes. As I said, I like what's happening. I've waited for this day for a long time—ever since O'Leary tried to look down on me because I didn't talk loud or try to act like the typical newspaperman. It's not revenge, but proof—proof to me that all good newspapermen don't have to be back-slappers or try to impress everyone with their personalities. We three here at PIO have donea [sic] good job, and I don't think anyone will deny that. The general has convinced the Divvy boys that they'd better notice it. Regimental PIO is going to build-up [sic] until each Regiment has one, and Division (that far-away thing) is passe [sic]. Wathc [sic] it. We've got the general on our side along with a nice guy who's head of division PIO. Now maybe the Marine Corps in Korea can get they [sic] publicity it deserves without personality holding the whole set-up back.

Man, that's a long paragraph! But it really rates it. It's accomplishment, hon, way over here in Korea. I'm proud of the whole thing. It lifts my spirit some to think that all this time isn't going to be wasted.

Tonight is a beautiful night despite all the world can do to it. Nature has done her best to give us occasionally a full moon, clear stars and a deep purple sky. The spotlights still try to penetrate it, the artillery blasts away at it. But if you can clothes [sic] your ears and eyes for a few moments to all that, you get a beautiful peace from just looking at such far-away beauty and contentment. It's wonderful, really.

About five o'clock this morning, 10 Chinese artillery rounds whined over the CP and crashed into the valley about 2000 yards away. I woke up more by instinct than anything else [sic] when I heard the first round come in. Richardson woke up too. We put on our clothes and waited. More came over, but all far enough away so they didn't worry us. We both went back to sleep eventually when friendly counter battery fire opened up in terrifying barrages. I sometimes wonder how the Chinese figure it's worth it to throw 10 rounds at us and catch 10 hundred in return. But I guess they know what they're doing.

It's been a busy, busy day and there were many foul-ups on the Ridgerunner. Radio was foulded [sic] up, mistakes galore, wrong date on today's paper, etc. But there are those days, and I'm sure that things will smooth out.

Darling, I love you and miss you with all my heart. I got the book today and have already started reading it—you know Dr. Spock's book on child care. I like it. Had to take no end of ribbing though. Give my love to our awful sweet little baby and tell her I love her loads ...

                  All My Heart And Love Forever
                  And Forever ... to wife and daughter ...
                  Al (and Boondocker)
                  XXXXXXXXXXXXXXXXX's
                      I love you—
                I forgot to enclose
                      these articles
                      I told you
                      about a
                      couple days ago [no enclosure present]

MZ 760

THREE. Cpl. Al Martinez, Combat Correspondent.... How About That!

January 20, 1952

(The first part of this letter is kinda gloomy, but read on. It gets happier. Love you—Al!)

Dearest Joanne, My darling—

I'm in a funny mood tonight, a crusading mood, a hurt mood. Something has built up in my mind that just won't quit—that has made me maddeningly restless, almost panicky. It's nothing physical, nothing immediate. Just a vague, confusing feeling that bothers me and bothers me. I just finished reading "Nightmare Alley."* You probably remember the picture a few years back. It's penetrating and ironic, sharpening a funny life to pin-point reallity [sic], and focusing injustice into a prism of light that doesn't make sense, that doesn't add up. All the social geometry of it is out of whack, and it seems to me that this whole damn world is out of whack and somebody's got to do something about it. You? Me? I don't know. But somebody, anybody, has got to change things for our children and a lot of other children.

I don't [know] what's the matter with me, Joanne. I guess the book had something to do with it. And a lot of other things. I'm a little tired of a lot of things. Korea, war, artillery, mud, snow—everything over here. I can see it clearly, all of it, war very much alive, very real, very physical. Why can't others see it? What's the matter with the world and why? What's the matter with me tonight?

The other day we got a clipping from one of Ayer's pen pals. Remember I told you that we wrote a letter to the Cinncinati [sic] Enquirer saying one of our buddies (ayers [sic]) wasn't getting enough mail. He didn't know about it. When he got all the letters he decided to write one woman and tell her it was all a big joke. She wrote back with disdain and anger, "I was shocked and hurt to find out ... why are you trying to make fools out of us?" Do you get that, Joanne? She was shocked and hurt. Shocked and hurt because because [sic] we were tired of sitting around and wrote a letter, and at the time—even now—the gesture seemed innocent enough to everyone concerned in relation to some of the things that transpire in a Korean war. But she was shocked and hurt because she felt someone had tried to fool her. Shocked and hurt because her vanity was altered a little and she discovered the solvent fact that somebody doesn't give a damn whether she writes or not. I wonder if she'd be shocked and hurt if she knew that Pete Mamaril was killed by a direct artillery hit and there wasn't enough of him left to scrape up? I wonder if she'd be shocked and hurt if she'd have seen a lot of nice guys die screaming? I wonder how many people who are shocked and hurt by a prank from Korea would be shocked and hurt by an incoming round of artillery that landed in front of you—a dud. And squeezed the breath out of you and stopped your heart and your life for a moment when you thought of what could have happened? Taking advantage of her? Yeah, that's funny. She's sitting back there not giving a damn what's going on in Korea, trying to fatten her ego by getting an answer from a Marine,

---

Nightmare Alley is a 1946 novel by William Lindsay Gresham. A film adaptation in 1947 starred Tyrone Power and Joan Blondell. The story concerns a con man who performs in a second-rate carnival and pursues a variety of scummy cons and tricks.

making her think she's helped the war effort, but she wants to know why we're taking advantage of her. I had a wounded buddy ask me the same thing only differently. All he said was "why?" and that took all the life he had to say it with. A lot of guys over here are wondering why, Joanne,—why they have to be here, why there has [sic] to be wars, why, why, why—a thousand times a day, a thousand questions—but no one seems to answer, to care, or to realize. But this woman, 7000 miles into the fog, is asking us why we had to make fools of them, the pomp and the living.... I'm just wondering why they can't let us live—just live.

I suppose this letter makes me sound dogmatic, bitter, frustrated. I'm none of those. I'm trying to answer a question to myself that has faced me so many times, and I want you to help me answer it. I've never been much of a student all of my life. If I have the potentialites [sic], I've not always employed them. I know it, I'm not kidding myself. But as far back as I can remember, I've studied: people, things, events. And I've tried to add them up, to put them together like a jig-saw puzzle, in more than just the substance of mathematics, or common reasoning, or two-and-two-makes four. I've tried to understand them, life, and make sense of it. I haven't. The questioned [sic] I've always asked myself and so many others is the great big "WHY?" Why does there have to be this when there could be this? Why are men different, what is the factor that makes them that way? Why is there war when with the flick of a brain cell there could be peace—hate, love, you can word the thing anyway [sic] you want. Am I a fool for asking? Will anyone ever find out? Am I just another somebody, without hope or future, with a restlessness that just asks "why?" I wonder and think all the time, Joanne, and it doesn't show up. I just think it, all of it, everything, and if I attempt to answer something it frustrates me, because I know I can't and it makes me mad to see someone else say he has the answer[,] the only answer, when I know he nor nobody else has. So I play their game, and I don't want to play it. I want to say I Don't Know, but I want everyone else to say it too. Because if they don't and I do, I'll be trampled under the natural acceptance of the cynic, cast out for not knowing and not pretending to know, called stupid and perhaps even insane, and that will be that and nobody will ever know, not even me ...

What am I trying to say that I can't say, darling? That I'm dissapointed [sic] in the world, that I feel insecure, that I want everyone to be honest and that I want everyone to be an idealist and say if it says the freedom of the press it is the freedom of the press and if everyone says there will be no more war there will be no more war? Is that what I want, Joanne? Or am I just confused tonight and pouring myself out because I'm so uncertain of so many things?

The outside right now, like life, is so inconsistent. It's snowing, softly, peacefully—not harshly. The clouds are moving over the face of the stars, hiding them, showing them, concealing and revealing in a game which is useful and beautiful. Then artillery is blasting, harshly, loudly, angrily, spouting flame from the muzzle and lighting up the valley in a brief, staring flash that leaves an impression in the sky that twists a moment a [i.e., and?] pulls itself even out of your mind's eye. And the purr of the generator motor is low and soft, lending itself to the contrast of war, with its peace and silent, sonorous contentment. But the spotlight is glaring, bending, rising[,] falling across an empty circumference in the sky, and it doesn't scare you from its source, but if you know where it's going then you feel its fear. Because the fear is here, very plain, very consistent with war and with artillery, out of place with the sky and the generator purr, with me and you and Cinthy and a lot of other kids in the hills tonight who are afraid and cold and who see the spotlight and just because of it they feel even more afraid, because they know what that enormous, unblinking eye is looking for out ther[e] in the shadows. And that makes them afraid, and they can't imagine what it's like to die.

Darling I love you and that matters a lot to me, and don't let this or any other letter I write upset you. Too often I become a slave to my own obsession, and if my sense of justice isn't the same as a lot of other people's, that's nobody's fault. Not even mine. I know, a lot of times I've considered some pretty important things to us as unimportant. Maybe my mind works on a larger scale, in wider dimensions, in concentric circles which encompasses [sic] the world and life in one great big sweep and I get blind to a lot of little things. I'm not trying to say I'm completely ignorant to details—you know better. But sometimes I overlook them, not always, but sometimes. I've just got a lot of [word omitted] to get off my chest, honey, and you're the only one who'll listen to me and not think I'm psycho. You know I'm sincere and I want you to know it. I've got a great many ideas and ideals, Joanne, and only now I'm beginning to introspect [sic] a little and understand them. Some of them I can't pin-point, because they're to[o] subjective, too reactional. Maybe I was just born 500 years too soon, and convention won't let my own mind accept their reallity [sic] or presence. I want to fight, Joanne, but not with guns or fists. I want to step into the crowd of the world and make them listen to me, and I want them to understand what they're thinking, because I'm going to tell them and they're going to settle down and not want to [word omitted] war anymore [sic], but move ahead, in vaste [sic] waves, progress that is so visible, like a clock, that if you watch it close enough and long enough you can see it move. Silly illusions, huh? I always did have a fantastic imagination. That's what everyone tells me, and instead of argueing [sic] myself into a frenzy against a piece of stone, I accept it and laugh with them. Maybe that's why I decided to be a writer, so when they said "you have a fantastic imagination" I could say, "yeah, that's why I can write." But I know I'm lying to myself there, and I don't like it. Oh, I love writing, don't get me wrong there. I've grown to love it more and more as a means of expression, but more than that because of the usefullness [sic] in it. I've come to understand it and that's important. Like a baby, like Cinthy. You can't do anything for her or make her grow or make her become stable and mature unless you understand and love her. You try to understand a baby for a long time, then unconsciously one day you do and you understand her more and more until it becomes a conscious, beautiful thing. That's the way with writing. Only now, I'm consciously beginning to understand it.

I guess you'll find a lot of mis[s]pelled, mistyped words in this letter but at the moment that's not too important. It won't wreck the world. Now watch some cynic leap up and say, "let me quote from history because I'm smart and like to call people down how a mis[s]pelled word one day almost wrecked an empire ..."

and he'll go on and on with his tongue wagging and his eyeballs growing bigger … while a couple of poor honest jerks, gullible as we are, sit in a foxhole and say he's right, he's right, he's right … now we know why we live and die. Then they die, and if they could speak after that, none of the poor dopes could answer as to why they died. They just listened but they didn't understand. That's propaganda …

I'm a little more relaxed now, honey, so you can smile your pretty smile and stop worrying about me. Cuz I know you are worrying. For awhile [sic] there I was all tight inside, and I was mad and didn't know at what. I felt like I said I did—so unable to answer all the questions inside me. I guess I have to blow off steam like this occasionally so I can take advantage of my new-found patience. This letter will probably come as a surprise, because it's been a long time since I've blown off steam or cried on your shoulder. I love you, Joanne, and I love our little Cinthy. I want things to be right for both of you and for the rest of the world. Sometimes events get a little hard to tolerate and I get keyed up trying to act civilized. I've past [sic] the stage of losing my temper. Now I just sit donw [sic] and pound a typewriter until the end of my fingers hurt, my arms get cramped and I relax. Sound[s] horrible, doesn't it? It's not. When Rich gets lonely, blue and hurt, he sits down and frantically draws a picture of his wife, the girl he loves and who left him, for hours and hours. Then when he's finished, the mood is past and he throws the picture away. Me? I pound a typewriter, only I send what I pound out to you—so you understand me better and love me anyway for what I am and can be.

What I described as the inconsistency of the outside is true. It really is inconsistency if you watch and listen. As for the woman who sent the letter—that's just one of those things. I really wasn't too upset about that. I was just upset about something tonight and that fit into the scheme of my mood. She also demanded an explanation. I've been half-way tempted to write her an explanation that would make her hair stand on end and make her see Korea so plainly that she'd see the kids who look too old staring her in the face. But then I decided against answering her at all. Let somebody else do it who doesn't fancy himself a martyr and who is less apt to get carried away than I. I've got enough worries without trying to smooth out the hurt ego of somebody so far away. But I love the public just the same and I love people. We don't see eye to eye all the time, but we like each other. Really.

The tent is real quiet now. Two of the fellows are writing and the others are lying wrapped up in their sleeping bags, half asleep or just resting. I've been typing steadily for more than an hour now, and the guys look at me once in awhile [sic] and remark as to what I'm doing or how I can go for so long. I wish I knew. If they could read the letter they'd add to the how-can-you-go-so-long, "and say nothing?"

You may be interested in the scuttlebut[t] which is currently circulating around here: I will leave Korea in February. It's become very strong for some reason, and I don't know why. Here's all of it: we are to go into Army reserve (the whole division) sometime in the middle of February; three replacement drafts will arrive in Korea, one the first of February, one the middle of February, one the end of February; up to the 8th draft will leave Korea by the end of February;

the 11th draft will be out by the end of April. Oh, guys say they heard this from the Colonel on down. It's all rumor, all scuttlebut[t]. I don't know if it's ture [*sic*], I have no basis for condemning or condoning it. I hope it's true, but I have not [*sic*] illusions. Remember—IT'S ALL RUMOR. Don't get your hopes up until I'm there in person, holding you close in my arms and telling you I'll never leave you again—and meaning it.

I think I'll make some bullion [*sic*] soup before I go to bed. Wonderful stuff, that bullion [*sic*]—I'd have never touched it in civilian life. But now it has a calming effect on me. Besides, it's the only thing we have to eat beside hard chocolate candy, and I'm getting a little tired of that.

Tonight I had a little run-in with 2nd Lieutenant Guice. He got word from the Col. that a March of Dimes article had to go in tomorrow's paper—which we put out tonight. The paper was all finished and they had started to run the stencils off. I got a little sore and asked him why it had to go in tomorrow's paper. There is no reason. The Col. just said so, and Guice[,] who is afraid of his own shadow, didn't have guts enough to tell him the paper was already finished. If he had, I have no doubt whatsoever that the Col. would have said, "then let it wait." But now, a boot second Looey who doesn't know his hole from a thing-in-the-ground, let the eagles shine in his eyes and he faded. I asked to talk to the Col. myself but he wouldn't let me. So the whole thing is being done over, but Hopkins is doing it. I'm a little fed-up with second lieutenants who try to tell me about Korea and my job when I've done both longer than he has. I'm not sore anymore [*sic*]. I just wish we had a PIO officer with a little more back-bone. It would help tremendously. As it is, I don't respect Gucie [*sic*]. To me he's the same as if he were a private and I still a sergeant.

Ever think I'd last this long? Fooled you, didn't I, cutie? You'd be surprised how much I have to say when I get started. On second thought, I guess you wouldn't be. You've heard me talk and seen me write too often. I love you, Muggins. Or, as I say when I hit the wrong keys, O ;pbr upi. ,ihhomd/ Cute, hey?

Well, the paper is out. We have the March of Dimes article in as you can see. [No enclosure present.] We had to transpose, use double stencils and everything else. But we did it. Did Guice appreciate it? No. Over the story there was a blank space. So he says, "gee, if there was only the one word 'GIVE' over the story it would make the Colonel happy." He wanted us to do the whole damn thing over again for the one word GIVE. It's exasperating. But we fouled [i.e., fooled] him. We WROTE the word "give" in ink on the paper. He was baffled how we ran off another stencil so fast. If he finds out, I don't care. Let him chew my behind. As I've began [*sic*] to philosophize, I've got lots of behind and he certainly can't chew it all off. It's been chewed off by bigger and better men than he. The paper I am sending you is circled in pencil where the word GIVE is written in for the Col, and Guice, and the Capt. etc. They say there have been many things tried in the Corps to fool the system. They also say that you can't buck city hall. Let it go on record as saying that PIO fooled the system so far and bucked city hall successful[l]y Tomorrow? We'll cross that bridge when we come to it. When Gucie's [*sic*] runner comes up and says the Lieut. wants to see me, I'll know what it's about. But then he can go ahead and chew. Like I said, there's plenty for all the 2nd Looeys in the Corps. LET THE GOOD TIMES ROLL!

Well, honey, after five pages, I feel much better, and can look back on tonight with typical Martinez humor. "Just one of those things," I can blandly say, and quote a little of Ogden Nash just to keep me on my toes. These guys around here don't know the difference. I could recite Nash's poem about The World's Most Prominent Bastards, and as long as I held a straight face, quivered occasionally, and pronounced the as "thy," they'd think it was Shakespeare. It's funny living, isn't it, hon? And I suppose it takes people like me to keep the world going 'round. The only trouble is, I wish I weren't so concscious [sic] of the world going around. Makes me dizzy ...

>All My Heart And Love
>Forever and Forever.
>   Al (and Boondocker)
>   XXXXXXXX's [sic] for the wife and
>   daughter I love forever ...
>I love you, darling!
>Honestly, I feel happier
>just writing to you!

MZ 766

February 1, 1952

Dearest Joanne, My Darling –

I just got off guard and feel like writing again because I spent time out there in the cold, cold night thinking of you. Do you realize, honey, that if the persistent rumor is true that I may be leaving Korea in one month? Do you realize that I may be home in less than two months, 8 weeks, 60 days? Is it as hard for you to realize as it is for me? I can't believe that after almost a year away from you I may be seeing you again. It's, it's just too hard to grasp. Geeee. Three months at the most. Darling, I'm goint [sic] to be home—home in San Francisco where the fog grows wild and the wind blows free through the Golden Gate from the Pacific Ocean. Home to you, my daughter and my city ...

As soon as I got off guard, the guys had something to show me: a picture story of San Francisco in Look Magazine called, "Why I Like San Francisco." Made me homesick.

Honey, I'd like to have you take another look at my diary through me. This page which I'm writing for you is one I've copied out of my diary. I've got about six typewritten pages from the diary. I'm going to try to retype it all in my spare time. Here's the page, hon. A part of Operation Pursuit. I think you can take it now:

"TUESDAY, JUNE 19: Moved toward the hard-to-take Objective 10. Easy Co. moved foreward [sic]. We waited. Mortars came in, killing one and wounding four. I helped carry the KIA (Killed In Action) down the hill, the heavy, lifeless

Three. Cpl. Al Martinez, Combat Correspondent.... How About That! 189

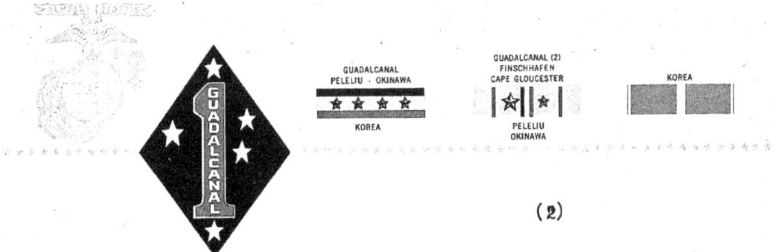

Al Martinez's drawings on the second page of his letter dated January 25, 1952. Boondocker, Al's toy turtle, wears his Purple Heart ribbon. The letter is not included in this book (The Huntington Library, MZ 772, p. 2). See the letter of November 20, 1951 (MZ 702) for Al's account of Boondocker earning the Purple Heart.

body. A young guy. About 23. I understand he liked to jitterbug. We waited long, expectant hours. The word came back, 'Marines on 10.' We could hear firing and grenades. Someone hollered 'corpsman' more than once—the battle-cry of the Seventh Marines ...

"We moved on 10 and secured it—a steep bluff with high rocky nose that we had to climb on our hands and knees. It has had 10 air strikes on it and artillery has pounded it for days. The trees are shrapnel cut and twisted at grutesque [sic] angles. The ground is charred and burned out. Shell craters are everywhere, as are the napalmed, fire-burned bodies of the enemy, with charred hands twisted into a half-closed death grip. The 3rd Bn. sent back these fighting words from across the valley on Objective 11: "We will take it if it takes us all night." They took it.

Mortars and artillery screamed over the bare ridge all night, killing the men set up below us in a small valley—our weapons co. We could do nothing but watch them die. Ever watch a man die? I have. Slow and careful, purposely and methodically until his breath flowed out with his blood and his heart stopped beating. I watched them die tonight.

God, I watched them die ...

Not pretty, honey. Not what a lot of the people would like to believe about the Korean skirmish. But real. As real as I saw and observed it, as I lived and thought it with my own eyes and thoughts. I think you believe me, darling. You know I'm a reporter. You know I can write very easily what I see. And I have.

I'm sending you three Ridgerunners [no enclosures present] for the days I've missed, including today's. I think I'll close now, baby, and write some more out of my diary. Love you, darling. With all my heart. Cinthy too.

All My Heart And Love
Forever and Forever ...
Al (and Boondocker)
I love you!

"Ronny Replacement," drawn by Al Martinez, in his letter dated January 25, 1952. The letter is not included in this book (The Huntington Library, MZ 772, p. 3).

MZ 777

THREE. *Cpl. Al Martinez, Combat Correspondent.... How About That!*

February 3, 1952
(same evening, about
two hours later)

Dearest Joanne—

A woman wanted to know how she could keep from getting pregnant all the Time [*sic*], so she went to see the doctor. "Do 10 pushups," the doctor advised, "in the evening." The woman hesitated, then blushed, asking, "before or after?" The doctor replied, "instead of."

One of the jokes I heard a little while ago which I thought was kinda cute, and which you could tell your friends. The other ones that were told, you can well imagine. Strictly MC jokes—definitely not for mixed crowds. Anyhow, I feel a little better now, so I thought I'd write more. Okay, sweetie?

You ever wonder how it feels to a man who stands watch 50 per cent of the night in a foxhole on the front lines? Wonder what he thinks about? It's strange, you know, sitting next to a sleeping buddy in a hole, looking out there until your eyes are strained and you're bored[,] disgusted, scared and tired. I thought I'd let you know how it feels a little more descriptively. I'll write it for you now ...

A foxhole isn't very deep. It's inadequate actually. But in it, you feel the strength of your own protection and the power of your defense. At night you have to depend on it. At night you can live in it, or you can die in it. You and one other person, protected from a terrible outside vengeance by a dirt parapet, 36 inches of earth, mounded in front of your front to stop a .30 calibur [*sic*]. At night you settle into it, one person awake, one asleep—you settle into it, feel the hard metal of your M-1, put your hand grenades in place, your helmet where you can reach it, and sink down into the close protection of the earth all around you ...

The night settles early in September. Slowly, but early. It creeps down over the facing rid[g]elines from the west, then closes in from your northern front, over the east, in back of you to the south; down over the skyline, the tree-tops, the valleys. It doesn't come quickly. It's there all the time, night in the air, but intermingled with a day that cheats you out of extra sleep. Day and night, in a geometry of movement and soft light. You watch the day change into twilight and the twilight into evening and the evening into another black, reproachful night. The men on your hill are silent. The camouflage of darkness is all-concealing. The young night passes slowly, but there is a long, [*sic*] period of quietness which doesn't disturb you. Then as your two[-]hour watch goes by, the noises begin—the snapping of a twig, the night pattern of mortar fire in the valley below you, the rustle of the wind through dead leaves, the scurrying of a chip munk [*sic*]. You stare intently into the shadows. Listen. A movement, a sound. You touch your grenades again, slide the safety of rifle forward.

Then it's time to go off watch, so you wake your buddy, a new replacement, wait until he sits up in the hole, wait until he's wide awake. You get into your bag, put your rifle down (where you can reach it), and settle back against the soft earth. For a long part of your two-hours sleeping time you lie awake, thinking and watching the new man stare straight ahead for a long time. His eyes droop, and you kick him in your sleeping bag. He starts then shakes his head. You sit up, pull him close to you by his jacket front and stare him hard in the face. "Tired of living, buddy?" you ask him. He shakes his head. You release him. "Stay awake then." For awhile [*sic*] you watch his unmoving body sitting on the side of the foxhole until it blends in the shadows. Sometimes he leans forward, watching or listening. You watch him until you feel he's awake, then nudge him again in soft confidence. "Don't be afraid to wake me up for anything," you whisper. You start to roll over on your side, then whisper back, "use grenades if you see anything …"

Two hours later he's shaking you. "Time for your watch."

You look at him angrily for a moment, then sit up suddenly reaching for your rifle automatically. Another second goes by before you realize that it's not trouble, just another two-hour watch. You try to clear your head and shake the sleep out of your eyes, wondering if the boy is cheating you out of sleep by setting his watch forward. But all this goes through your mind quickly as you get up. The night is colder now, and you watch the new man get in his sake [i.e., sack] with envy. You pull your jacket up close to your ears. Then as you settle donw [*sic*] on the edge of the foxhole the sharp chatter of an automatic weapon spins you off the edge of the hole and down into it. You crouch there, the safety off your rifle, breathing hard, staring to the distance where the shot came from. The new man is struggling desperately to get out of the sack, making too much noise. You slap a hard grip on his shoulder that hurts him. He understands and stops struggling, rising quietly instead to a sitting position beside you, his rifle in his hand. You point to the back of the hole, and he understands and faces that way, watching the ridgeline for the enemy straggler, the line-crosser.

The silence wears on. You feel the presence of others in foxholes next to you, all wide awake, looking down the same valley, testing the optical substance of a shadow or a tree that seemed to move. There are no more shots. In the distance, artillery opens up. They whish over your head and crash into the valley in front of you, probing the valley for Gooks, slamming in the midst of whatever is there, lighting the night in an orange ball that errupts [*sic*] with a thick crash and sharpness, then dies a quick death into silence. The pattern fire of artillery stops, then 81 mortars sends [*sic*] flares over the hills. The light of the last flare is barely receding, and you see it. A human form, 30 feet to your front, crouching behind a bush, looking up at you, staring with deadly eyes that says [*sic*] you're going to get it next. The new man doesn't see it, but as you duck quickly into the hole, he does too. A maddening moment passes while you feel the parapet in the dark for a hand grenade. Your hand closes about it, and you carress [*sic*] the hard, pocked lead—but only for a moment. Your other hand is groping for the pin. It comes out, and only a spoon clamped to the grenade, holding it from exploding. Then you throw it. A snap in the air, a pin-point of light as the primer strikes the fuse chain. You look over the edge of your hole for a second in time and the human form is still there. Four seconds later, the grenade explodes in a quick furry [*sic*], throwing shrapnel whining over the top of your head. You look cautiously over the top of the foxhole. There's nothing there now, and you wonder if there ever was. There is no sound then. Only a stillness that seems to laugh at you, and say there never was anything there. But you know better. And because you know better, you smile at the new man and squeeze his shoulder. "Get some sleep," you say. He hesitiates [sic] for a moment, ready to argue and tell you it's his turn for the watch. But he doesn't. He lays his rifle donw [sic] next to him and slips into his sleeping bag. He lays for a moment, but his confidence is high, his eyes are heavy. It isn't long before he's breathing deeper, and you're alone again.

Artillery opens another barrage.

Two more watches pass. There are shots fired, but you hear no return fire. At 4 a.m., you wake up and decide you'll take the watch until dawn. Your eyes burn, your head aches from lack of sleep. It isn't your watch, but you know the enemy too well, and the hour of banzai is at hand. You'd rather be awake, than have to have a new man face it. This time he doesn't argue. His eyes are heavy too. He's asleep quickly, looking up at you once, faintly smiling his thanks. You smile back at him without saying a word. He's alright, you think, and you're glad he's part of your fire team. And you decide right there you're going to take care of him.

The morning wears on colder, and the blackness gets blacker. A wind starts up and you curse it, watching the sky all the time for the faint light that says you've lived for another day. You laugh to yourself—"They'll never catch me asleep," you think, remembering the ones they had caught in a sleeping bag, and how they looked.... You shiver. It's cold, too cold. And it's quiet, too quiet.

For a moment you think the hollering is a part of your mind. Then it breaks into sharp clarity, contrasting hard against the silence, and you remember thinking before you spin down into a crouch again, that they actually did holler Banzai! The hollering grew [sic] louder, and the new man is up, by you again, fear grabbing wildly at him. "They're quite aways [sic] away," he pants half-reassuringly to himself. "No." you say. He knows in a minute. The hollering is still going on across the valley, or maybe down in the valley, it's hard to tell.... But the crashing of the grenades and the high-curved pitch of the a [sic] Gook gun is right in front of you, next to you, behind you, in an instant of confusion that finds grenades flying from your hand, the rounds leaping from the new man's rifle in a crack that defeans [sic] you and makes you wince ... in timeless periods that hears [sic] the light machine guns open up, the M-1 smash into human flesh, the screams, the crashing in the shrubbery below you, the empty clip flying out of a rifle, the burp gun again ...

You're only vaguely aware of thinking "it was almost morning, we were almost safe ..." Mortars cough in back of you, arc high above the earth, then crash into the valley, thundering in the sharp air, hurling back whatever enemy might be coming up behind the first wave. Artillery enters the fight and far, far behind you roars in a constant barrage for minutes that seem like hours. Seconds later they land, into the valley again, and you wonder why they mess with the damn valley when the gooks are up there, right next to you.... The confusion grows, and the .30 caliber shells streak in the early morning darkness, kicking aside the brush and the twigs ... machine guns are talking down the burp buns with their superior, heavy stutter.... For a moment you ease up on your trigger ... everyone else does at the same minute ... the enemy that you never saw, never really heard, doesn't fire back. And in the infinite moment of silence that follows, you know you've beaten him back, you know his dead are out there and you'll find them in the morning. The infinite silence grows deeper …

Then, as an afterthought, a dying voice calls feebly, "Corpsman …"

You look at the new man. He's had his babtism [sic] of fire a rough way to get it, but at least he's alive. You smile a little to yourself as you watch him staring wild-eyed, almost eagerly down in front of you, fingering his rifle nervously, breathing fast. You touch his shoulder only lightly. His head snaps to you, and his rifle almost comes up. Then he looks at you, like he wants to ask you it [sic] everything is alright, and lowers his rifles [sic]. He's young, you think. Too young. "It's okay now," you say. They're gone. "Hit the rack," you say. This time he looks at you incredulously. You order this time: "hit the rack!" He knows better than to argue. In his sleeping bag, he lays his rifle down gently. He twists for awhile [sic], touches his rifle again, then lies still. You know that no matter how afraid a man might be, how nervous, you can only take so much. The kid is asleep. You look at him again and reach down. "Damn replacements," you say fondly.

You snap the safety of his rifle on …

The first faint glow of morning touches the eastern ridgelines, the bustle of a late dawn moves all about you, but it's okay. The night is sinking away, back into the shadows and the corners of the earth where those who enjoy it can have it. Quickly the morning comes, almost loudly, crashing into the cold air webbing the sky with light where there is still darkness, brushing aside all the fears of the night, all the emptiness of the black, tearing away mortal awareness of sound, making you comfortably sleepy for the first time in 12 hours. You take out your wallet, look at the picture of a girl, your wife—and at the tiny small [word omitted] of your daughter. You smile at them, and it's a tired smile, but it's a happy one, because the damn slant-eyed peoples haven't gotten you yet.

The replacement is sleeping easily. You look down at the place where you had thrown the one grenade. A tree stump is bent. It looks almost like a human form crouching there …

Suddenly it's morning.

##########

That's it, hon. And I couldn't have written it more graphically, if I'd've pounded a typewriter for three weeks. I don't know why, but it comes easily just now. For about two hours I haven't stopped typing, haven't lifted my head from my desk. What you have just read is the product. Right now while it is in my mind, I like it. When I re-read it, I'll probably find all kinds of errors and poor structure and want to tear it up. But it tells what I want to tell you anyhow. I want you to know what the kids in the hills are doing … what I did up there. The incident is true, it happened to me in the September attack when I had a new man in my fire team and decided I'd better keep him with me the first night. Tell me what you think about it, baby. And even if you don't like it, tell me if you understand what I'm trying to say, because I want you very much to know … and I know you want to know.

That's all for now, darling. I feel a lot better now. I guess I haven't changed much since my civilian days. I'm still a writer, deep down inside me, and whenever my unconscious mind has a story it wants me to tell, I get restless and nervous and irritable. Then when I tell it I'm relaxed—not usually satisfied, but relaxed. Love me even if I am a writer, darling? Hope so. Because I love you with all my heart and soul and will always and forever. You know that, Joanne. You know how deeply I love you. And how much I love our little Cinthy. I won't disappoint you when I get hom[e], sweetheart. I Promise. I love you ...

All My Heart And Love With [sic]
And For All My Life,
    Al (and Boondocker)
I love you!
XXX's [sic]

P.S.—Just reread the story. Oh, well.
I can work on it when I get home.
    love you, honey!
        Cinthy too!

MZ 779

February 4, 1952

Dearest Joanne, My darling—

Received two letters from you today, darling, and thanks for the compliment. I remember the letter I wrote about asking questions, and I don't possibly see how you could have figured it out, but you're an exceptional girl—er lady, however you care to have yourself addressed. And you're right. About several things, I mean. You're right about thinking of the little things, about the imlportance [sic] of a comprehended [sic] education, about asking questions to yourself and to the world even though a direct answer may never be forthcoming. I liked your letters, hon. As I always do.

Buy whatever you want to, darling. I trust entirely your good sense, and will never question anything you see fit to purchase. You found a poem (or "thing" as you called it) I wrote about not wanting you to undress in front of me? Darling, I swear by everything that's sacred, by all my God-granted rights of self-expression and humanity, I cannot at the moment think of anything I would rather see than you undressing in front of me. To be even more blunt, I'll probably leap at you like a tiger and help you undress faster than you have ever done so in all your 21 years of lovely life on earth. Consider, baby doll, I haven't seen you for a year already, and before I get home it will probably be 14 months! As I recall you undressing in front of me now, and I recall it quite vividly at times, you were beautiful—such a figure, such a, a, a—now see what you've done. As for thinking—as for EVER thinking—of you as ugly in the morning—impossible. I think you're beautiful anytime [sic] of the day, anywhere. I love you, honey, and my strongest emotions are so humanly strong towards you that sometimes I can't stand them. I love you—and the day you undress in front of me again will be like the first night we were married. But this time, I promise, I'll be a little gentler. I've never forgotten the sting of your insinuation that I "raped" you that night. I've learned my lesson. I love you.

Pvt.—or PFC, whatever he is—Hobel seems to have made out grandly as far as the Marine Corps is concerned. In fact, he has it knocked. I never mean to imply that, as you caustically said, "...the worst always gets the best is just not true." But I will say this, despite the fact that I like Alan and have told you so—it isn't fair. I do not by any means think that I am the most capable man in Korea. And by the same token, I do not think Alan is the most capable one at El Toro. We are all expendable, Alan as well as I. And that's why I think that every Stateside Marine SHOULD unless he is physically incapable serve his tour of duty overseas. I believe I say that broad-mindedly, and with fairness to everyone concerned. There were a lot more intelligent men than Alan serving with the infantry who were killed. I do not wish that fate, or even the Korean tour of duty, on anyone. But Pete Mamaril didn't wish it on himself, nor did I, nor did a lot of other guys. I hold the Marine Corps personally responsible for the lack of fairness in the outfit. To Alan, I say—More power to you. The longer you can stay next to the one you love, the more I am for you. To the Marine Corps I say, show me your method and reason of choice, and I'll show you a hundred thousand errors. But I like Alan and am sincerely glad he got a good deal, even though it may not sound like me. My tour of duty is almost over, and I got a break. I wish I could say the same for a couple other fellows who made the one-way trip ...

Gee, I wish I could have been there to see your Dad and Blendeena.* It would have been wonderful. But time is certainly not dead, nor is a trip to Michigan impossible. I will see him before too long, I know. I did write him a letter thanking him for the package. I think he's a wonderful person and regret that I can't be there to tell him so. But my thoughts are always there at 2023 as I so graphically said on page one of this letter ... oh, to have you by my side in a nice warm ... stop torchoring [sic] yourself, Marintez [sic] ... (Martinez, is the name, Al Martinez, M-A-R-TON-E-Z—nuts! I'll be damned if I can't spell my own name! M-A-R-T-I-N-E-Z, There.)

Our little darling sounds like she's really making all-out attempts to motivate [i.e., move?] under her own power. Such a sweetie-pie. And I challenge your dad's saying that Cinthy is a much nicer baby than you ever were. I think you're both sweet, evn [sic] though (even is the word I believe) I have never seen either of you as a baby. Well, that's all of your two letters, darling, so I shall ramble on.

After I wrote that description to you last night I called Night Watch, I showed it to Rich thinking that he might be interested in it since he pulled 8 months on the lines. Honestly, I've never had such a pumped-up ego as I did then. He raved. So then I showed him what I had typed from my diary. That did it, and I felt like Ogden Nash last night, with a thousand people applauding me. He, and others have said the same thing, want me to make carbons of all that stuff I type. I would be glad (personally) to oblige but figured it is not good business since I plan to

---

*Blendeena married Joanne's father.

Three. Cpl. Al Martinez, Combat Correspondent.... How About That! 197

sell this stuff some day [sic]. He has made me promise that I will send him a book, however. The one I write. Tsk.

Nothing unusual has happened today, so I think I'll just ramble on like I did last night. It kept me occupied for awhile [sic] and I enjoyed it. Hope you did too. But if you didn't, just say so, and I'll stop ... think I'll turn the page and start this off. I think I'll tell you about a page from my diary, a little more detail, a little more descriptive ...

The stalling was torture to every man in the company. The hill was ahead, but it was easier reaching it, taking it, then [sic] digging in. Out there on the open ridge there was no protection from the incoming rounds, from the flat-trajectory 76,* from the high-arcing mortars.

As it was, there was no movement. The company commander studied his map. The platoon leaders crowded around him, and if you watched them all closely you could tell which way you were going. They looked at the map then looked up. The Company commander pointed. If you watched closely, you could see the hill. If you watched there [sic] faces you catch the deep-creased frowns, the smiles or the worried stare. You could always tell how rough the objective was going to be. But that didn't matter. Only half of your time was spent watching them. The other half you spent listening, listening intensely, until your ears rang with the strain, for the sound of the incoming. Sometimes you listened too hard and the sound of a person's voice scared you ...

The Company moved on.

Out of the protection of the lower ridges and the sheltering branches and toward the high ground. The bare ridges, where the rockets and the napalm had done their jobs well. That's where you expect it every moment—the incoming. And you're usually not disappointed.

The air rang with the silence one minute. The next it was sliced it [sic] two, cut like a sheet of hard ice with the heavy swoosh and the cracking impact of a mortar. You could see out of the corner of your eye where it hit, and you wondered why everyone took so long to hit the deck. The black smoke rose, the stench of powder was heavy in the air. No one had been hit, you could tell by the lack of commomtion [sic]. Or else he'd been hit directly and there wasn't enough left of him to call corpsman for. The smell of earth was heavy in your nostrils, and it tasted cool and fresh in your mouth. A small bug crawled in front of your open eyes. You might have been afraid of bugs at one time. You weren't then. You envied him.

Some[one?] shuffled to his feet. It was the Company commander. "Moving out," he hollered back over the heads of the column. No one moved for a moment. "On your feet," he commanded, "let's go." The scurrying was simaltaneous [sic]. Each man was on his feet, but he hunched low where he stood, eager to remain close to the earth when the next one came in. You had a chance to study the faces then. The white, blank one, pasty with a fear that made no pretense of courage; the hard and experienced one that just listened and showed no emotion; the look

---

*Al refers to the flat-trajectory 76 anti-tank gun.

of patient, willing disgust, that objected to it all, but that accepted fate with sarcasm; the determined one, that swore he'd last out every mortar round that could be thrown; the smiling indifferent, the joker, the clown, the one that only got hit on special occasions. You wondered what you looked like. You were afraid, sure, but not like that one guy—not mortally, panickly [sic] afraid. You were just normally afraid. Who were you trying to kid.

Your stomach was in a knot.

The company moves out, the interval wide, the column cutting off to the reverse slope. Another round comes in. Everybody flinches, no one hits the deck. Two more scream over your heads and crash down into the gulley below you. You keep moving. Then the company commander, who has been leading the column, stops. You know you're near the objective. He calls your platoon leader forward and orders the others to disperse their men. You're on a nose above a dip in the ridgeline. On the other side of the dip the ground rises quickly. There are bunkers on either side of the point leading to the top; nervously inhabitated [sic] bunkers, with fresh earth and live men in them.

The platoon leader confers with the company commander. Friendly artillery slams into the hill in front of you over your head, drowning out anything you might have been able to overhear from the conversation. It's cold.

The hill is rocky and steep that you are to take. It's objective 8, hill 749.* There are no full trees on it. There are only half-trees and large shell craters; burned earth ... and bunkers. You take all this in in one quick glance. Then you study it from flat on the ground. It's 200 yards away, maybe 300, and you haven't drawn fire yet. Out of the corner of your eye you see the company commander smile at the platoon leader and squeeze his hand.

You drop your pack automatically, and the rest of the company moves back to a rise for overhead and supporting fire. Your platoon is alone, and the platoon Sgt. calls the squad leaders up. The squad leaders call the fire-team leaders. That's your que [sic]. The squad leader explains the approach route of the assault; your squad goes right through the middle, the first and second come around the sides. The plt. sgt. hollers "move out." And before you move the squad leader says as an afterthought, to you,

"Take the point."

The rumble of friendly artillery stops. You move slowly, all the pins on your grenades free to slide out quickly, the safety of your rifle off and the trigger ready to pull by command or reaction. You hunch low, send you[r] scout out and start forward. The squad leader walks behind the last man in you[r] fire team. You're the expendable team.

The walk is long and slow. Someone behind you hollers commands that you don't really hear, but comply with automatically. You start thinking of everything, but mostly of your wife and your kid. You wonder if it will hurt when it hits you ...

You move ahead.

---

*Hill 749 was one battle in the larger battle of the Punchbowl. Al's Fox Company, in the 2nd Battalion of the 7th Regiment, was central to this operation and suffered heavy casualties.

You hear them go off, indistinctly, way off in the distance, out of hearing range actually, but you hear them cough. Five of them, and you wonder if they're … you're [*sic*] question is answered before it materializes. Five enemy mortars slam into the tail of the platoon. Direct hit! Someone screams, then somebody else and you recognize a couple voices. You wonder how many, then scream, "move out!" to your fire team as the scout hesitates to look back. You hear the Corpsman run up behind you. More mortars pile into the platoon and somebody else hollers. You want to turn back, but you're afraid. Afraid to move ahead, afraid to stop, afraid to move back. But you haven't hesitated.

Then it happens.

Your scout is out of sight before you know what happens and a grenade explodes. Then a burp gun, a Russian BAR, a machine gun. The platoon scatters to the sides of the nose, and another scream. But this time he isn't screaming from pain. That's the signal. The assault.

Your mouth opens and you scream until your throat hurts! Your rifle is kicking in your hands like something gone made [*sic*] and the other two supporting platoons open up over your heads. A clip flies out of your M-1, another and another. You start to trot, then you're moving faster, faster, faster until your mouth is wide open scream [*sic*, word or words missing?] out a strange sort of hell, and your throat is gagging from the dust. You listen to yourself and almost laugh. The other two squads are moving fast towards the bunkers that kick out shells. One brown-clothed Gook makes a break for it from his bunker. Your scout takes off the back of his head. He crumples in the dust and never moves again. The two squads on your flanks are moving faster, and you have to step it up.

You're half way up the slope, bunkers are being equalized on both sides. Bullets fly out of a position to your direct front. You skirt the trail and race towards it. Your BARman [*sic*] comes straight at it, pinning down the trapped occupants. The assistant BARman [*sic*] throws .30 calibers into it, the scout approaches it from the other side. For a minute the live grenade is hard in your hand. The next, it[']s snapping near the bunker then falls out of sight into it. Short seconds pass. You expect the grenade to come back, but someone didn't move fast enough. It explodes in the bunker, and the gun is quieted.

The screaming stops when the first prisoner comes out hands up. Someone lets a round go, and he drops holding his side. More prisoners come out from everywhere, more than you expected. Your squad moves to the ridgeline and spreads out, waiting for a counter attack that never comes. The hill is secured, the prisoners are stripped and sent to the rear. The wounded are evacuated. The other two platoons move up.

The high ground is yours.

#######

Halfway through that I was interrupted by a very pleasant surprise. My fitness report. I told you about the last one I got which every NCO (sgt[.] and above) gets when his section leader leaves. When Major Sedewick [*sic*] left, I got one then. The one I got today was the regular semi-annual one. The last one was pretty good, but this one is far better than I ever expected. NONE of my marks were below EXCELLENT and most of them were outstanding. It's so much better than the last one it's frightening. And GUICE marked this one. He recommended me for promotion to staff sgt. with the added notation of PIO. In the place of "comments" he wrote, and I quote, "Newspaper background and present assignment qualifies him for PIO work. His abilities and interest in this field would be invaluable to the Corps." For my general rating value, I was marked "excellent." Everything was good, even the remark, "glad to have him in my command." Honey, I'm so surprised and pleased I don't know what to do. I'm the one who's always arguing with Guice, making him know that I know my business better than he does, snowing him with words he's never heard and I know he doesn't understand. I don't know what I did to him, but he gave me the best fitness report in the S-1 section. It makes me feel good, especially since I'm getting my Marine Occupational Speciality [sic] number changed from 0311 (combat infantry) to 4312, Combat Correspondent. Honey, I'm in like Flynn. If I'm ever called in the Corps again, I'll come in as a PIO man, and nothing else. All they have to do is refer to my record book for proof of my past work—and there isn't a thing in my book that is a disadvantage to me. I've seen my last of the infantry. I'm a PIO man—gold framed yet. Proud of me, honey? Hope so.

Well, darling, another day has gone, another night is ahead and I can't be too PO'd with the Corps. I guess it's the same story all over for a long time to come yet, and I fall into that old pattern: the Marine Corps isn't a good outfit, but there's not a better one in the world. And until a better one comes along, I'll settle for the globe and anchor. It's a hell of an outfit—but I love it, even though I'll leave it first chance I get. I love you, our daughter and the challenge of civilian life more. I miss you with all my heart …

All My Love Forever And Forever,
Al (and Boondocker)
I love you!
XXXXX

[Drawing of man (Al) in profile, with a set of sergeant's stripes visible on the sleeve; an arrow points to the stripes from the caption:] how would that look

MZ 781

February 17, 1952

My Darling wife—

Just received two very wonderful, wonderful letters from you and was quite surprise[d]—not because your letters were wonderful (they always are) but because we got mail. Certainly didn't expect it. Sounds like you're having loads of fun developing my film. Hmmmmmmmm. The process of learning the art of photography and developing, they say, is long and tedious. I hope some pictures do turn out though. I'd like to see my mistakes and profit by them. Develope [sic] all my film yourself, darling—or I should say all OUR film. Because it does belong to both of us. I'm counting on you to get me hep on the art of developing when I get home.

I love you too, angel, you know that. Keep loving me. And missing me.

You asked me about what situation will confront me when I return to the United States. I will be released to inactive duty in the reserves—not even having to attend meetings. Since my enlistment is up in the reserves April 29th of this year, my COG (convenience of government, one year extension) year will be up one year hence—April 29, 1953, and I will be discharged from the United States Marine Corps Reserve. I will be out completely. But I will be released from active duty when I get home unless there is a radical change. I've gotten letters from buddies who have been released to civilian status when they returned home. If there is no war by April 29, 1953, and if the government doesn't extend me another year, I will be completely out of the Marine Corps. Oh, joy. And, s'helpmehanna, I'll never, no never, join another reserve outfit again. I mean that. I made a mistake once, but I won't make that same mistake again. But, as you cautioned, I am not going to count on getting out or anything else. When I set foot in the United States I will say I am home. When I see you, I will acknowledge the fact of the moment. When I have a complete discharge paper in my hand, I will say I am out of the Marine Corps. I know this outfit too well to count on anything. I will eat the crumbs as they fall, and put off counting the chickens until they hatch. So much for the Corps and clichés.

I like the comments you wrote on my description of a night watch. And you are perfectly right. I do tend to build up words into a series of climaxes in one story. I think that's a [sic] rather amateur in my attempt to create interest all the way through a story. I'm too conscious of what I'm doing. Instead of working toward a goal I go off in all directions at once (as is actually the case in combat), but I don't put it across. You ever hear the word "monotapoetic [sic]"?* It means putting the exact sound of an object in words. Poe did that in his poem "The Bells"—where his meter was the meter of swinging bells, etc. I tried to do more or less the same thing in my story—to creare [sic] a confusion in words that took place in actuality—to create a mood of shifting thoughts, hazy memory, moving darknes[s] with words that shift and are vague and unreal and moving. I suppose I haven't done too well at that, but I like the idea. Combat is one of the easiest things in the world to write about because the confusion and the objects of the confusion are so real. And yet it is the hardest thing in the world to write for people to believe. Combat is so concrete and real, that the ideas formed about it are concrete and fixed. Everyone has his own idea about it, right or wrong. And when a person writes about what it actually is, if it's not filled with pathos and guts, hard men and killer Marines, it isn't worth a damn. It's got to be stereotype for the public. And I have absolutely no idea of writing imaginary things about it. I want to tell the truth about this thing over in Korea, about what the guy up on the lines sees, and I think if it's good enough it will sell. But I've got to get out of the word rut I'm getting in. I've got to begin striving for plot, organization, movement in the stories without early or post or anti climatic heads. You've got to help

---

*The correct word is onomatopoeic, the adjectival form of onomatopoeia, which is the formation of a word from the sound it describes, e.g., plop, gulp, hiss.

me alot [*sic*], that's why I want your advice. The fellows who read my stuff like it for the plot alone because they know it's true, they know it's real because they've seen the same things I have. Now it's the public I've got to convince and I'm going to do it. I don't just "think" I'm going to do it, I know damn well I'm going to. I've made too many verbal promises to you, and to[o] many silent ones to kids like Pete Mamaril to let any of you down. I think that speaks for itself.

You mentioned that the people in my stories are too nice. That's what I mean about it being true over here, and the public not accepting it because of their built-up theories. I've never seen closer friendship in my life than I have overseas—I've never seen men closer to each other, being nicer to each other, thinking more of each other, than the men of Fox Co. and every other company. I felt like a father to my fire team and there wasn't a thing in the world I wouldn't do for them. When I got a new man in my fire team I felt it my job to look after, protect him and teach him until he was combat-wise enough to do it for himself. Really, Joanne, I can't emphasize enough the closeness over here. If it were that way in real life, we would have no worries about war. I've seen—and have myself—men risk their lives to look after thier [*sic*] buddies who were wounded. I've seen a man put his lips to his buddy's face and breath[e] into his mouth when he was dying because he though[t] it might save his life. I've seen Corpsmen run through mine fields and certain death to get to a wounded Marine—and that isn't just duty. It goes beyond duty and reaction and hits very close to the heart. Men are foolish animals, and they react unpredicatbly [*sic*] in combat. Tears are common and so is bravery. Fox company risked its damn neck to save two men who were trapped in a valley. But we got them out. The whole second battalion jumped off into the Chinese Main Line of Resistance and into artillery barrages to save Able company last June in Yang-gu valley. These things are real, so real and so moving that it takes the subtlest type of writing to portray them to make them sound real and not made up, I don't know if I'm the man for that job right now or not. But I know damn well I'm going to try and get that down until I am the man who can tell that story. I'm going to make it sound so real—the soft toughness of men looking after one another, the gruff comfort one gives a wounded Marine—that those who read it are going to live through 12 months of Korea right with me. Because these—war and combat—are the things that make differences in the future of the world and I believe I have a right to exploit my art to make the public read it. It's a test of my ability and one that I'm working to make come true. Keep your advice coming, darling. It's what I need desperately.

Honey, I'm not mad at you and never have been. I though[t] you were angry at me for a long time and can't figure it out—rather "couldn't" figure it out. I couldn't be mad at you, not as long as I'm over here. Look through my desk all you want, sweetheart. That certainly doesn't bother me. I want you to look at what I write and see what you think of them and me at that time in my life. As for marriage being a partnership.... I don't like that word and never have. It's more than that, a lot more than that. I'm from the old school and believe that it's a blending of two lives into one, in every way, mind, body and soul. I believe it's the ultimate in the physical and spiritual unity of a man and a woman and I can never consider it on the plane of just a "partnership." It's more than the simple sharing of thought and life. It goes far deeper. I don't mean to sound like I'm correcting you, but simply stating what I think in answer to you[r] question, "what is marriage?" I wish you did feel a little more possessive. It doesn't make me feel real modern (or whatever the term they use now) to know I'm free to do as I please. I don't, as you, consider marriage as two individuals. I consider them as ONE family. I wish you felt a little differently about it, because I won't [sic] to feel as though you love and want to possess me as much as I do you. I hate feeling like a complete idiot, wanting you with all my heart and soul and not having that returned. You stated that I am free to do and think as I please. I, too, agree with a person thinking as they please. But I wish you'd think a little more about that doing as I please: are you just saying that or does it actually exist in your mind that you'd let me do as I please without argument? Darling, I'm not angry, mad, annoyed, or anything else now. It's silly, I know, but I want you to possess me in your heart anyhow. The definition of possess would disprove anything I think about marriage, I know. It means complete possessiveness, jailing thought and action and killing happiness. But I think of possessiveness between two married people as the wanting of him or her with all your heart and life. I wanted to marry you, so I can be trusted to do as I want, without doing the wrong thing. But I don't think there's a sincere husband in the world (or a wife) who doesn't want to be utterly and completely possessed by the person he loves. You're right, darling. I am possessive concerning you, but only because I love you extremely. But it's possession in my definition. And if that's wrong, then so is my whole idea of marriage. Possess me, darling—I'd love it. I hope you understand what I mean. And I'm not a bit angry. I love you and just want you to understand and love me as much as I love you.

Honey, that little extra note you put in your letter was very, very sweet and wonderful, you know. I can see where you would get annoyed with me. I'm a rather confused person and a lot of times say things I don't even begin to mean. It's my impetuousness, and one which will take time to get out of. I want normal reaction from you, darling. When I say something to get you annoyed, I want to hear about it. I don't want to feel like a damn freak because I happen to be one of the anonymous "boys overseas." That's what I love about you, and that's why I know I will have no trouble becoming adjusted again to civilian life. Because you're as sweet and as sensible as you are. Keep loving me, and I'll be a better man when I return than I was when I left you. I suppose I'm just human, and like to know that I'm love[d] and missed. 'Specially by you. As long as you can become just humanly annoyed with me and love me nonetheless, then I know our marriage is on a firm and very wonderful foundation. I love you, darling. Very, very much.

This light meter I have is a DeJur, made by Ansco corporation. I understand it's better than Westinghouse because it gives light in relation to distance, the object, shutter speed and stop opening. It is definetly [sic] more complicated than a Westinghouse, but once I master it (which I haven't done yet), I think it will be a valuable asset in photography. Incidentelly [sic], this is an American light meter, not a Japanese model.

Well, darling, that about answers both your letters, so I'll go on to other things. Less important, but the happenings of the days in Korea. Oh, yes—one thing you said is not to think about when I'm coming home, but just to think about that it will be soon. I wish I could do just that. But I'm afraid it's a little hard. That's about all I think about now is when I'm coming home. It had better be soon, or I'll be a nervous wreck just thinking about it. I'm getting shook.

Hon, don't take too much stock in what I write if I sound annoyed in one of my letters. It's not you, it's just things. Sometime[s] Korea gets a little hard to bear, but once I blow off steam I'm okay. It's very natural over here, and certainly not serious. I know you understand.

Right now far, far in the distance there is the rumble of the artillery—incoming artillery. It isn't hitting back here, however, but up on the lines—in the hills where the guy in the foxhole is sweating it out for another dark night. Then there's the comforting roar of our own 105's [sic] and 155's [sic] and 8 inchers, talking [sic?] down that weak barrage in the miles. There's not a man in Korea that can say he didn't have good support from artillery. They're the finest in the world, and I'm sure the Chinese would never question that word. There's too many of thier [sic] bodies lying in the hills.

About this sotry [sic] (story, that is) I wrote on night watches. I see what you mean about not narrowing the plot. It should be narrowed down into definite form, substance and climax. Without the usual "darkness is falling" stuff. How could I narrow it down? How could I make you feel that you were there in the night, in the gray dawn, watching and listening with me, feeling the strain of the night and the impulse to cry...

I almost started to write another short descriptive story then, hon, but I've been interrupted so often ("How do you spell 'passion,' Al?["]) that I've lost the trend of what I was thinking in the first place. The incoming artillery is getting a little too close for comfort as it has all day, and if I spend the rest of the night in a bunker it wouldn't surprise me a bit. That's the trouble with being in the rear—you feel so safe and cocky, but actually it's more dangerous because they throw artillery at you when you least suspect it. I don't think I told you this, but the second day I was back in PIO they practically wiped out [word omitted?] regiment with artillery: 21 men wounded in action, some seriously. They even got a direct hit on Regimental sick bay. It's not even safe in the rear anymore [sic]. Got to get home, that's all there is to it. You won't hit me, will you, darling?

Well, baby, I've cried on your shoulder, adviced [sic], commented, loved you and everything else in five typewritten pages, so I guess it's time to stop. Let this be a hint for you to write me a nice long letter sometime ... just kidding, sweetheart. I love your letters no matter how short or long they are. Just keep telling me you love and miss me and I'll be happy. And don't be angry at my ideas on marriage. I think we both feel the same way about it, but just have different ways of expressing our feelings. Am I right? Love me? I love you. Miss me? I miss you. Want Me? I want you? Feel sexual to me? I feel sexual to you. Love Cinthy? I love her[,] to[o]. What the devil [word omitted? are?] we talking about[,] we agree on everything. Haven't we got a wonderful life to look forward to? You, Cinthy and I—and 11 more when I'm able to support them. I never have forgotten "Cheaper

By The Dozen"* and the fun they had raising their family. I haven't met a good sergeant yet who couldn't handle the masses. Or a good father. And I'm going to be the best father and husband in the world. Let's have a million children. But just one wife and husband ...

> I love you with All My heart!
> All My Love Forever And
> Sincerely to the Most
> Wonderful Wife in the World ...
>   Al (and Boondocker)
> XXXXXXXX   XXXX's [sic]

MZ 794

> Feb. 22, '52

Dearest Joanne—

About two of the "old" guys I knew in Fox were actually the only ones I remembered from the May-June campaign, Yang-gu, etc. The rest had gone home, been wounded or knocked off. These two were the last that remained & both had been in my fire team. Now, the old Fox Co. is gone for me. Because these 2 men are.

The way I read it from official reports was this: the 2nd plt. (my plt.) of Fox had an outpost. My old fire team was on a knoll all by itself. In the morning, one of the guys by the name of Weitman walked about 25 yds. in front of his position. He was jumped & dragged away after a struggle. The men saw it but didn't fire[,] afraid of hitting Weitman. So they started after the Gooks. Mortars came in an[d] killed 2 Marines—a lieut. I didn't know & one of the other guys I was talking about, PFC Raymond G. Siedel [sic]. And that's what I mean when I say the last of the old Fox is gone—one captured, perhaps dead; the other blown to eternity by a mortar.

Weitman was a 6th drafter, due to go home in about 2 weeks. His injustice is irony all the way through—not a scratch until now –missing in action. Siedel [sic] was an 11th drafter, a fat Cornhusker from Nebraska—careless & not too bright but a nice guy. He's the one I wrote about in my story of an [sic] night watch. Weitmann had a girl in Ohio—she use[d] to send pictures & letters with lipstick on them. Siedel [sic] was a lazy guy—but I just couldn't get too mad at him. When I left they gave Weitman my fire team. I feel a little sorry now that I didn't teach him a little more because as his fire-team leader it was my responsibility. Siedel [sic] was a peon & always would be—one of the guys "who'd never get it."

    Cpl. Albert W. Weitmann
    PFC Raymond G. Siedel [sic]

I want to remember those names along with a lot of others. It makes my

---

Cheaper by the Dozen is a 1948 novel by Frank Bunker Gilbreth, Jr., and Ernestine Gilbreth Carey about their childhood in a family with twelve children. Al had probably seen the 1950 film based on the book.

future more set & my drive more determined. They were my buddies. They were nice guys. I'm going to miss them—

All My Love –
Al

(P.S.—I'm sorry about such a rotten letter, hon. It's just the way I feel—pretty damned rotten & pretty damned ashamed of the human race!)

MZ 800

March 4, 1952

Dearest Joanne, My darling—

Baby, don't be so perturbed. The letter I got from you tonight sounded so blue and annoyed, and—oh, I don't know. Waiting, I agree, is one of the hardest things to do in any war. But consider, darling, that now we are waiting for the time when I will be home—not when I'll be leaving. Bear up, sweetheart, and it won't be too long. The latest "semi-official" scuttlebut[t] (that's what the Sgt. Major calls it) is that the 6th and 7th drafts will be leaving Korea MARCH 15 or 18! Darling, that['s] not more than 13 days! The reason I'm so excited is that the Sgt. Major is about the most non-committal person I know—never passes out bum scoop, doesn't believe in spreading rumors, and just never says anything unless he feels it's halfway true anyhow. Of course, this could be just bum scoop. I don't know for sure, and no official word has come via Regiment, of that I am sure. So let's leave it there, darling—close your eyes, cross your fingers and pray …

I certainly know what you mean about those days when nothing—but <u>nothing</u>—seems to go right. I've had those days. In fact I'm still having them. But I chalk that up to Korea. Nothing ever goes according to Hoyle* over here. But I've learned to take the set-backs with a bit of well-worn philosophy—things could be worse. Kind of like, "I complained that I had no shoes, 'till I met a man who had no feet." It does hit home sometime[s]. I've got no kick coming.

This Christine sounds like an aggravating person. If she annoys you, she probably will me too. But then, after Korea, I doubt if anything short of reactivation to fight Russia will faze me. We shall see … won't we?

My present has aroused my curiosity to the point of longing. I never could have a present kept from me for too long before I start asking for "just one little hint." When I was a kid, I use[d] to approach Harry when he was drinking and usually ask for and get the scoop on what I was getting for Christmas. Of course, this annoyed my mother no end, but I always found out what I was getting. Nosey, nosey me. Journalistic instinct, I reply when somebody calls me nosey.

Uninformed? You? Who are you trying to kid? I don't know Allen Jaeger now, and consequently [sic] can't say how well informed he is. But I know you are very

---

*To say that something is "according to Hoyle" means that it is according to the rules, or the way something is normally done. The phrase comes from a book of rules for card games written by Edmond Hoyle (British, 1672–1769).

well informed and conscious of the situation around you. What I call being well informed is not just knowing what's going on everywhere in the world. It's more than just that. It's <u>realizing</u> what the consequences will be and specualting [*sic*] on the possibilities. Right at the moment[,] as far as the world situation is concerned, I am probably better informed than I ever have been in my life. And I am close to what appears to be a world trend—war. But I'm not miserable. I'm skeptical sometimes, sure. But I can't see a person crying in his beer. I'm hopeful, and anxious and awful willing to theorize. You're a lot more informed than you think you are, muggins, by a wide margin. I know you. If anyone should be having a hard time living in the world, I think I've got a pretty good reason. But if life is just looking on the dark side, then it certainly isn't a very progressive life. Be it far from me to advice [*sic*] someone like Allen, but I'd advice [*sic*] him (if he asked me) to look on the brighter, more promising side of life and do a little hoping for a brighter fut[u]re—and a lot of work towards it. The world is too much troubled today with a sort of telepathy that rings of war. Uncertainty is with [word omitted], sure. But even from uncertainty can spring peace. I for one, despite the fact of Korea, am willing to believe that life can be, and will be, better.

Hon, when I was on the lines and feeling pretty low down, you wrote me a letter and asked me to smile. At that time I didn't have much to look forward to except 8 more months in the infantry and maybe even a lot [*sic*] plot of ground all my own somewhere in those damn nameless hills. That letter did a lot for me, because I learned a part of your philosophy, and I learned to smile a lot harder when everything was blacker than the insides of a bunker. Now, things are a lot more promising. I have a month at the most to go in Korea, I'm in the rear, I'm a lot more of a man than I ever was. So I want to ask you the same thing, under better circumstances. Darling, give yourself a big smile for me, will you? It makes a lot of difference. I love you, sweetheart. That made a lot of difference to me too when you wrote it—it still does.

The night outside is still and calm. "Laura" (the song)* is on the radio, and everyone is quiet. No snow, no wind, not even too much cold. The mud is forming on the ground, and the snow is melting quite fast on the mountains. The cycle of the seasons is completing itself, and spring is touching the ends of a troubled, dying winter. The snow is getting dirty, the rivers muddy. It brings back memories of my trudge up the first Korean hill, and those walks on the muddy, muddy roads to Chunchon [*sic*].† Like the song—I'll remember April.... Yeah, I'll always remember April—1951. Just like I'll remember this coming one—in 1952.

Right now[,] Korea looks like yesterday. I say yesterday, because I'm in a reminiscent mood, and my cruise in the land of the many hills is closing. Not climaxing, because the climax came the day I got my transfer. Since then it has been a dull decline and a long wait until now or then—when I get home. It seems like

---

*The film *Laura* (1949) was a romantic mystery starring Dana Andrews, Gene Tierney, and Clifton Webb. The movie's theme song "Laura" was composed by David Raksin.
†Chuncheon is the capital of the South Korean province of Gangwon. Much of the city was destroyed in the Battle of Chuncheon, at the beginning of the Korean War.

such a long time since I joined Fox company on the Kansas line. Stone, Keen, Jenkins, King, Wertman, Rod, Swenson—the newness of it all, the stretch ahead of me. The quantico line, the blue line, the brown line, Hayes line, Operations Mousetrap, Pursuit, killer, Punchbowl—Yang-gu, mortar hill, Banzai hill, 749, objective 10, the patrols, the fire fights, the mortar barrages, the valleys, the ridges … all gone in a passing parade that never makes me miss them.

It's like then now. Because the mud is on the roads, the dead smell of Korea is in the air, stiffling [sic], ugly, thick. The air is cold and wet, the opposing troops are getting ready for the attack, because the snow is melting on the hills. When I look at a replacement now, I try to find one that looks like me, or acts like me. Because in a way, one new member of Fox company is joining by filling in my footsteps when I came here last April. He has the same anticipations, the same fears, and the same burning curiosity to see what it's really like. Some dumb kid is going to climb his first hill just a boy, and come down a man when he sees his first buddy killed. He's going to learn a humility he's never before had, a humbleness, a belief in God, a faith in man—he's going to emerge from the hills and the valleys with a strong will to live and see that something like Korea never happens to his kids. He's going to be a dreamer with a rough touch of realism—a dreamer that dodges hand grenades and prays in a foxhole. He's going to dream and fight in one magnificent motion.

The kid that replaces me in a foxhole up on the front lines is gong to get a break. He'll get transferred, but not without first gaining a deep insight into life, his surroundings and the world he lives in—without reading a single book. He won't have a chip on his shoulder or any bitterness in his heart. He'll be able to keep the bitterness out of his heart toward our "crazed enemy"—because he's seen our crazed enemy—a 17[-]year[-]old kid, crying because he had a hole in his body. And how can you be bitter at a kid, slant eyes or not?

I'm looking for him in the crowds of the replacements that stumble with fear-ridden faces through regiment who watch us and try to copy our actions. I'm looking for this pug-nosed adolescent, because he's going to help me tell a story when he gets home that I won't be around to see. I'm looking for my replacement. I wonder if I'll find him …

> I'll love you forever!
> All My Love Forever And
> Forever And Always …
>   Al (and Boondocker)
>   XXXXXXXXX
>   XXXXX

[Drawing of a face, Joanne's? with the caption:] SMILE! [A second, smaller face is probably Cinthy]

MZ 811

Thursday
March 28

My darling—

The rotation list is out. And on it is the name of one Sgt. Al Martinez, 1056679 USMCR—due for release to inactive duty in April & due to leave Korea around April 8th. I have about 11 days left in Korea, sweetheart. Eleven of the longest days of my life. Then on about April 30th I'll be kissing my two darlings, holding them close, shutting out the bad memories of 12 months of Korean duty and bringing in the happiness that only my wife & our little girl can bring.

The list came out this morning & the Sgt. Major showed it to me. I've been a new man all day. I'm coming home on reserve release rather than regular rotation. I could make it on either one actually, but they like to put you on the reserve roster—makes the Corps look like they're treating their boys good. Doesn't make a damn to me as long as I get there. I'll always know I did my time in Korea.

We're settled for awhile [sic] in our reserve area after a week of making about 4 moves. We are now engaged in making the area look good! What a laugh! Atlas Const. Co. couldn't make this mudhole look good. The way they're putting the tents up is ridiculous. These salty 16th drafters haven't been around for the rainy season yet. But come the rain, their tents will be floating around on the road somewhere. Oh, well—I'll be in a warm home then. This war will be theirs then, & they can run it however they please.

We are on the Western front now, about 3 miles from Munsan, 10 miles from Kaesong, 5 miles from Panmunjom—all neutral zones. The land over here is the flattest I've seen in Korea. Long flat valleys with the low hills rising out of the mist in the many-miled distance. The vallies [sic] are criss-crossed with barbed wire & treacherous with mines. This is the land the Marines fought so hard for on the scarlet road to Seoul—the land the Army couldn't hold. They expect a big push here by the Gooks—thus the reason for the Marines shifting from East to West. Now tell me the 8th Army doesn't respect the Corps. Where there's Marines, there's a strong line or a rough attack. Even a rear-echelon doggie told me yesterday that he could sleep night[s] now without wondering if the line would switch from 10 miles north to his back yard. You see, the 3rd Army Division was here before. And they have a reputation—a <u>fabulous</u> reputation—for retreating.

The Gooks have held a couple air strikes on this country. But if they can get by the 1st Air Wing's Corsairs—they deserve a lot of credit. This is also tank country. But there are so many anti-tank roadblocks, I doubt if they'd get far.

Panmunjom is a circus of balloons, signs & guards in the day, & all kinds of spotlights at night. That's to protect the neutral zone. One of our Service Bns. is in part of the neutral zone, & it's a general court martial to fire a round. The guards stand post with fixed bayonets. One shot fired there could excite an international incident.

Not much more to write, darling. So I'll close. Love ya loads & loads am anxious to be with my 2 sweethearts. Won't be long now. Almost on my way!

All My love forever
Al (& Boondocker)
XXXX

MZ 827

April 3

Dearest Joanne—

Am I sorry we had a girl? Silly! There is nothing sweeter in the world than a pink, soft little girl baby. I think they're the most adorable little creatures alive. As pert and mischievous as a baby kitten, as much a master of the art of their prescious [sic] sex as anyone could hope to be. I could never be sorry we have a daughter. Our little Cinthy couldn't be sweeter, I know it. Don't ask such silly questions. Sorry? I'm damned proud to have a little daughter.

Another day is fizzling out to the west, and there's the smell of pine-needles, burning grass & Korea in the air. The mountains are brown and the long stretch of vallies [sic] are [sic] brittle & gray under the sun. In a short while I know it will be dark, but the change will come quickly, without notice or warning. A lot of the men are outside playing baseball now. There is hollering and laughing. War seems a million miles away now.

There is peace in the air.

Last nite there was danger. We were at the movie when the call came: all corpsman [sic] report to the forward aid station. Stretchers were gathered. Trucks were alerted & readied to move the gear instantly. Phones buzzed and the tension mounted. The rumors started: there was a breakthrough on our flanks; the Gooks were pushing; we were being pulled out of reserve & committed on line … but they were all just rumours [sic].

The whole thing started yesterday. Our forward elements above Panmunjom got a tremendous amount of incoming artillery. Movement was observed & the Gook air waves were busy. It could have just meant re-enforcements for them, troops being relieved or anything. But the scuttlebut[t] of a jump-off shook everyone & the panic button was pushed. Radio jeeps hummed. Activity caught the CP. But this morning the sun showed us our empty panic. It was nothing at all. Nothing. But they'd better get me out of here before I flip my lid over "nothing." I've got short-timeridus [i.e., short timer-itis], as the Sgt/Major said last nite. I was a nervous wreck.

I heard the Colonel ask Guice today if the draft was still going to leave <u>Sunday</u>. I was standing there & Guice didn't want to say much. But the CO seemed pretty certain that we're leaving Sunday, April 6. That's 6 more days. The CO could be wrong, as he doesn't always get the scoop on things like that. But I'm sure hoping. Even if it is the 10th, that's only 7 more days—<u>one week</u>! Glory hallelujah! I understand we're leaving from Inchon. Kind of symbolic …

Well, darling, the light's about gone & it's getting hard to see, so I'll stop. I'm really counting the days until we can be together, dearest. Imagine, darling, after 13 months we'll be able to live & love as we please. Right now, I couldn't ask for more. I've had my fill of war, Korea & the USMC! See you the end of this month, darling! Cinthy!

All My love & kisses through
letters for now, in person in
four weeks! I love you both!
Al (& Boodocker)
XXXXXX

MZ 832

April 8, '52

Dearest Joanne—

Last nite <u>may</u> have been my last full nite in Korea. There is very persistent scuttlebut[t] that the draft will leave here tomorrow morning around 2 a.m. I asked the Sgt. Major about it and he said "there's a very good possibility." This could mean absolutely nothing. Then again, it may be a good indication that the scuttlebut[t] is straight scoop. Can't say. We filled out our change of address cards this afternoon. And they're stamped "transferred to Conl US"—Continental United States. I never thought I could love the US as much as I do now.

Took another shower this morning and got all clean clothes—from skivvies to dungarees. I've got a set that fits now.

Last nite we spent our time talking and drinking beer. You know, there are quite a few buddies I'm leaving behind. <u>Good</u> buddies, like I could never have in civilian life. There is nothing in Korea that can stand in the way of friendship, because money & material belongings loose [sic] their value. I could go out right now & borrow a $100 with only the spoken promise that I'd mail them the money back. I could bob to the next tent & drink their beer, and nothing would be said. We've eaten the same food out of the same can, with the same spoon. We've used each other's toothbrushes, soap, razor & shirt. I've cried on their shoulders, they've cried on mine. We've climbed hills together, bitched together, fought together, & slept together. We've protected each other's life on nite watch, worried about each other in combat, risked our lives for each other. How far does friendship go? 'Way past the line that divides life & death.

When the 7th draft pulls out, with it will go the memory of the big jump last April, the trap at the Quantico line, a regiment alone holding the line, the withdrawal to Chunchon [sic]. With it will go Operations Ripper & Mousetrap. And the later replacements will enshrine the memory in awe as we did with Inchon & the Pusan perimeter.

I guess I'm getting nostalgic, but I can't help it. I've been through a lot with the Big Seven, and it's always taken care of me. I came to Korea with my eyes wide open, but still a boot. Fox Co. took me in & watched over me with a vigilant eye, until I developed the sharp senses a man needs to stay alive in war. And when the company moved you could never mistake it for another; the point was far in front, an officer led, and the hills we took were high. When Fox fought, it was the hardest battle in Korea, when it won it was the greatest victory, when its men died, it was the greatest loss. I remember Fox by its officers who cried "fix bayonets & purple hearts, we're going up!" when we assaulted Sugar Loaf hill; "what the hell are we running for!" when we were trapped on 673; "we're gonna hold this f_cken hill!" when they banzaied [sic] us on 749. I remember Fox by its officers because if they were afraid, they didn't show. And when they died, the men had to go <u>forward</u> to recover their bodies. Stone, Nester, Phalen, Buchman, Lathem, Minor, Cody—I want to remember those names.

And I remember the Company by its peons, the citizens of the Corps, the family of Fox. We use[d] to call ourselves the Little Foxes—hot to trot. I remember it by people & phrases, Bert Jenkins & "I wonder what the poor people are doing;["] little "Guts" Nunn & his standard phrase, "they're coming tonight." I remember them hunched low & sharp-eyed moving up the crest of a hill; digging in on a taken objective; lying face flat on level ground when the shells were incoming; tired & dirty along a dusty road—suddenly exhausted when they went in reserve.

That was Fox, bearded, tough, young & cocky. It's a great company!

The replacements now are younger than the earlier drafts were. Most of them are regulars, so the civilian breed of reserves are going home. The war will take on a professional tint, because the bitch of the "weekend warrior" won't be there. But it won't make any difference ...

But I guess you know all about that stuff, hon, from the 3 or 400 letters I've written you from Korea. You'll probably hear all about it again when I get home. Then when I've told you about it and written about it, we can forget it. If we can ...

I love you, darling. Give Cinthy a big kiss for me & tell her daddy will be home soon.

All My love forever
to wife & daughter –
Al (& Boondocker)
XXXXXX's [sic]
all you want!

MZ 836

April 27

Dearest Joanne—

One of the things I'll always place among my most wonderful thrills is the sound of a soft voice coming to me over the phone after 13½ months—yours. I'll remember it for its sweetness, for its tremble & for its excited happiness that only you can convey to me.

This morning when we pulled within eyesight of the continental United States I experienced a nostalgia & a feeling of pride which is inevitable when one realizes that with all its stubborn pride, with all its arrogance, with all its impudence—the United States is still the finest nation in the world. I could never quite explain the sight of the land rising out of the mist, the pointed fingers of the morning sun touching it with roses, and the spirit of God over America which is visible even in a physical sense.

And when we actually pulled into San Diego, the rising cheer of 500 waiting mothers, wives, sons, fathers—did something to you that the war had failed to do—humbled you & brought tears to your eyes. The sound of the band, the voice of the general ... "your country & the Marine Corps are proud of you ..." These are experiences which happen only once or twice in the course of a lifetime.

But hearing your voice like I heard it this afternoon is a thrill that happens just once.

So Korea is behind, darling, and in a week you & I will begin reliving the life we started almost three years ago on States St. Korea was an interlude—one which has taught me well of life & human misery—as well as human hope. Because even at war there is hope—a more violent hope never existed.

Darling, I love you. More than life, ambition or all the fallibilities of men. I've found you as I've had to—with the same eyes that bore the wound of war, & now needs the healing balm of you.

Korea is gone. I'm home, darling, I'm home—<u>just as I promised</u>!

        All My Love
        forever & forever –
        Al XXX

MZ 837

        San Diego, Cal.
        May 1, '52

Dearest Joanne—

It's a lovely, balmy 7:50 p.m. at the Marine Corps Recruit Depot. There's a blueish light in the evening & a softness in the air. It might as well be spring.

I suppose I should be happy now, lying on my behind inside the Continental limits of the US, waiting to be released from active duty with the Corps. But I'm not altogether so. I want to be with you & Cinthy, in San Francisco, not in this scourge of the State called Southern California. All this processing is taking too damned long to suit me. We should get out of here Sunday, but I'm not going to bet on it. I wouldn't bet on anything the MC promised. Death & taxes inclusive.

I just came from the base theatre which probably accounts for the present mood. The picture I saw was "The Sniper"*—about a sex criminal (<u>this</u> doesn't account for the mood), filmed in S.F. (<u>this</u> does). Richard Geyer† (I think that's his name) had a bit part in it. He's the one who taught at State & married Poly Poulson. The one you liked. All he said was "You're early" or something to that effect.

Thus far in our processing we have undergone a dental & physical examination, a couple lectures and some other BS. Under the latter, we were asked if we

---

 *The Sniper (1952) is a film that tells the story of a sniper who kills young women and of the police who try to identify him. The stars of the film are Arthur Franz and Adolphe Menjou.
 †Richard Glyer had a bit part in the film.

wanted to re-enlist. There I had the extreme, if not sadistic pleasure, of turning on the Sgt troop handler & laughing squarely & directly in his face. Once for me & once for the 7th Marines in Korea.

Yesterday after noon chow I was standing in back of the mess hall wondering what to do with my spoon, knife & fork when I became aware of the most pitiful "sir" I have ever heard. Looking to my right, my eyes fell upon a stiffly-at-attention, hat-too-big-for-him boot. "I'll take your silver, sir," he said scairdly [sic], and when I handed it to him, he took off like a scaird [sic] rab[b]it. I guess the combination of three stripes, a hashmark & campaign ribbons on a uniform were a little more than he could take.

It's hard to think that I'm only a year and a half removed from the plight of these hopeless boots. It's like looking at yourself in your childhood. That was me? Oh, no! But I guess it was. I guess a boot is the lowest thing in the world after all.

See you Sunday, darling! Unless this letter gets there Monday. Then I'll see you yesterday!

All My love to you,
Cinthy, & Boondocker!
Al

MZ 838

Afterword

After his return to the States in 1952, and after being mustered out of the Marines, Al Martinez enrolled in the University of California, Berkeley, but soon left to begin his career in journalism at the *Richmond Independent*. In 1955, he moved on to the *Oakland Tribune*, where he worked as a reporter and columnist. In 1971, the *Los Angeles Times* enticed him to head south, and he joined the paper as a reporter, accepting his own column in 1984 as a featured writer. For the next 23 years, his columns appeared regularly, earning him three (shared) Pulitzer Prizes in journalism, a National Headliner Award for the best column in the United States, a National Ernie Pyle Award, a lifetime achievement award from the California Chicano News Media Association and numerous other distinguished awards. In his own apologia, Al wrote, "Editors and publishers come and go, typefaces change, formats shift, columns move from here to there. I endure, writing the words and singing the songs, prowling like an old alley cat through the lives of those I father into my paragraphs."*

When the *Times* released him in a cost-cutting move in 2007, scores of his readers stormed the editorial offices with calls, emails, and letters, protesting his dismissal. The paper's management reinstated him but ultimately let him go 18 months later, in January 2009. Soon, he began writing a column for the *Los Angeles Daily News*, and his final piece appeared in March 2013. He also wrote columns for the LA Observed website and for his hometown paper, the *Topanga Messenger*. In addition to producing columns and essays, he taught writing workshops and seminars until shortly before his death.

In the 1970s to 1990s, Al carved out a second career writing for television. His credits include scripts for episodes of *Hawaii Five-O* in 1978; *B.A.D. Cats* in 1980; and *Out on the Edge*, a series starring Rick Schroder for which Al received an Emmy nomination in 1992. *Jigsaw John*, a 1976 television drama starring Jack Warden, was based on a profile Al had written for the *Times* about John St. John, a one-eyed Los Angeles homicide detective.

Al wrote several books, including *Rising Voices: Profiles in Hispano-American Lives* (1974, revised and reissued in 1993), *I'll Be Damned If I'll Die in Oakland: A Sort-of Travel Memoir* (2003), *Barkley: A Dog's Journey* (2006), and two novels:

---

*Al Martinez, *I'll Be Damned If I'll Die in Oakland* (New York: Thomas Dunne, St. Martin's Press, 2003), 190.

Joanne and Al Martinez at their home in Topanga, California, 2011. Photograph by John Sullivan for The Huntington Library and used in the Al Martinez exhibition (DSC 1290).

The Last City Room (2000), and *City of Angles: A Drive-By Portrait of L.A.*(1996). He also produced compilations of his columns: *Ashes in the* Rain (1989), *Dancing under the Moon* (1992), and *Reflections(* 2003).

Al and Joanne had three children. The eldest, Cinthia, was born on May 31, 1951, while Al was deployed in Korea. She died from cancer in 2011. They also had a son and second daughter: Allen Martinez and Linda Bach.

As noted in the Preface, in 2012 The Huntington Library mounted a major exhibition, "Al Martinez: Bard of L.A.," that presented highlights of his life and career and that included a sampling of his letters from Korea.

Al and Joanne continued to reside in their long-time home in Topanga Canyon, where Al wrote freelance pieces for a variety of publications and taught writing seminars, and where Joanne hosted grandchildren and tended an ever-changing flock of pets, including dogs, cats, and at least one goat. Al passed away from complications of COPD in February 2015, and Joanne died of lung cancer on April 5, 2021.

The Korean War never completely left Al. He wrote a number of columns and essays about the war, remembering the war even as he looked forward and went about his daily life as a journalist and columnist. In 1992, Al and Joanne traveled to China and Korea on one of a series of tours for veterans of the war and their families, in the Revisit Korea Program. On the trip, Al looked back to his own experiences and watched as his fellow veterans relived their own moments of battle and loss, and as the widows, sons, and daughters of the fallen stood on the ground where their soldier or Marine gave his life to an unfathomable war. Afterward, in several columns, Al wrote poignantly of the memories evoked by his visit, recalling his Marine buddies who didn't make it home.

On July 27, 1995, the Korean War Memorial was dedicated in Washington, D.C., and Al traveled there to be part of the opening ceremonies and to write about the event and its meaning. As with his return visit to Korea, this brought back a flood of memories that found expression in his columns and essays.

The Korean War would remain with Al for the rest of his days both as deeply-felt memories of his lived experience and also as influences that helped shape the humanity and compassion that became the hallmarks of his life.

Glossary

*People, Places, Events, Phrases,
Abbreviations, Military Terms*

America's Town Hall Meeting of the Air—a public affairs radio program that ran from 1935 to 1956.

Aztec Stadium—home to the San Diego State University Aztec football team.

"Bali Hai"—a song from the Rodgers and Hammerstein musical *South Pacific* (1949). Bali Hai is an island paradise, visible but always out of reach.

Banzai Hill—no battle found by this name. It is likely Al's private name for a battle.

Battle of Hoengsong—see Massacre Valley.

Bloody Ridge—part of the Battle of the Punchbowl, q.v.

Blum, Art (d. 2003)—known as the "king of public relations" in San Francisco, representing a wide variety of clients.

Bn.—battalion.

Boondocker—a small toy turtle Al carried throughout his time in Korea. Joanne sent it to him, and Al wrote on May 20, 1951, to thank her.

Boondockers—the lace-up field boots worn by Marines.

Boot—a newcomer to the Marine Corps. The term carries both positive and negative connotations. It can also denote a Marine new to a rank or an assignment and can describe a Marine who has not been in combat.

Btn.—battalion.

Buchman (or Buchmann, or Buckman) Ridge—there appears to be no ridge by this name. It is probably Al's private name for the ridge where a platoon leader named Buchman distinguished himself. Similarly, Al named Hamlin Hill for Sergeant Hamlin, who had shown considerable bravery.

Caen, Herb (1916–1997)—a long-time, legendary daily columnist for the *San Francisco Chronicle* whose columns treated social and political affairs, with a generous sprinkling of puns.

Camp Matthews—named for Calvin V. Matthews. It was the Marine Corps rifle range in La Jolla, near San Diego, and served as a Marine corps base from 1917 to 1964.

Castillo, Ferdinand (1917–1993)—raced and taught swimming. In 1942 he joined the

Marines and saw battle in the Pacific. He fought again when he re-enlisted in the Korean War. Al knew him at San Francisco State.

The Castro—a district in San Francisco whose character changed over the years. It became a working-class neighborhood in the 1930s and over the next several decades it developed into a gay community. Presumably, Al and Joanne would have strolled the area and sampled the night life.

Charles, Ezzard—on September 27, 1950, Ezzard Charles beat the favored Joe Louis in the fifteenth round of a heavyweight boxing match.

Cheaper by the Dozen—a 1948 novel by Frank Bunker Gilbreth, Jr., and Ernestine Gilbreth Carey about their childhood in a family with twelve children. Al had probably seen the 1950 film based on the book.

Childress, Ted—a sergeant and mail clerk. He went to high school with Al. Al ran into him at the PIO.

Chink—a pejorative term used in referring to people of Chinese extraction. It was also used for Asian people in general.

Chosin Reservoir—a battle occurring from November 27 to December 13, 1950. UN forces had to withdraw after being surrounded by Chinese troops. The withdrawal was spearheaded by the Marines, who fought valiantly, saving many lives. They became known as "the Chosin Few."

Chuncheon—the capital of the South Korean province of Gangwon. Much of the city was destroyed in the Battle of Chuncheon, at the beginning of the Korean War.

Clement, William T. (1894–1955)—served with distinction in the Marines during World War II. In September 1949, he became commander of the Marine Corps Recruit Dept in San Diego, retiring in 1952.

Cliff House—a building on the cliffs north of Ocean Beach, San Francisco, part of the Golden Gate National Recreation area. Since 1863, it has featured restaurants with ocean views.

C.O.—commanding officer.

Col.—colonel.

Corsairs—the type of plane flown by Marines.

C.P.—command post.

Cpl.—corporal.

Diamond, Lou (1890–1951)—a career Marine who rose to the rank of gunnery sergeant, serving in both world wars. He was known for his exploits in battle.

Doggies—a derogatory term for soldiers in the U.S. Army, slang from the World War I term "dog face."

Douglas, Paul (1907–1959)—an American actor who performed on Broadway and in films.

Eisenhower, Dwight D. (1890–1969)—became the Republican candidate for president in 1952, defeating both Earl Warren and Robert A. Taft in the primary, and he was elected president, serving from 1953 to 1961. He had served as a five-star general in the U.S. Army in World War II and as the Supreme Commander of the Allied Forces in Europe, in charge of the invasion of France and Germany. He was popularly known as "Ike," especially during his presidential campaign.

Fagan, Paul—businessman and owner of the San Francisco Seals.

"File 13"—the name of Al's column in the *Golden Gater*, the campus newspaper at San Francisco State.

Fire team—the smallest group in a military unit, smaller than a company or a platoon, typically made up for four men.

Galo, Frank—friend of Al at San Francisco State. He wrote for and became managing editor for the *Golden Gater* while Al was serving in the Marines.

Geyrene—Al's spelling of Gyrene, q.v.

Glyer, Richard—an actor who had a bit part in the film *The Sniper*.

Golden Gater—the campus newspaper at San Francisco State.

Gook—American troops used this racist, pejorative term to identify Asians from World War II through the Korean and Vietnam wars. Its origin is uncertain. David Halberstam notes in *The Coldest Winter* (p. 110) that it arose from guerrillas in the Philippines who were called "niggers" or "gugus" (or "goo-goos"), a name for tree bark used as shampoo. In *The Last Stand of Fox Company* (p. 12), authors Bob Drury and Tom Clavin place its origin with American soldiers who heard Korean children say what sounded like "Me gook" while pointing at the Americans. Drury and Clavin note that "the Korean word 'gook' means 'country,' and the children's use of the phrase 'Me gook' was probably a complimentary reference to the United States as a 'beautiful country.'" From there, the word "gook" acquired its pejorative connotation.

Guice, Henry B.—Al's lieutenant in the PIO, who approves each issue of the *Ridgerunner*.

Gung ho—a phrase that denotes people possessing overly zealous military enthusiasm. It is from a Chinese term meaning to work together.

Gung ho hat—a cloth cap with a visor.

Gyrene—slang for a U.S. Marine. The word probably originated by combining "GI" for "government issue" and "Marine."

Hamlin Hill—there is no record of this hill in accounts of battles. This is likely Al's private name for the hill, in recognition of the action that took place under Sgt. Hamlin.

Hamlin, Sgt.—a member of Al's unit. He saved a number of lives on a patrol and was recommended for the Navy Cross.

Hava-no or havano—the English-language rendering of the Korean mispronunciation of "have no," meaning "don't have any."

Hearst, William Randolph (1863–1951)—founded the largest newspaper chain in the United States. His papers emphasized sensationalism and led to the term "yellow journalism" to describe this approach.

Heartbreak Ridge—part of the Battle of the Punchbowl, q.v.

Highway 101—one of two major arteries that span nearly the full length of California.

Hill 749—see Punchbowl.

Holiday Rhythm—a 1950 film starring Mary Beth Hughes and David Street. It tells the story of a young man who hits his head, passes out and dreams of the show he is trying to convince an airline to sponsor.

Hoyle, Edmond (1672–1769)—the British author of a book of rules for card games. The phrase "according to Hoyle" means that something is according to the rules, or the way something is normally done.

Hwachon (or Hwacheon) Dam—a battle that took place between April 22 and 26, 1951.

In like Flynn—this expression was probably based on the actor Errol Flynn, whose womanizing and drinking were legendary. To be in like Flynn denotes that one has attained a goal quickly and easily. The phrase can also refer specifically to sexual accomplishments. The title of the film *In Like Flint* (1967) is a play on the phrase. As a result, people often erroneously use the phrase "in like Flint," rather than the correct, original one.

Inchon—the Battle of Inchon began on September 15, 1950, and involved an amphibious landing at Inchon Harbor. General Douglas MacArthur urged this action against the strong advice of his advisors. Against all odds and despite the extreme challenges of the inhospitable harbor, the landing succeeded, and UN troops marched on Seoul and took the city from the North Koreans.

Inje—a county in Gangwon Province, South Korea.

Itchy Pup—probably a stuffed animal Joanne had. In his letters, Al occasionally mentions Itchy Pup, often in conjunction with reference to Boondocker.

Jenkins, Bert—Al's buddy and often his foxhole mate, a 19-year-old from Kentucky. Al mentions him frequently in his letters.

Kaesong—a city in the southern area of North Korea. It was the site of peace talks beginning on July 10, 1951, but these moved to Panmunjom on October 25, 1951.

Kansas Line—a defensive line, a few miles north of the 38th parallel.

The Keyhole—a periodical, but there have been several with the same name, so it cannot be determined exactly which of them Al referred to.

Kildare, James—a fictional physician created in the 1930s by Max Brand, a writer whose real name was Frederick Faust. Several motion pictures and television series featuring the character have been made.

Laine, Frankie (1913–2007)—an American singer and performer.

Laura—this 1949 film was a romantic mystery starring Dana Andrews, Gene Tierney, and Clifton Webb. The movie's theme song "Laura" was composed by David Raksin.

LeBaron, Eddie—lieutenant in the Marines in Korea. He was an All-American quarterback at College of the Pacific and later played for the Washington Redskins and Dallas Cowboys.

LeBlanc, Earl—Al's buddy and fire team leader in boot camp, from Texas.

The Lemon Drop Kid—starring Bob Hope, Marilyn Maxwell and Lloyd Nolan, it was a 1951 film about a swindler who must raise $10,000 by Christmas to repay a gangster.

Lesser, Jean—a writer for the *Golden Gater*.

Lieut.—lieutenant.

MacArthur, Douglas (1850–1964)—a five-star general in the U.S. Army who had a distinguished career as superintendent of the U.S. Military Academy at West Point and as a combat veteran of both world wars. During World War II he served as commander of the U.S. Army Forces in the Far East, and he officially accepted Japan's surrender on September 2, 1945. Initially placed in charge of the United Nations' troops in the Korean War, he was later removed by President Harry Truman in April 1951.

Mamaril, Pete—Al's buddy, killed in action. Al mentions him in several letters.

Martz, Ernie—worked with Al at regimental PIO but was transferred soon after Al joined PIO.

Glossary

Massacre Valley—the Battle of Hoengsong took place February 12–13, 1951. It was one of the worst defeats suffered by the U.S. military during the war. Angry Marines placed a sign along the road where their comrades had fallen, reading "Massacre Valley, Scene of Harry S. Truman's Police Action. Nice going, Harry!"

Mauldin, Bill (1921–2003)—an American editorial cartoonist, receiving two Pulitzer Prizes. He was best known for cartoons of soldiers in World War II.

Mausert, Frederick—a sergeant in the Marines in Korea. He earned the Medal of Honor for multiple acts of heroism and for ultimately sacrificing his life at the Battle of the Punchbowl on September 12, 1951.

Merritt, Dixon Lanier (1879–1972)—the author of the limerick "The Pelican," which has often been attributed to Ogden Nash. The classic version of the verse reads: "A wonderful bird is the pelican / His bill will hold more than his belican, / He can take in his beak / Enough food for a week / But I'm damned if I see how the helican!"

Mnts.—mountains.

Mortar Gulch—no battle found by this name. It is likely Al's private name for a battle.

Nash, Ogden (1902–1971)—the supposed author of "The Pelican."

NCO—noncommissioned officer.

The Next Voice You Hear—a film made in 1950 starting James Whitmore and Nancy Davis. She later married Ronald Reagan and was the First Lady of California (1967–1975) and of the United States (1981–1983). A voice claiming to be God interrupts all radio programming for six days. The script was adapted from a short story by George Sumner Albee.

Oakland Oaks—a minor league baseball team that played from 1903 to 1955 in the Pacific Coast League.

Objective 10—part of the Battle of the Punchbowl.

O'Doul, Francis Joseph "Lefty" (1897–1969)—the manager of the San Francisco Seals following a career as a player in major league baseball.

Operation Clam-up—a period of absolute silence by the Marines, beginning on February 7, 1952, designed to fool the opposing troops into thinking nothing was going on, when in reality the UN troops were preparing for an offensive. This action began on February 15, 1952.

Operation Killer—began the second major battle against the Chinese Communists and the North Korean Army, from February 20 to March 6, 1951. It was planned by General Matthew Ridgway.

Operation Mousetrap—in May 1951, the 7th Marines were airlifted to an area in advance of the front lines in order to lure the Chinese troops into a space where they could be attacked by troops from either side.

Operation Pursuit—unidentified battle action.

Operation Yo-Yo—in June 1950, the North Korean government claimed the entire Korean Peninsula as its own territory. The United States fought back along lines that stretched all the way from Pusan at the south end of the peninsula to the Chinese border, changing constantly between those two areas. Hence, the fighting in the first year of the war was known as "Operation Yo-Yo."

Panmunjom—the location of peace talks from October 25, 1951. Previously, the talks had been held in Kaesong.

PFC—private first class.

PIO—the Marines' Public Information Office.

Plt.—platoon.

P.O.'d or P.O.'s—pissed off, or pisses off. Al often wrote that someone or something "P.O.'d me" or "P.O.'s me."

Poge or pogue—someone in the military who works in the rear, in a noncombat role. Among front-line Marines and soldiers, it was common to view such personnel in a negative light, or even with scorn.

Polk Gulch—the area around part of Polk Street in San Francisco. The name stems from an old stream under the street. It was the city's primary gay area for about thirty years beginning in the 1950s.

Prisoners in Petticoats—a 1950 film that starred Valentine Perkins as a naïve young pianist who becomes unwittingly involved with a gang of mobsters.

Punchbowl—the Battle of the Punchbowl took place from August to September 1951 and encompassed the Battle of Bloody Ridge and the Battle of Heartbreak Ridge. Marine forces controlled the hills north of the Punchbowl. Hill 749 in this area would be taken by the 7th Marines. Fox Company (Al's group) was central to this operation and suffered heavy casualties.

Pyle, Ernie (1900–1945)—a famous American journalist in World War II who wrote about ordinary soldiers. Winning a Pulitzer Prize in 1944, he was killed by enemy fire in the Battle of Okinawa.

Rayder—it is unclear whether Al's mention of Rayder refers to a person or is a misspelled reference to Marine Raiders.

Rich—see Richardson, Bob.

Richardson, Bob—cartoonist who worked with Al on the *Ridgerunner*.

Ridgway, Matthew B. (1895–1993)—had a distinguished career in the U.S. Army. Following service during and after World War II, he became the commander of the 8th U.S. Army in Korea. After President Truman removed General MacArthur as commander of all United Nations forces in Korea, Ridgway replaced him.

ROK—the acronym for Republic of Korea. Al and his fellow Marines referred to the South Korean soldiers as ROKs, pronounced "rocks."

Roper, Don—in Korea. His wife is Pat, and Joanne seems to know them. He is in the 2nd Battalion.

Salty—slang used to describe a Marine or sailor who has had considerable experience and is tough as a result. The term could also be used ironically to denote new Marines who wanted to appear more tough and experienced than they were, and it could be used to describe a Marine whose uniform was visibly old, worn and distressed by age and use.

San Francisco Seals—a minor league baseball team that played from 1903 to 1957 in the Pacific Coast League.

Scout—Marine scout snipers are highly skilled marksmen, but Al uses just the term "scout," so it is unclear exactly what he means.

Sgt.—Sergeant.

Shelter half—essentially, half a pup tent, used for shelter over a foxhole.

Smoker—an unauthorized fight or boxing match.

The smoking lamp is lit—this phrase is used in the Navy and Marine Cops to grant permission to smoke.

The Sniper—a 1952 film that tells the story of a sniper who kills young women and of the police who try to identify the killer. The stars of the film are Arthur Franz and Adolphe Menjou.

Spock, Benjamin—Dr. Spock's *The Commonsense Book of Baby and Child Care* was the most popular book on the subject beginning with its first publication in 1946. Joanne writes to Al about it and then sends him a copy.

Stone—"Mr. Stone" was a lieutenant with Al's Fox Company in Korea.

Taft, Robert, Jr. (1917–1993)—sought the presidential nomination in 1952, his third unsuccessful try. He was a Republican Congressman from Ohio, 1963–1965, and a U.S. Senator, 1971–1976.

30 or Thirty—in journalism, the number "30" was once typed at the end of copy to signify the end of the article. It is not used much today, as "end" or "###" is preferred.

Thomas, Gerald C. (1894–1984)—appointed commander of the 1st Marine Division in Korea in April 1951.

Tip-toe tanner—presumably a dance step, but its meaning has proven elusive in searches of dance terminology. Joanne Martinez suggested that it was probably a term that Al invented.

Up the gigi, or up the giggy—a slang term referring to the gigi as the anus. The phrase would be similar to "up the wazoo," a slang phrase meaning to excess, or as much as one can handle.

Verducci, Joseph—San Francisco State's football coach and athletic director in the 1950s and early 1960s.

Warren, Earl (1891–1974)—served as governor of California (1943–1953) and was appointed Chief Justice of the U.S. Supreme Court (1953–1969). In 1948 he was the nominee of the Republican Party for vice president, running with Thomas E. Dewey. He unsuccessfully pursued the Republican nomination for president in 1952.

Weiland, Don—with Al in boot camp.

Wichita Line—a battle line in the middle of the Korean Peninsula, in the hills north of the 38th Parallel. A series of four hills (1179, 983, 940, and 773) occupied a ridge running parallel to the Wichita Line. From August 18 to September 5, the Battle of Bloody Ridge took place on these hills.

Winchell, Walter (1897–1972)—a well-known American newspaperman and radio figure. Winchell's son, Walter Jr., committed suicide, not at Parris Island, and not while in the Marines, but in the family garage on Christmas night, 1968. According to Herman Klurfeld's biography, *Winchell: His Life and Times*, Walter Jr. joined the Marines after dropping out of school. Leaving the Corps, he traveled to Africa, returning home to speak of his misery in the Marines and of his adventures in Africa. His behavior was erratic, and he began seeing a woman he identified as the daughter of a Nazi general. After their marriage, he wore a Nazi uniform in public, goosestepping and crying out "Heil Hitler!" He eventually received psychiatric treatment, but it apparently did little good, and he drifted from one low-end job to another until he took his life in 1968.

The Woman on Pier 13—a film made in 1949 starring Robert Ryan, Laraine Day, and John Agar. It told the story of a man blackmailed by the Communist Party into spying for it.

X-Ray—It is unclear whether this is a named battle or location, or Al's private name for part of the Punchbowl. Battle.

Yanggu—a county in Gangwon province, South Korea.

Yankees—presumably, the New York Yankees. The team name appears in a letter that mentions several teams from the Pacific Coast League, but there doesn't appear to have been a Yankees team in that league in the early 1950s.

Further Reading

The Korean War

Baldovi, Louis. *A Foxhole View: Personal Accounts of Hawaii's Korean War Veterans*. Honolulu: University of Hawai'i, 2002.
Ballenger, Lee. *The Outpost War: U.S. Marines in Korea, Volume I, 1952*. Washington, D.C.: Brassey's, 2000.
Barron, Leo. *High Tide in the Korean War*. Mechanicsburg, PA: Stackpole Books, 2015.
Blair, Clay. *The Forgotten War: America in Korea 1950–1953*. New York: Times Books, 1987.
Brady, James. *The Coldest War: A Memoir of Korea*. New York: Thomas Dunne, St. Martin's Griffin, 1990.
Cumings, Bruce. *The Korean War: A History*. New York: The Modern Library, 2011.
Drury, Bob, and Tom Clavin. *The Last Stand of Fox Company*. New York: Grove Press, 2009.
Estes, Kenneth W. *Into the Breach at Pusan: The 1st Provisional Brigade in the Korean War*. Norman: University of Oklahoma Press, 2012.
Fehrenbach, T.R. *This Kind of War: The Classic Korean War History*. Dulles, VA: Potomac Books, 1963.
Freedman, Ron. *Love Letters to Pete: A Korean War Memoir*. Lady Lake, FL: Court Jester, 2013.
Halberstam, David. *The Coldest Winter: America and the Korean War*. New York: Hachette, 2015.
Hanley, Charles J. *Ghost Flames: Life and Death in a Hidden War, Korea, 1950–1953*. New York: Public Affairs, 2020.
Harrison, Carlos. *The Ghosts of Hero Street: How One Small Mexican-American Community Gave So Much in World War II and Korea*. New York: Berkley Caliber, 2014.
Jager, Sheila Miyoshi. *Brothers at War: The Unending Conflict in Korea*. New York: W.W. Norton, 2013.
Leckie, Robert. *Conflict: The History of the Korean War, 1950–53*. New York: Da Capo Press, 1996; originally published New York: Putnam, 1962.
Millett, Allan R. *Their War for Korea: American, Asian, and European Combatants and Civilians, 1945–1953*. Sterling, VA: Potomac Books, 2004.
Millett, Allan R. *The War for Korea, 1945–1950: A House Burning*. Lawrence: University Press of Kansas, 2005.
Millett, Allan R. *The War for Korea, 1950–1951: They Came from the North*. Lawrence: University Press of Kansas, 2010.
Mills, Randy K. *"Honoring Those Who Paid the Price": Forgotten Voices from the Korean War*. Indianapolis: Indiana Historical Society Press, 2002.
Montross, Lynn, et al. *U.S. Marine Operations in Korea, 1950–1953, Volume IV: The East-Central Front*. Washington, D.C.: Headquarters, U.S. Marine Corps, Historical Branch, G-3, 1962.
O'Donnell, Patrick K. *Give Me Tomorrow: The Korean War's Greatest Untold Story—The Epic Stand of the Marines of George Company*. Cambridge: Da Capo Press, 2010.
Peters, Richard, and Ziaobing Li. *Voices from the Korean War: Personal Stories of American, Korean, and Chinese Soldiers*. Lexington: University Press of Kentucky, 2004.
Rees, David. *Korea: The Limited War*. New York: St. Martin's Press, 1964.
Rice, Douglas. *Voices from the Korean War: Personal Accounts of Those Who Served*. Bloomington: iUniverse, 2011.
Richardson, William. *The Valleys of Death: A Memoir of the Korean War*. New York: Berkley Caliber, 2010.
Russ, Martin. *Breakout: The Chosin Reservoir Campaign, Korea 1950*. New York: Penguin, 2000.
Russ, Martin. *The Last Parallel: A Marine's War Journal*. New York: Fromm International, 1999; originally published New York: Rinehart & Co., 1957.
Sides, Hampton. *On Desperate Ground: The Marines at the Reservoir, the Korean War's Greatest Battle*. New York: Doubleday, 2018.

Sloan, Bill. *The Darkest Summer: Pusan and Inchon 1950: The Battle That Saved South Korea—and the Marines—from Extinction.* New York: Simon & Schuster, 2009.
Stokesbury, James L. *A Short History of the Korean War.* New York: William Morrow, 1988.
Tomedi, Rudy. *No Bugles, No Drums: An Oral History of the Korean War.* New York: Wiley, 1993.
Weintraub, Stanley. *A Christmas Far from Home: An Epic Tale of Courage and Survival During the Korean War.* Boston: Da Capo Press, 2014.
Wilson, Marc. *Hero Street: The Story of Little Mexico's Fallen Soldiers.* Norman: University of Oklahoma Press, 2009.

General Reference Sources

Crawford, Danny J., et al. *The 1st Marine Division and Its Regiments.* Washington, D.C.: History and Museums Division Headquarters, U.S. Marine Corps, 1999.
Elting, John R., et al. *A Dictionary of Soldier Talk.* New York: Charles Scribner's Sons, 1984.
MacMillan, Margaret. *War: How Conflict Shaped Us.* New York: Random House, 2020.
Millett, Allan R. *Semper Fidelis: The History of the United States Marine Corps.* New York: The Free Press, 1991.
Samet, Elizabeth D. *Looking for the Good War: American Amnesia and the Violent Pursuit of Happiness.* New York: Farrar, Straus and Giroux, 2021.
Samet, Elizabeth D., ed. *World War II Memoirs: The Pacific Theater.* New York: The Library of America, 2021.

By Al Martinez

Ashes in the Rain: Selected Essays. Berkeley: TQS Publications, 1989.
Barkley: A Dog's Journey. Santa Monica: Angel City Press, 2006.
City of Angles: A Drive-by Portrait of Los Angeles. New York: St. Martin's Press, 1996.
Dancing Under the Moon. New York: St. Martin's Press, 1992.
I'll Be Damned If I'll Die in Oakland. New York: Thomas Dunne, 2003.
Jigsaw John. New York: Avon, 1976.
The Last City Room. New York: Thomas Dunne, 2000.
Reflections: Columns from the Los Angeles Times. Los Angeles: Los Angeles Times Books, 2003.
Rising Voices: Profiles in Leadership. Glendale, CA: Nestle USA, 1993, a revised version of the 1974 book.

Index

Agar, John 63
"Al Martinez: Bard of L.A." (exhibition) 4, 216
Albee, George Sumner 41*n*
"All the Lonely People" 8*n*1
America's Town Meeting of the Air (radio show) 156, 156*n*
Andrews, Dana 207*n*
"Anniversary Song" 64
Arden, Eve 152
armistice 11
Associated Press (AP) 150, 150*n*, 165, 166
Aztec Stadium, San Diego 46, 46*n*

B.A.D. Cats (television show) 215
Balboa Park, San Diego 47
"Bali Hai" 84, 84*n*
Banzai Hill 172, 172*n*
Battle of Bloody Ridge 12, 69
Battle of Heartbreak Ridge 11, 12, 69–70, 140, 140*n*
Battle of Hoengsong 117, 117*n*
Battle of Inchon 10, 12, 69
Battle of Mortar Gulch 172, 172*n*
Battle of Mortar Hill 172
Battle of the Bulge 89*n*
Battle of the Chosin Reservoir 10, 12, 69, 171
Battle of the Hwachon Dam 69, 154, 171
Battle of the Punchbowl 11, 12, 69, 140*n*, 154, 158*n*, 163, 171, 172, 188, 198, 198*n*; Hill 749 70, 198, 198*n*, 212; Objective 10 172, 172*n*, 188
Battle of the Yanggu Valley 154, 171, 172, 202, 205
Battleground (film) 89, 89*n*
Blondell, Joan 183*n*
Blum, Art 180, 180*n*
Boondocker (turtle) 71, 73, 73*n*, 91, 131, 172; purple heart 161; reproduced 189

Brady, James 11
Brady, James: *The Coldest War* 11*n*
Brand, Max 25
Buchman (also spelled Buckman and Buchmann), platoon leader 92–93, 212
Buchman Ridge 172, 172*n*

Caen, Herb 34, 34*n*, 55, 102
California Chicano New Media Association award 2, 215
Camp Matthews 45, 47, 47*n*, 50, 51
Camp Pendleton 3, 12, 62
Carey, Ernestine Gilbreth: *Cheaper by the Dozen* (novel) 204–205, 205*n*
Castillo, Ferdinand J. 106, 106*n*
The Castro, San Francisco 60, 60*n*
Charles, Ezzard 30, 30*n*
Cheaper by the Dozen (film) 204–205, 205*n*
Cheaper by the Dozen (novel) 204–205, 205*n*
Childress, Sgt. Ted 151
China 10, 14, 79
Chinese (people) 6
Chinese (troops) 39, 80, 87, 89–93, 96, 99, 112, 118, 119–120, 125–126, 141, 142, 156, 182, 192–194, 202
Chosun 8
Chuncheon 207, 207*n*
Cincinnati Enquirer 183
Citera, Joe 14, 124, 172
Clement, Gen. William T. 44, 44*n*
Cliff House, San Francisco 26, 26*n*
Cold War 10
The Coldest War 11*n**
College of the Pacific 157, 157*n*
combat action 10, 11, 12, 16–17, 71, 76–77, 78, 80–84, 87, 89–90, 92–93, 96, 97–98, 99, 100–102, 103–104, 106, 119–120, 133, 138, 140, 141–142, 152–153, 156, 171–173, 182, 188–190, 191–194, 197–199, 204, 205, 210, 212
The Commonsense Book of Baby and Child Care 167, 167*n*
comradeship 7, 12, 49, 76, 147, 152, 153–154, 167–168, 193, 194, 202, 211–212
Conrad, Paul 4
Corsairs *see* United States Marine Corps: Corsairs

Day, Laraine 63
Demilitarized Zone 11
Democratic People's Republic of Korea troops 141, 142, 165–166, 192–194, 209
"Desert Song" 108
Dewey, Thomas E. 163*n*
Diamond, Lou 172, 172*n*
A Dictionary of Soldier Talk 29*n*
Douglas, Paul 178, 178*n*
drawings by Al Martinez: mentioned or described 3, 5, 15–16, 21, 27, 73, 79, 80, 91, 103, 110, 130, 200, 208; reproduced 101, 131, 168, 189, 190
drawings by Bob Richardson: mentioned or described 5, 170; reproduced 161, 165, 166; *see also* Richardson, Bob

Eisenhower, Dwight D. 163, 163*n*
Elting, John R.: *A Dictionary of Soldier Talk* 29*n*
Emmy Award 2, 215
Ernie Pyle Award *see* National Ernie Pyle Award
USS *Essex* 152

229

Fagan, Paul 85, 85n
Fair Employment Practice Committee 7
Faust, Frederick *see* Brand, Max
File 13 37, 37n, 79, 91
Fisk, Alfred G. 173, 173n
Flynn, Errol 81n
four feathers 133
The Four Feathers (film) 133n
The Four Feathers (novel) 133n
Franz, Arthur 213n
future of the world 15, 16, 17, 61, 167

Galo, Frank 29, 29n, 34, 36, 37, 39, 48, 91, 92, 99, 116, 128, 137, 137n, 138, 149, 160
Gangwon Province 109n, 117n, 207n
Geyer, Richard *see* Glyer, Richard
Gilbreth, Frank Bunker: *Cheaper by the Dozen* (novel) 204–205, 205n
Glyer, Richard 213, 213n
"God Bless America" 108, 108n
The *Golden Gater* 12, 22, 22n, 37, 37n, 91, 160
Gordon, Gale 152
Gresham, William Lindsay: *Nightmare Alley* 183
Guice, Lt. Henry B. 169, 170, 177–178, 187, 200
"The Gypsy" 104

Hamburger Hill 16, 102
Hamlin, Sgt. *see* Hamlin Hill
Hamlin Hill 172, 172n
Hammerstein, Oscar 84n
Hawaii Five-O (television show) 215
Hearst, William Randolph 35, 35n, 150n
Hill 673 212
Hill 749 *see* Battle of the Punchbowl: Hill 749
Hodiak, John 89n
Holiday Rhythm 43, 43n
Hongcheon 87n, 109, 109n, 149, 154
Hope, Bob 105, 105n, 107
Hotel San Clemente 65
Hoyle, Edmond 206, 206n
Hughes, Mary Beth 43
The Huntington Library 4, 5, 216

In Like Flint 81n
Inje 117, 117n
Itchy Pup 73, 73n, 161, 169

Jaeger, Allen 129, 137, 206–207
Jaeger, Barbara 129
Jaeger, Eric 162
Japan 10
Jenkins, Bert, "Jenk" 7, 85, 85n, 86, 95, 98, 103, 104, 111, 139, 147, 153, 154, 170, 208
Jigsaw John (television show) 215
Johnson, Van 89, 89n, 160, 212

Kaesong 11, 14–15, 71, 113, 113n, 125, 140, 209
Kansas line 154, 171, 208
The Keyhole 74, 74n
Kildare, Dr. James 25, 25n
Klurfeld, Herman: *Winchell: His Life and Times* 88n
Kobe, Japan 72, 73
Korda, Zoltan 133
Korean children 75, 83, 108, 111–112, 132, 167
Korean people 5–6, 75, 111–112, 132

L.A. Observed (website) 215
Laine, Frankie 59
Land of the Morning Calm 8
Laura (film) 207n
"Laura" (song) 207, 207n
Leatherneck 145, 156; Pacific edition 145
LeBaron, Eddie 157, 157n
LeBlanc, Earl 85, 85n, 98
The Lemon Drop Kid 105, 105n, 107
Lesser, Jean 36, 37, 99
Lewis, Sinclair 74
Looking for the Good War 11
Los Angeles Daily News 215
Los Angeles Examiner 34
Los Angeles Times 4, 6, 215
Louis, Joe 30, 30n

MacArthur, Douglas 10, 39, 39n, 89n, 91, 163, 163n
Mamaril, Pete 14, 93, 97–98, 170, 179, 183, 196
Marine Recruit Depot, San Diego 21n, 44n, 213
Martinez, Al: "All the Lonely People" 8n
Martinez, Cinthia Louise 5, 13, 17, 58, 71, 90, 91, 94–95, 98, 99, 100, 116, 126, 128, 130, 133, 134, 137, 138, 149, 153, 155, 158, 161, 164, 196, 210, 216; Al's letter to Cinthia 135–136
Martz, Ernie 149, 150, 151, 152
Mason (reserve area) 94, 94n

Mason, A.E.W.: *The Four Feathers* 133n
Massacre Valley *see* Battle of Hoengsong
Mauldin, Bill 145, 156n
Mausert, Frederick 158, 158n
Maxwell, Marilyn 105n
Medal of Honor 158, 158n
memory of the war 12, 13, 14, 16, 17, 88, 120–123, 205–206
Menjou, Adolphe 213n
Merritt, Dixon Lanier: "A wonderful bird is the pelican" 163, 163n
Montalban, Ricardo 89n
Munsan 209

Nash, Ogden 163n, 188, 196
National Ernie Pyle Award 2, 215
National Headliner Award 2, 215
The Next Voice You Hear 41, 41n
Nickerson, Col. Herman 121
Nightmare Alley (book) 183, 183n
Nightmare Alley (film) 183, 183n
Nolan, Lloyd 105n
North Korean troops *see* Democratic People's Republic of Korea troops

Oakland, CA 12
Oakland Oaks 41, 41n
Oakland Tribune 215
Objective 10 *see* Battle of the Punchbowl: Objective 10
O'Doul, Francis Joseph "Lefty" 85, 85n
O'Leary, Lt. 159, 166
On Desperate Ground 1
Operation Killer 172, 172n
Operation Mousetrap 69, 89, 100, 154, 172, 211
Operation Pursuit 104, 104n, 188–190
Operation Ripper 211
Operation Yo-Yo 172, 172n
Our Miss Brooks (radio show) 152, 152n
Out on the Edge (television show) 215

Pacific Coast League 41, 41n, 84n, 85n
Panmunjom 11, 14–15, 71, 113n, 166, 209, 210
peace talks 11, 14–15, 71, 105, 109, 110, 112, 113n, 118, 125, 140
pejorative language 5–6, 71

Perkins, Valentine 43
poetry by Al Martinez: "The Fly" 16, 96–97; "Give me the strength to live, oh Lord" 127; "The hills tear open with the flame!" 119; "I'm missing you, that's all I say" 48; "The purple liquid twilight pours" 118–119; "Starlight, starbright [sic]" 134
poges 178
Power, Tyrone 183*n*
Prisoners in Petticoats 43, 43*n*
Pulitzer Prize 2, 84, 156, 215
Punchbowl 106; *see also* Battle of the Punchbowl
Pusan 10, 72, 73, 87, 132
Pyle, Ernie 84, 84*n*

Quantico line 154

racism 5–6, 7
Raksin, David: "Laura" (song) 207, 207*n*
Reagan, Nancy *see* Davis, Nancy
Reagan, Ronald 41*n*
"Remembering the Forgotten War" 1*n*
Republic of Korea troops 87, 113, 117
Revisit Korea Program 216–217
Richardson, Bob 182, 186, 196; *see also* drawings by Bob Richardson
Richmond Independent 215
The Ridgerunner 3, 12, 144, 145, 148, 149, 150, 151, 153, 157, 158, 169, 170, 176–178, 181, 182, 187–188; issue reproduced 174–175
Ridgway, Gen. Matthew B. 89, 89*n*, 108, 110, 140, 141, 166
Rodgers, Richard 84*n*
ROK *see* Republic of Korea troops
Roosevelt, Franklin D. 7
Roper, Don 154, 155
Runyon, Damon 107
Russo-Japanese War 10
Ryan, Robert 63

St. John, John 215
Samet, Elizabeth D. 2, 11; *Looking for the Good War* 11*n*; *World War II Memoirs* 2*n*
Samson 102, 102*n*
San Francisco 20*n*, 55, 60, 96
San Francisco Chronicle 34*n*
San Francisco Examiner 34

San Francisco Seals 84, 84*n*, 85*n*
San Francisco State College 12, 22, 34*n*, 79, 106, 173*n*, 213
Seabloom 168, 179
Sedgewick, Maj. 154, 166, 199
Seidel, Raymond G., PFC 199
Seoul 10, 110*n*, 209
Sides, Hampton: *On Desperate Ground* 1; "Remembering the Forgotten War" 1*n*
Smith, Jack 4
Smith, Kate 108, 108*n*
The Sniper (film) 213, 213*n*
South Korean troops *see* Republic of Korea troops
South Pacific 84*n*
Soviet Union 8, 10
Spock, Benjamin: *The commonsense Book of Baby and Child Care* 167, 167*n*, 182
"Stardust" 104
Stars and Stripes 145, 156, 181
Sterling, Jan 178, 178*n*
Street, David 43
Strickland, Bob 14, 163
Sugar Loaf Hill 212
Swain, Norma 160

Taft, Robert, Jr. 1163, 163*n*
thirty (or "30") 1090, 109*n*, 114
38th parallel 11, 39, 77
Thomas, Gen. Gerald C. 154, 154*n*, 181
USS *Thomas Jefferson* 69, 72
Tierney, Gene 207, 207*n*
Topanga Messenger 215
Treasure Island, CA 20, 20*n*
truce *see* peace talks
Truman, Harry S. 7, 39*n*, 63, 89*n*, 91, 100, 117*n*, 163, 165, 166

United Nations 8, 39*n*, 89*n*, 133
United Press International (UP or UPI) 150, 150*n*
United States 10, 20, 63–64, 212–213
United States Air Force 117
United States Army 10, 39, 75, 77, 89*n*, 117, 130, 142, 209; doggies 70, 82, 93, 209; 1st Cavalry Division 140; 2nd Division 109, 117, 140; 3rd Division 209; 7th Division 117; 24th Division 878th Army 110, 166; 101st Airborne Division 89*n*
United States Marine Corps 7, 8, 10, 12–13, 22, 27, 27*n*, 33, 34, 70, 82, 139, 141–142, 173, 200–201, 209; battalions (1st Battalion, 7th Regiment [1/7] 110, 157*n*; 2nd Battalion, 7th Regiment [2/7] 12, 79, 81, 89, 105, 106, 107–108, 110, 118, 132, 137, 155); boot camp 19–25, 27–41, 43–57, 61–63, 65–68; companies (Able Co. [2/7] 202; Charlie Co. [2/7] 69, 92; Dog Co. [2/7] 103, 106; Easy Co. [2/7] 133, 152; Fox Co. [2/7] 7, 12, 69, 76, 92, 97, 98, 106, 112, 113, 114, 116, 120, 121–122, 133, 137, 139, 146, 147, 148, 155, 160, 163, 168, 171, 202, 205, 208, 211–212); Corsairs 80, 80*n*, 117, 172, 209; criticism 12–13, 19, 35, 38, 40–41, 57, 62, 66–67, 68, 72, 121–122, 201; decorations 173; Distinguished Service Citation 170–171; divisions (Air Wing 117; 1st Division 87, 109, 145; Public Information Office [PIO]) 159, 166, 178, 181; Special Services 178); esprit de corps 13, 43, 44, 46, 49–50, 51, 93, 120–123, 200; evacuating the wounded 160, 160*n*; Presidential Unit Citation 105 (3rd Battalion, 7th Regiment [3/7] 190; Howe Co. 165); regiments (1st Regiment 89, 133, 140; 5th Regiment 89, 93, 97, 110, 133, 140–141, 145, 152; Public Information Office [PIO] 3, 12, 37, 37*n*, 106, 113–114, 114*n*, 124, 125, 130, 137, 144, 145, 146, 147, 148, 149, 154, 156, 159, 164, 169, 176–178, 181, 200; 7th Regiment 12, 74, 93, 97, 103, 104, 120–123, 129, 140–141, 142, 145, 147, 149, 150, 152, 169, 179, 214)
United States Marine Corps Reserves 12, 164, 209
United States Military Academy 39*n*
United States Navy 129; swabbies 6, 46*n*, 152–153
University of California, Berkeley 41, 41*n*, 215

Valentine, Percy Friars 79, 79*n*
Verducci, Joseph 34, 34*n*
Vietnam War 1, 11, 20

W.A. Balinger's 26
Warden, Jack 215

Warren, Earl 163, 163*n*
Webb, Clifton 207, 207*n*
Weiland, Don 20, 20*n*, 27, 27*n*, 61, 178
Weitmann, Cpl. Albert W. 205
"We'll Be Together Again" 59, 104
"Whispering" 104
Whitmore, James 41*n*
Wichita Line 129
Winchell, Walter 23, 23*n*, 87–88, 88*n*
Winchell, Walter, Jr. 88, 88*n*
Winchell: His Life and Times 88*n*
The Woman on Pier 13 63, 63*n*
"A wonderful bird is the pelican" 163, 163*n*
Wonju 110, 110*n*
World War II 5, 10, 11, 14, 20, 84n, 141, 156n

World War II Memoirs 2*n*1
writing ambition 63, 88, 102, 124, 125, 127, 185, 202

Yalu River 69, 84, 132, 142
Yanggu 117, 117*n*; *see also* Battle of the Yanggu Valley

Zoot Suit Riots 7

www.ingramcontent.com/pod-product-compliance
Lightning Source LLC
Chambersburg PA
CBHW060340010526
44117CB00017B/2906